THE WOODS

JAMES **TYNION IV** • MICHAEL **DIALYNAS** • JOSAN **GONZALEZ**

VOL. 2
THE SWARM

THE WOODS Volume Two, May 2015. Published by BOOM! Studios, a division of Boom Entertainment, Inc. The Woods is ™ & © 2015 Boom Entertainment, Inc. Originally published in single magazine form as THE WOODS No. 5-8. ™ & © 2014 Boom Entertainment, Inc. All rights reserved. BOOM! Studios™ and the BOOM! Studios logo are trademarks of Boom Entertainment, Inc., registered in various countries and categories. All characters, events, and institutions depicted herein are fictional. Any similarity between any of the names, characters, persons, events, and/or institutions in this publication to actual names, characters, and persons, whether living or dead, events, and/or institutions is unintended and purely coincidental. BOOM! Studios does not read or accept unsolicited submissions of ideas, stories, or artwork.

A catalog record of this book is available from OCLC and from the BOOM! Studios website, www.boom-studios.com, on the Librarians page.

BOOM! Studios, 5670 Wilshire Boulevard, Suite 450, Los Angeles, CA 90036-5679. Printed in China. First Printing.

ISBN: 978-1-60886-495-9, eISBN: 978-1-61398-349-2

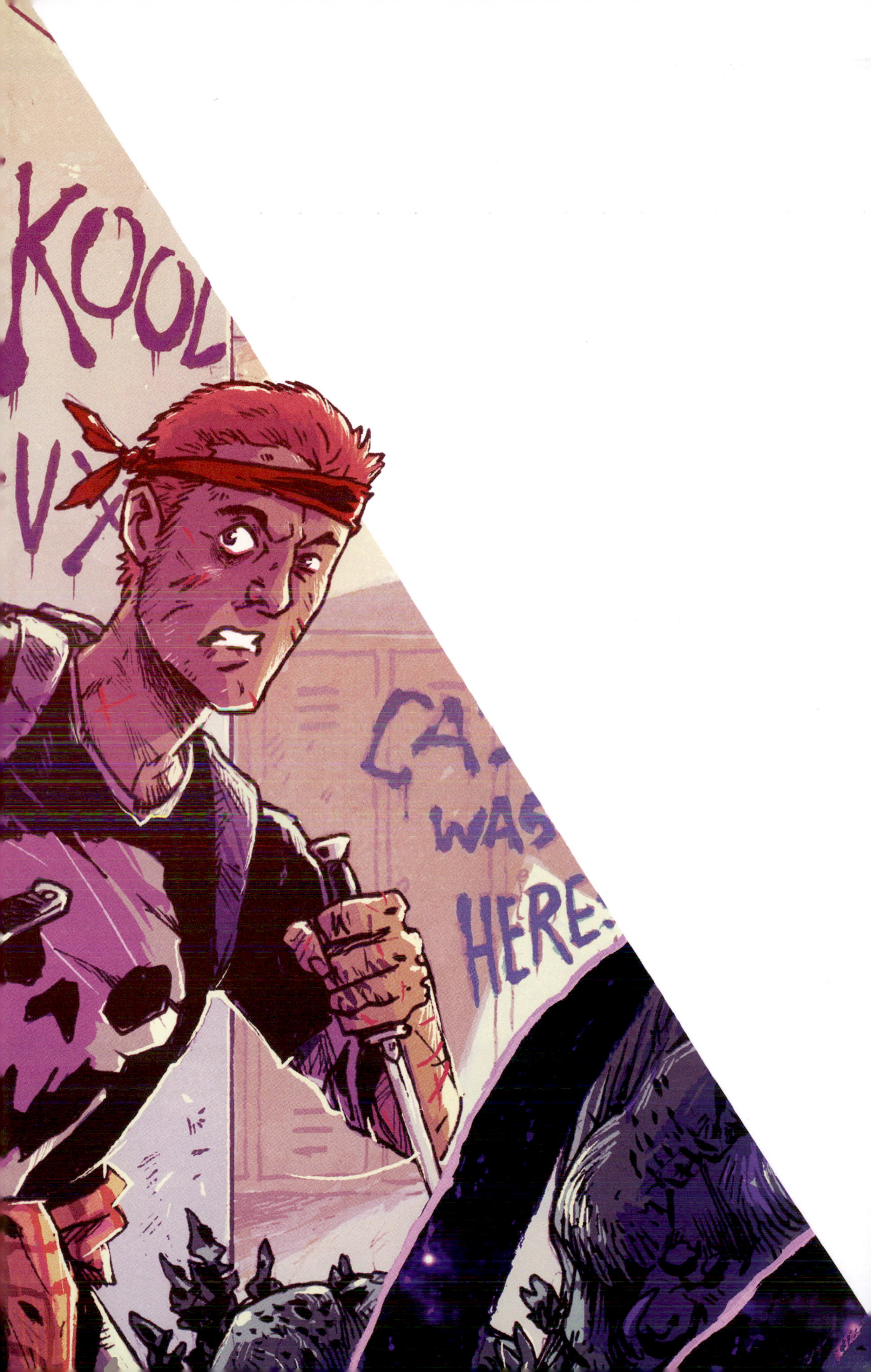

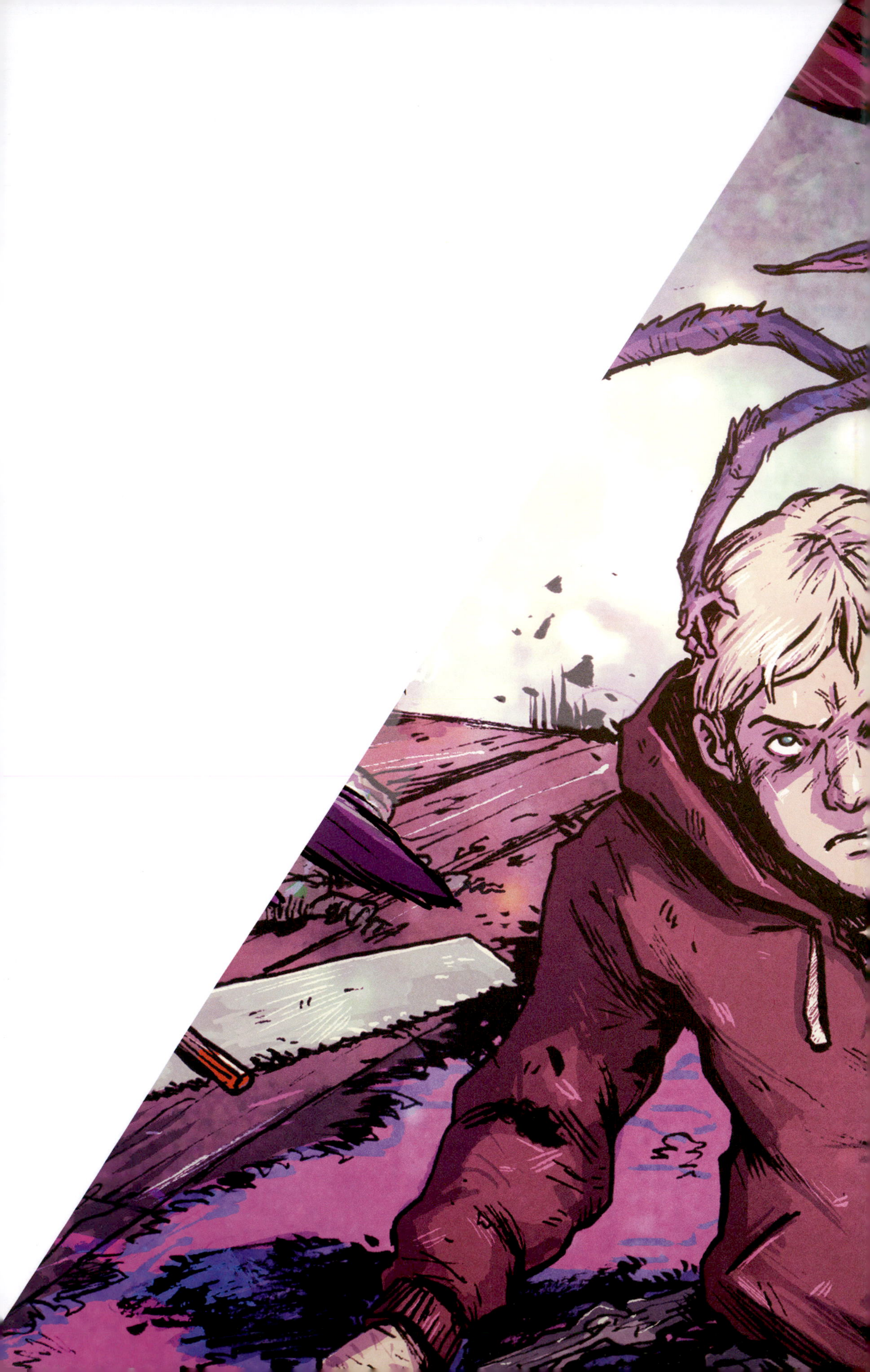

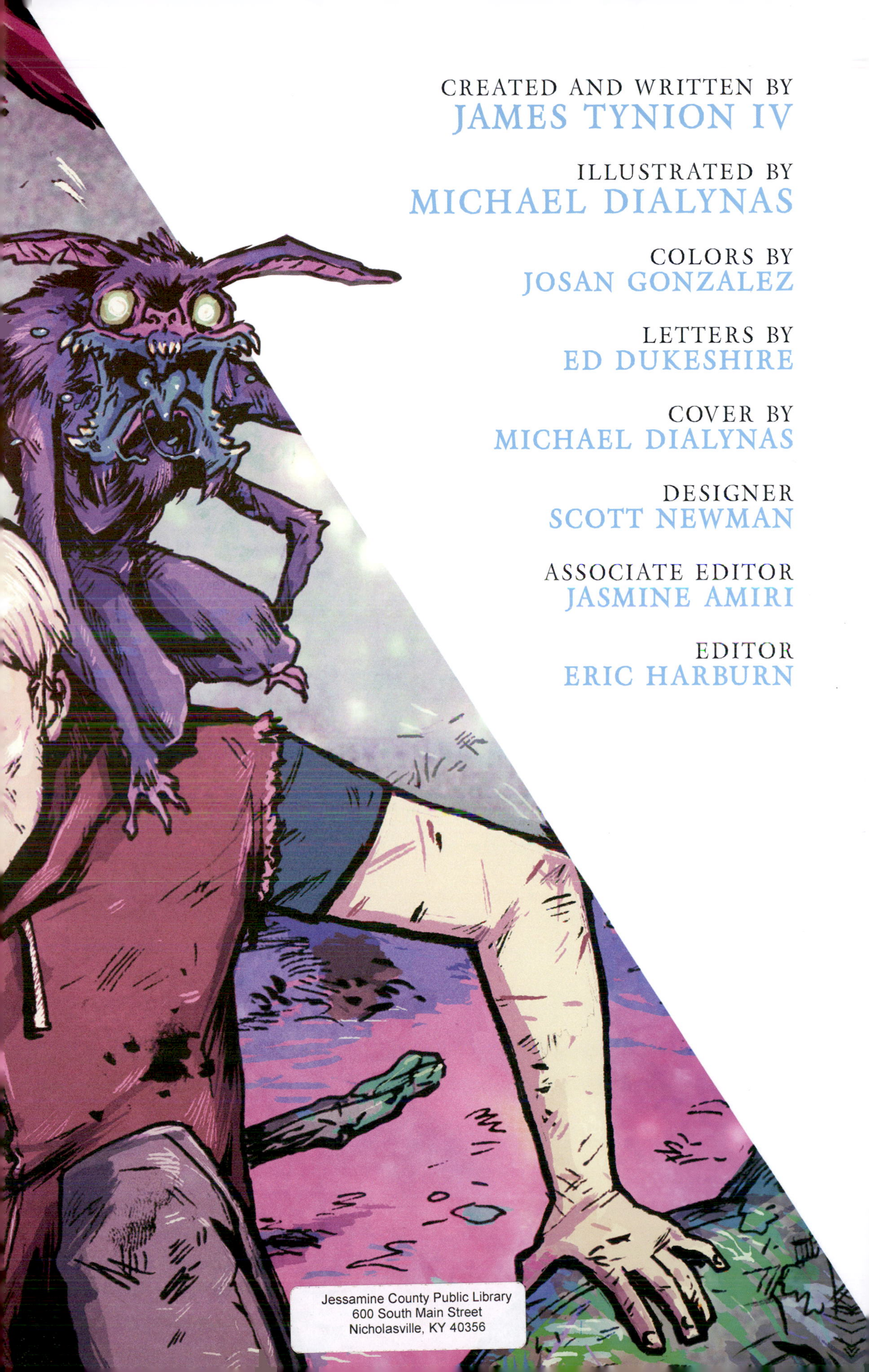

CREATED AND WRITTEN BY
JAMES TYNION IV

ILLUSTRATED BY
MICHAEL DIALYNAS

COLORS BY
JOSAN GONZALEZ

LETTERS BY
ED DUKESHIRE

COVER BY
MICHAEL DIALYNAS

DESIGNER
SCOTT NEWMAN

ASSOCIATE EDITOR
JASMINE AMIRI

EDITOR
ERIC HARBURN

CHAPTER FIVE

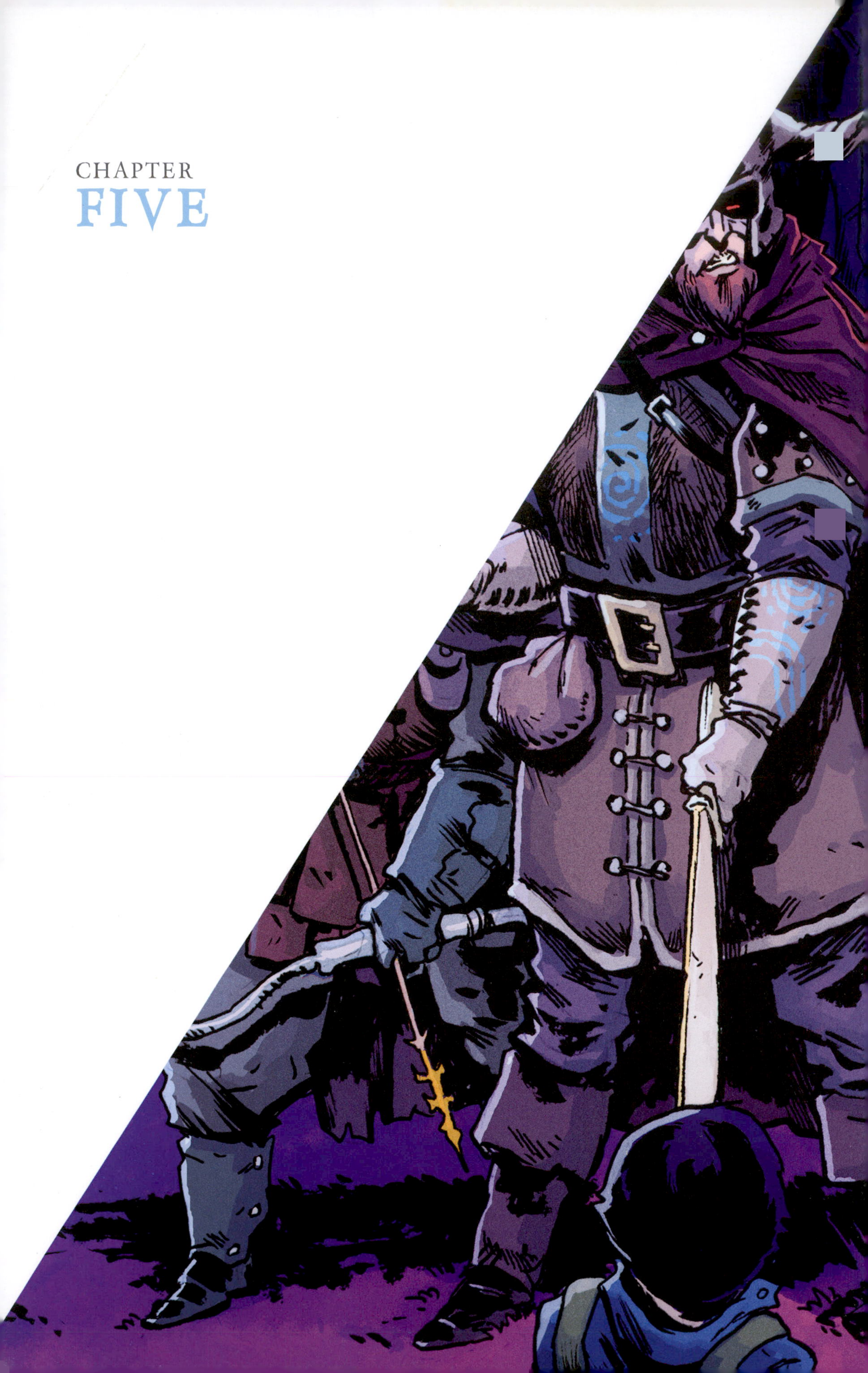

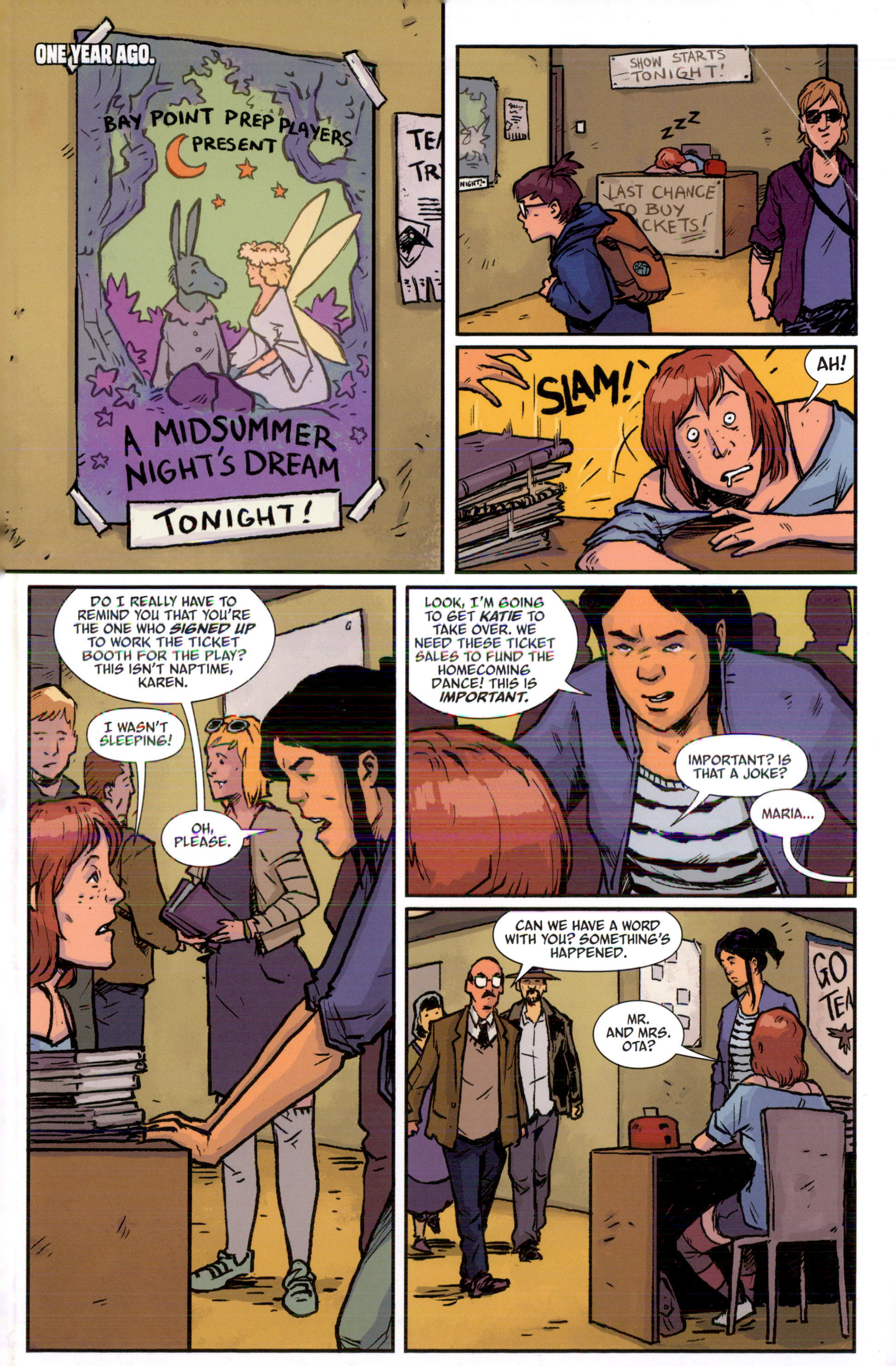
ONE YEAR AGO.
BAY POINT PREP PLAYERS PRESENT
A MIDSUMMER NIGHT'S DREAM
TONIGHT!
SHOW STARTS TONIGHT!
ZZZ
LAST CHANCE TO BUY TICKETS!
SLAM!
AH!
DO I REALLY HAVE TO REMIND YOU THAT YOU'RE THE ONE WHO *SIGNED UP* TO WORK THE TICKET BOOTH FOR THE PLAY? THIS ISN'T NAPTIME, KAREN.
I WASN'T SLEEPING!
OH, PLEASE.
LOOK, I'M GOING TO GET *KATIE* TO TAKE OVER. WE NEED THESE TICKET SALES TO FUND THE HOMECOMING DANCE! THIS IS *IMPORTANT.*
IMPORTANT? IS THAT A JOKE?
MARIA...
CAN WE HAVE A WORD WITH YOU? SOMETHING'S HAPPENED.
MR. AND MRS. OTA?

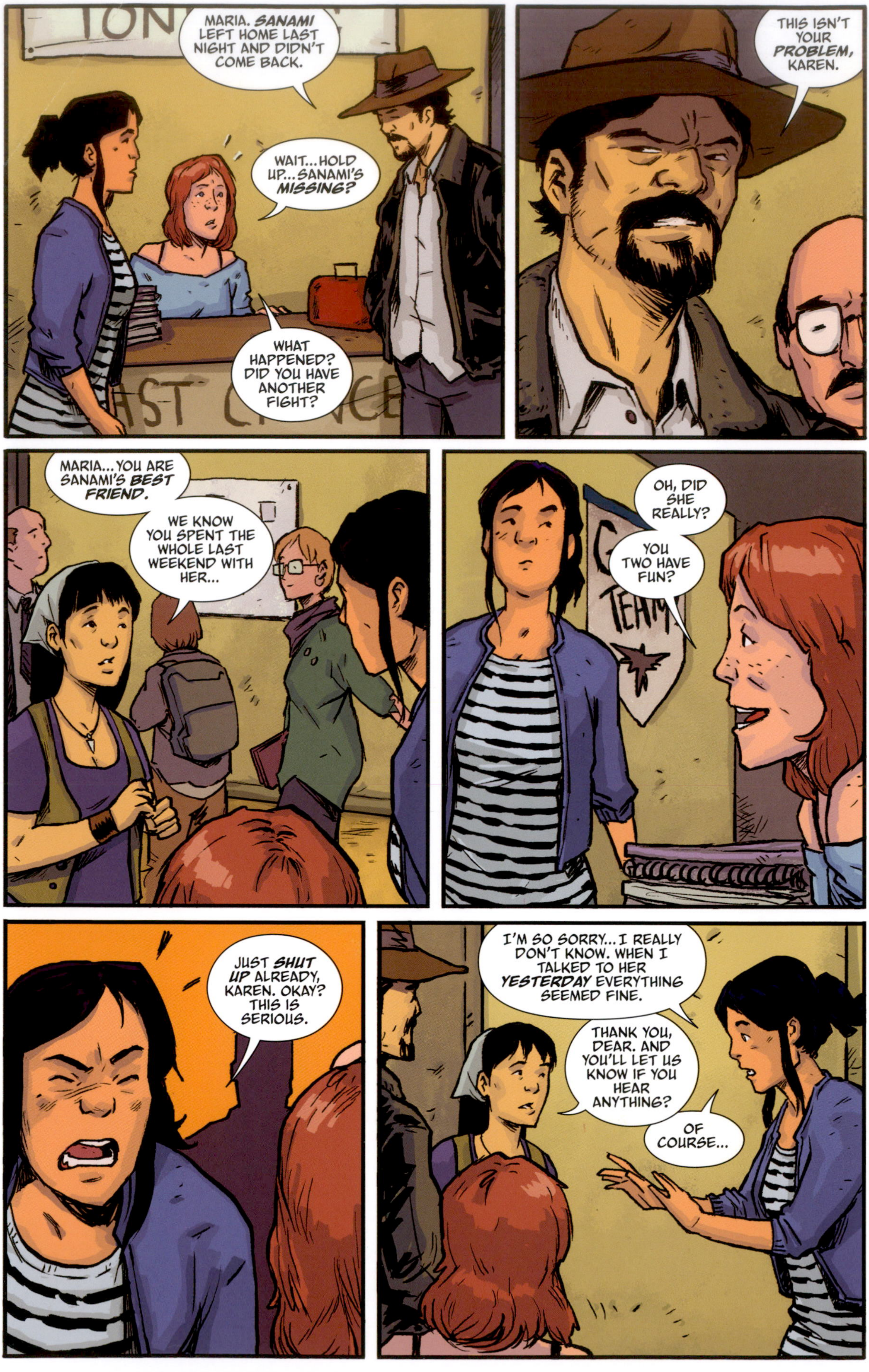
MARIA. SANAMI LEFT HOME LAST NIGHT AND DIDN'T COME BACK.
WAIT...HOLD UP...SANAMI'S MISSING?
WHAT HAPPENED? DID YOU HAVE ANOTHER FIGHT?
THIS ISN'T YOUR PROBLEM, KAREN.
MARIA...YOU ARE SANAMI'S BEST FRIEND.
WE KNOW YOU SPENT THE WHOLE LAST WEEKEND WITH HER...
OH, DID SHE REALLY?
YOU TWO HAVE FUN?
JUST SHUT UP ALREADY, KAREN. OKAY? THIS IS SERIOUS.
I'M SO SORRY...I REALLY DON'T KNOW. WHEN I TALKED TO HER YESTERDAY EVERYTHING SEEMED FINE.
THANK YOU, DEAR. AND YOU'LL LET US KNOW IF YOU HEAR ANYTHING?
OF COURSE...

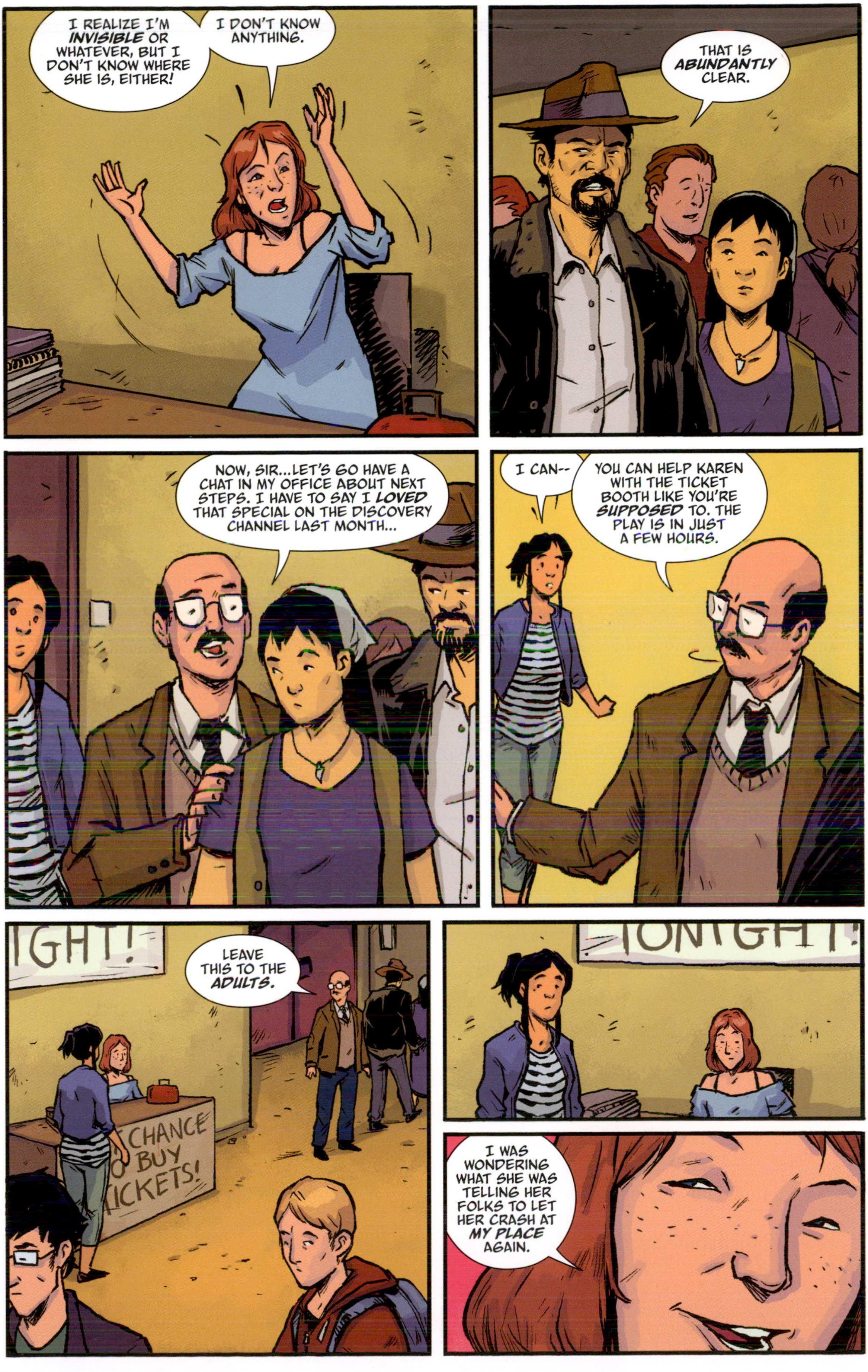
I REALIZE I'M *INVISIBLE* OR WHATEVER, BUT I DON'T KNOW WHERE SHE IS, EITHER!
I DON'T KNOW ANYTHING.
THAT IS *ABUNDANTLY* CLEAR.
NOW, SIR...LET'S GO HAVE A CHAT IN MY OFFICE ABOUT NEXT STEPS. I HAVE TO SAY I *LOVED* THAT SPECIAL ON THE DISCOVERY CHANNEL LAST MONTH...
I CAN--
YOU CAN HELP KAREN WITH THE TICKET BOOTH LIKE YOU'RE *SUPPOSED* TO. THE PLAY IS IN JUST A FEW HOURS.
IGHT!
LEAVE THIS TO THE *ADULTS.*
CHANCE
BUY
ICKETS!
TONIGHT!
I WAS WONDERING WHAT SHE WAS TELLING HER FOLKS TO LET HER CRASH AT *MY PLACE* AGAIN.

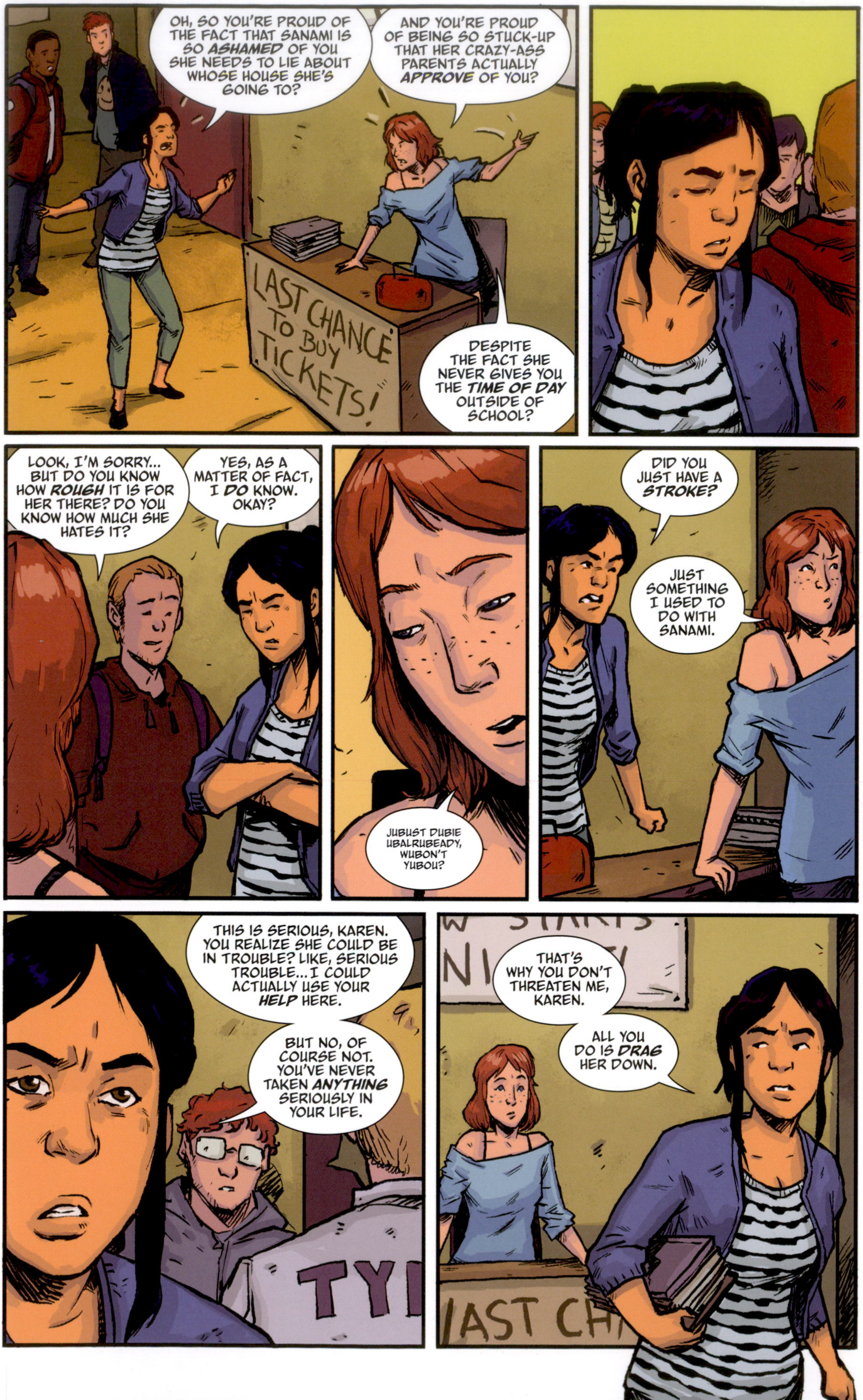
OH, SO YOU'RE PROUD OF THE FACT THAT SANAMI IS SO ASHAMED OF YOU SHE NEEDS TO LIE ABOUT WHOSE HOUSE SHE'S GOING TO?
AND YOU'RE PROUD OF BEING SO STUCK-UP THAT HER CRAZY-ASS PARENTS ACTUALLY APPROVE OF YOU?
LAST CHANCE TO BUY TICKETS!
DESPITE THE FACT SHE NEVER GIVES YOU THE TIME OF DAY OUTSIDE OF SCHOOL?
LOOK, I'M SORRY... BUT DO YOU KNOW HOW ROUGH IT IS FOR HER THERE? DO YOU KNOW HOW MUCH SHE HATES IT?
YES, AS A MATTER OF FACT, I DO KNOW. OKAY?
JUBUST DUBIE UBALRUBEADY, WUBON'T YUBOU?
DID YOU JUST HAVE A STROKE?
JUST SOMETHING I USED TO DO WITH SANAMI.
THIS IS SERIOUS, KAREN. YOU REALIZE SHE COULD BE IN TROUBLE? LIKE, SERIOUS TROUBLE... I COULD ACTUALLY USE YOUR HELP HERE.
BUT NO, OF COURSE NOT. YOU'VE NEVER TAKEN ANYTHING SERIOUSLY IN YOUR LIFE.
THAT'S WHY YOU DON'T THREATEN ME, KAREN.
ALL YOU DO IS DRAG HER DOWN.

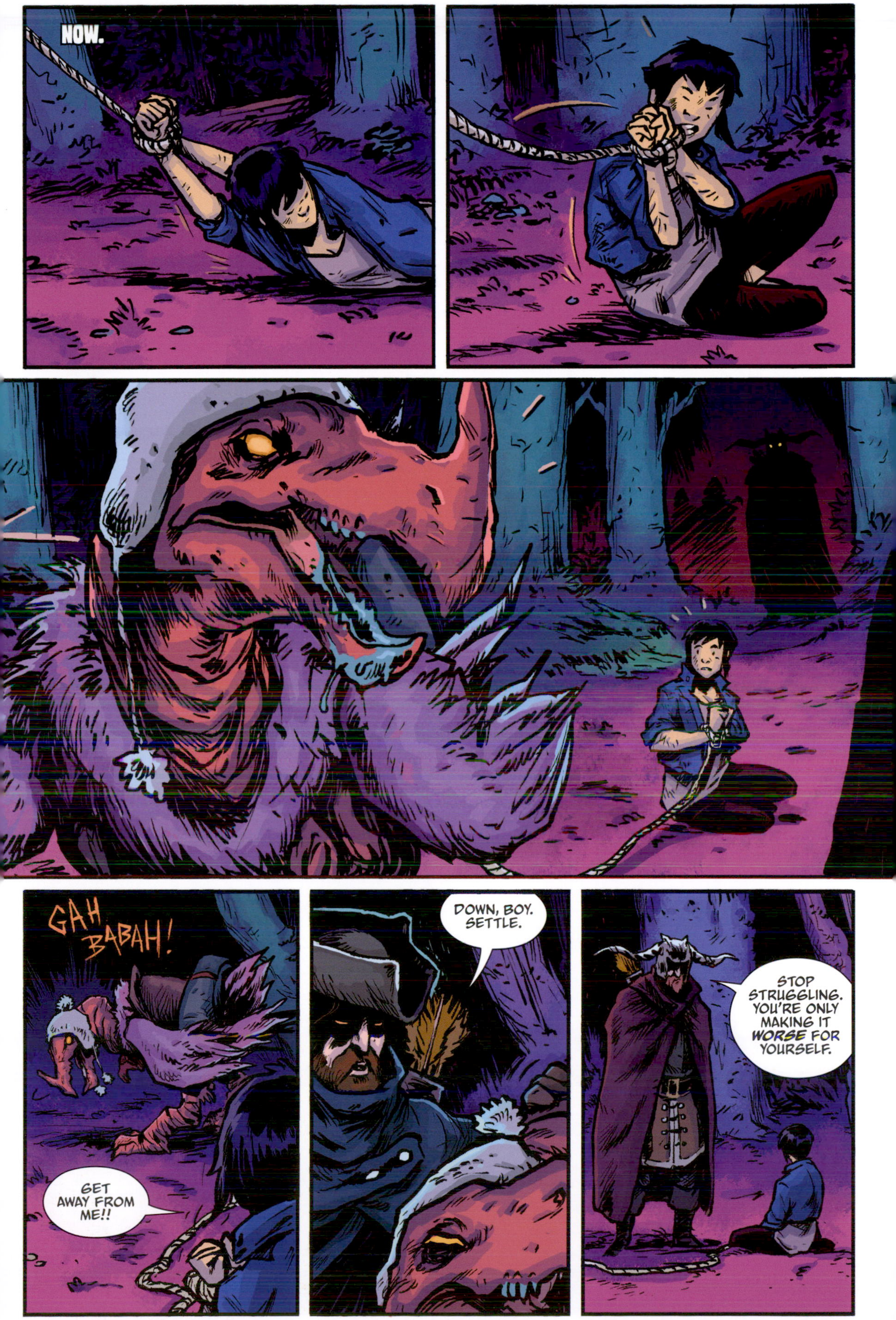
NOW.
GAH BABAH!
GET AWAY FROM ME!!
DOWN, BOY. SETTLE.
STOP STRUGGLING. YOU'RE ONLY MAKING IT WORSE FOR YOURSELF.

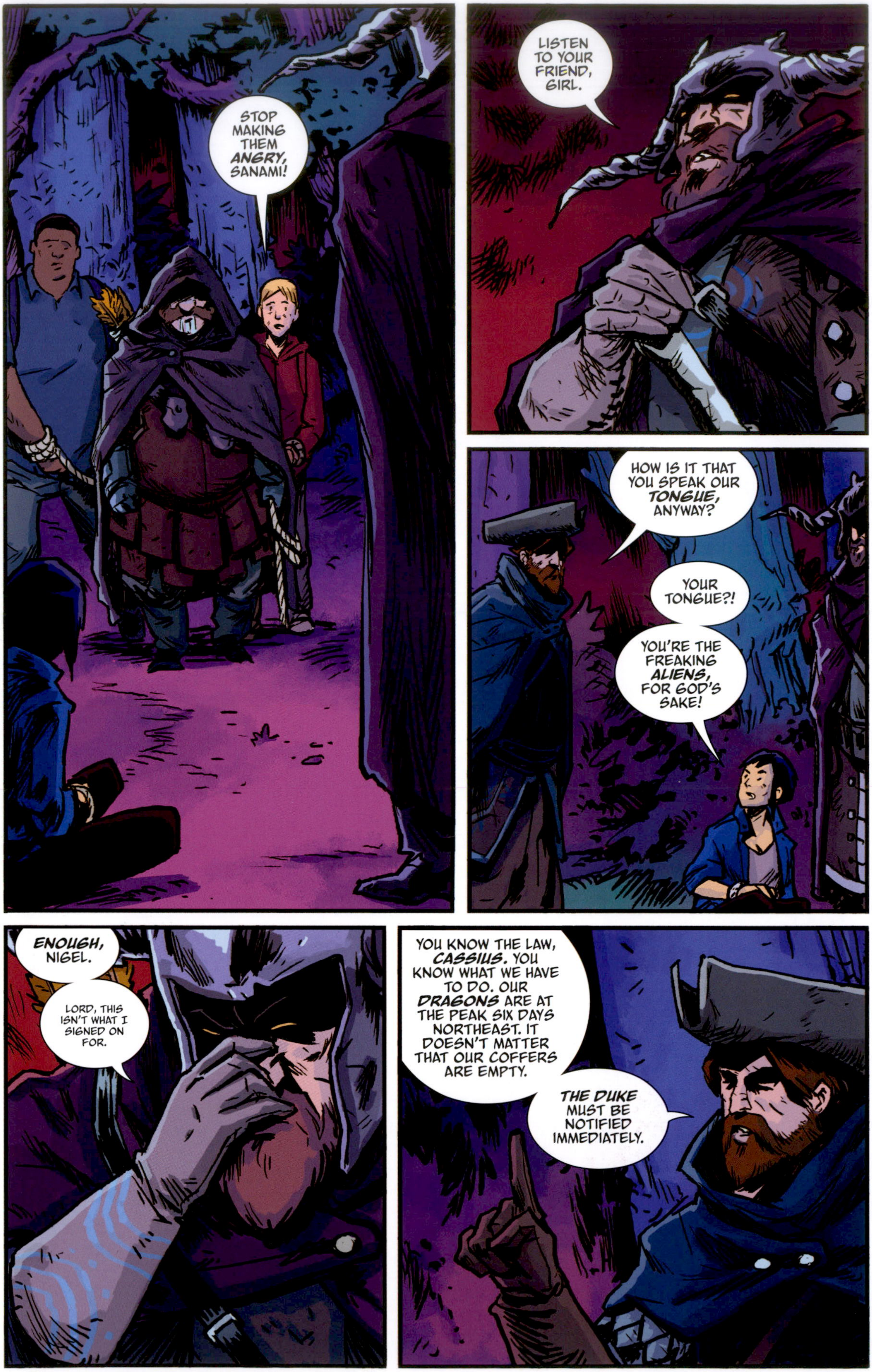
STOP MAKING THEM ANGRY, SANAMI!
LISTEN TO YOUR FRIEND, GIRL.
HOW IS IT THAT YOU SPEAK OUR TONGUE, ANYWAY?
YOUR TONGUE?!
YOU'RE THE FREAKING ALIENS, FOR GOD'S SAKE!
ENOUGH, NIGEL.
LORD, THIS ISN'T WHAT I SIGNED ON FOR.
YOU KNOW THE LAW, CASSIUS. YOU KNOW WHAT WE HAVE TO DO. OUR DRAGONS ARE AT THE PEAK SIX DAYS NORTHEAST. IT DOESN'T MATTER THAT OUR COFFERS ARE EMPTY.
THE DUKE MUST BE NOTIFIED IMMEDIATELY.

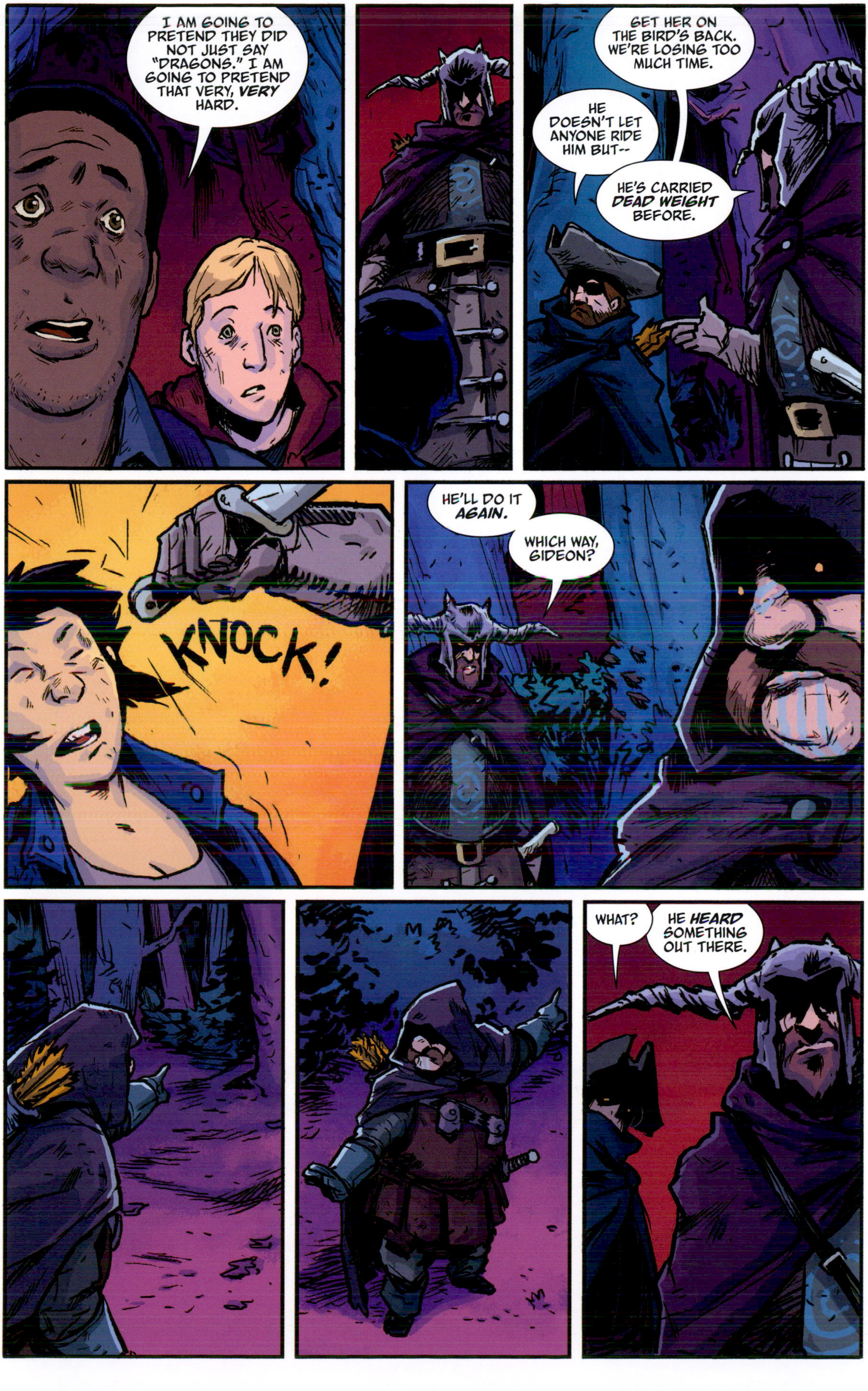
I AM GOING TO PRETEND THEY DID NOT JUST SAY "DRAGONS." I AM GOING TO PRETEND THAT VERY, VERY HARD.
GET HER ON THE BIRD'S BACK. WE'RE LOSING TOO MUCH TIME.
HE DOESN'T LET ANYONE RIDE HIM BUT--
HE'S CARRIED DEAD WEIGHT BEFORE.
KNOCK!
HE'LL DO IT AGAIN.
WHICH WAY, GIDEON?
WHAT?
HE HEARD SOMETHING OUT THERE.

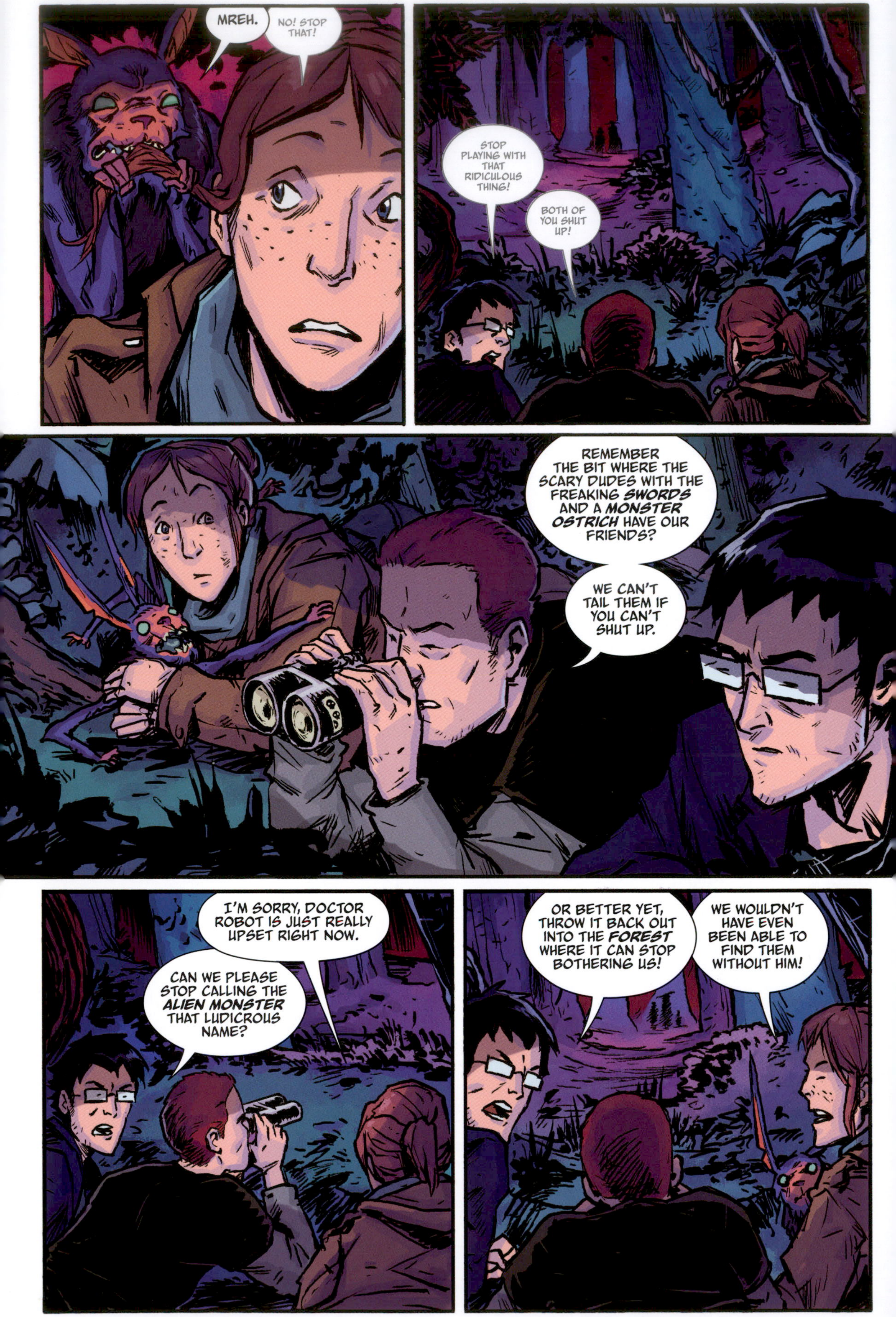
MREH.
NO! STOP THAT!
STOP PLAYING WITH THAT RIDICULOUS THING!
BOTH OF YOU SHUT UP!
REMEMBER THE BIT WHERE THE SCARY DUDES WITH THE FREAKING *SWORDS* AND A *MONSTER OSTRICH* HAVE OUR FRIENDS?
WE CAN'T TAIL THEM IF YOU CAN'T SHUT UP.
I'M SORRY, DOCTOR ROBOT IS JUST REALLY UPSET RIGHT NOW.
CAN WE PLEASE STOP CALLING THE *ALIEN MONSTER* THAT LUDICROUS NAME?
OR BETTER YET, THROW IT BACK OUT INTO THE *FOREST* WHERE IT CAN STOP BOTHERING US!
WE WOULDN'T HAVE EVEN BEEN ABLE TO FIND THEM WITHOUT HIM!

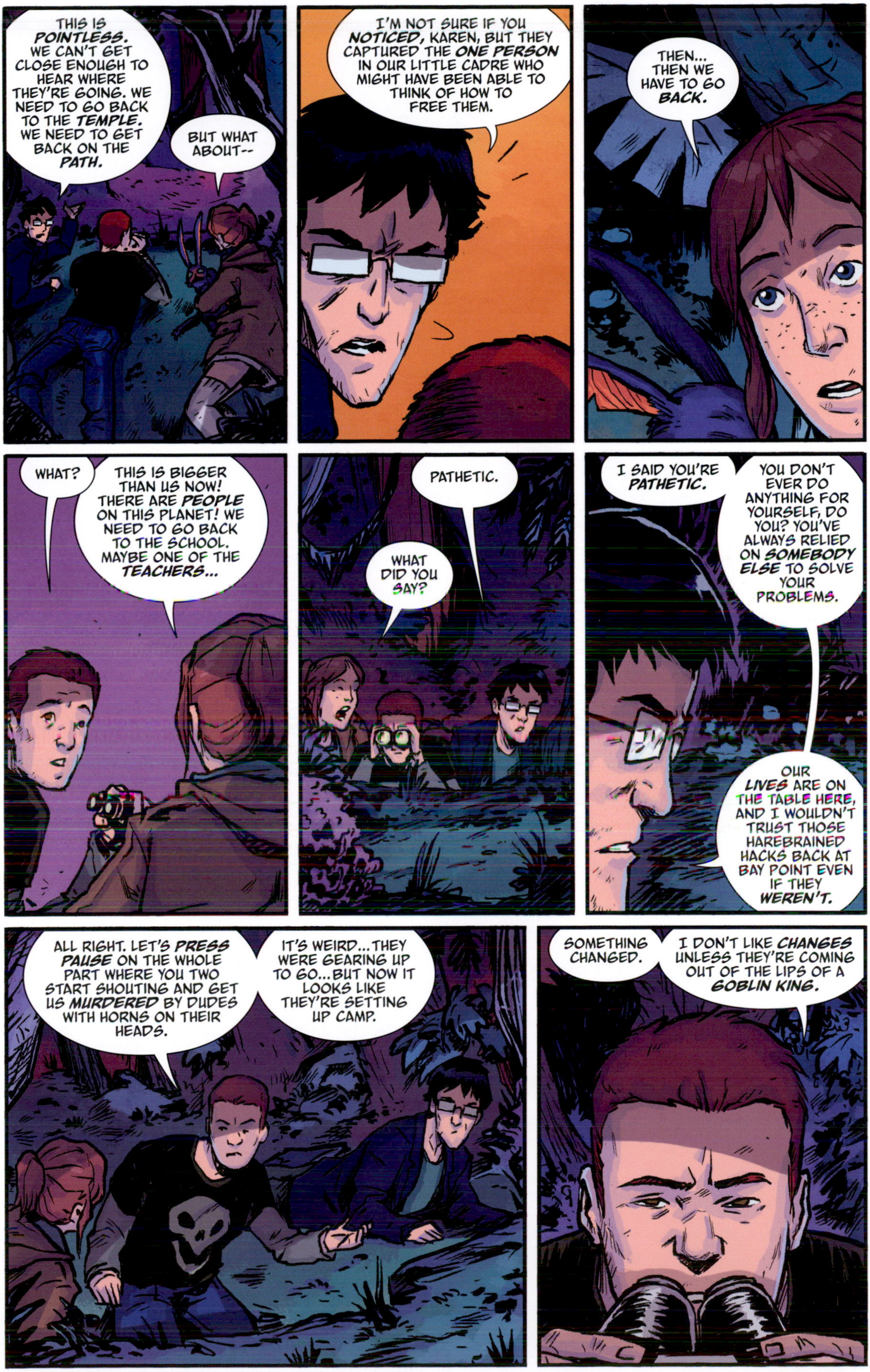
THIS IS POINTLESS. WE CAN'T GET CLOSE ENOUGH TO HEAR WHERE THEY'RE GOING. WE NEED TO GO BACK TO THE TEMPLE. WE NEED TO GET BACK ON THE PATH.
BUT WHAT ABOUT--
I'M NOT SURE IF YOU NOTICED, KAREN, BUT THEY CAPTURED THE ONE PERSON IN OUR LITTLE CADRE WHO MIGHT HAVE BEEN ABLE TO THINK OF HOW TO FREE THEM.
THEN... THEN WE HAVE TO GO BACK.
WHAT?
THIS IS BIGGER THAN US NOW! THERE ARE PEOPLE ON THIS PLANET! WE NEED TO GO BACK TO THE SCHOOL. MAYBE ONE OF THE TEACHERS...
PATHETIC.
WHAT DID YOU SAY?
I SAID YOU'RE PATHETIC.
YOU DON'T EVER DO ANYTHING FOR YOURSELF, DO YOU? YOU'VE ALWAYS RELIED ON SOMEBODY ELSE TO SOLVE YOUR PROBLEMS.
OUR LIVES ARE ON THE TABLE HERE, AND I WOULDN'T TRUST THOSE HAREBRAINED HACKS BACK AT BAY POINT EVEN IF THEY WEREN'T.
ALL RIGHT. LET'S PRESS PAUSE ON THE WHOLE PART WHERE YOU TWO START SHOUTING AND GET US MURDERED BY DUDES WITH HORNS ON THEIR HEADS.
IT'S WEIRD... THEY WERE GEARING UP TO GO... BUT NOW IT LOOKS LIKE THEY'RE SETTING UP CAMP.
SOMETHING CHANGED.
I DON'T LIKE CHANGES UNLESS THEY'RE COMING OUT OF THE LIPS OF A GOBLIN KING.

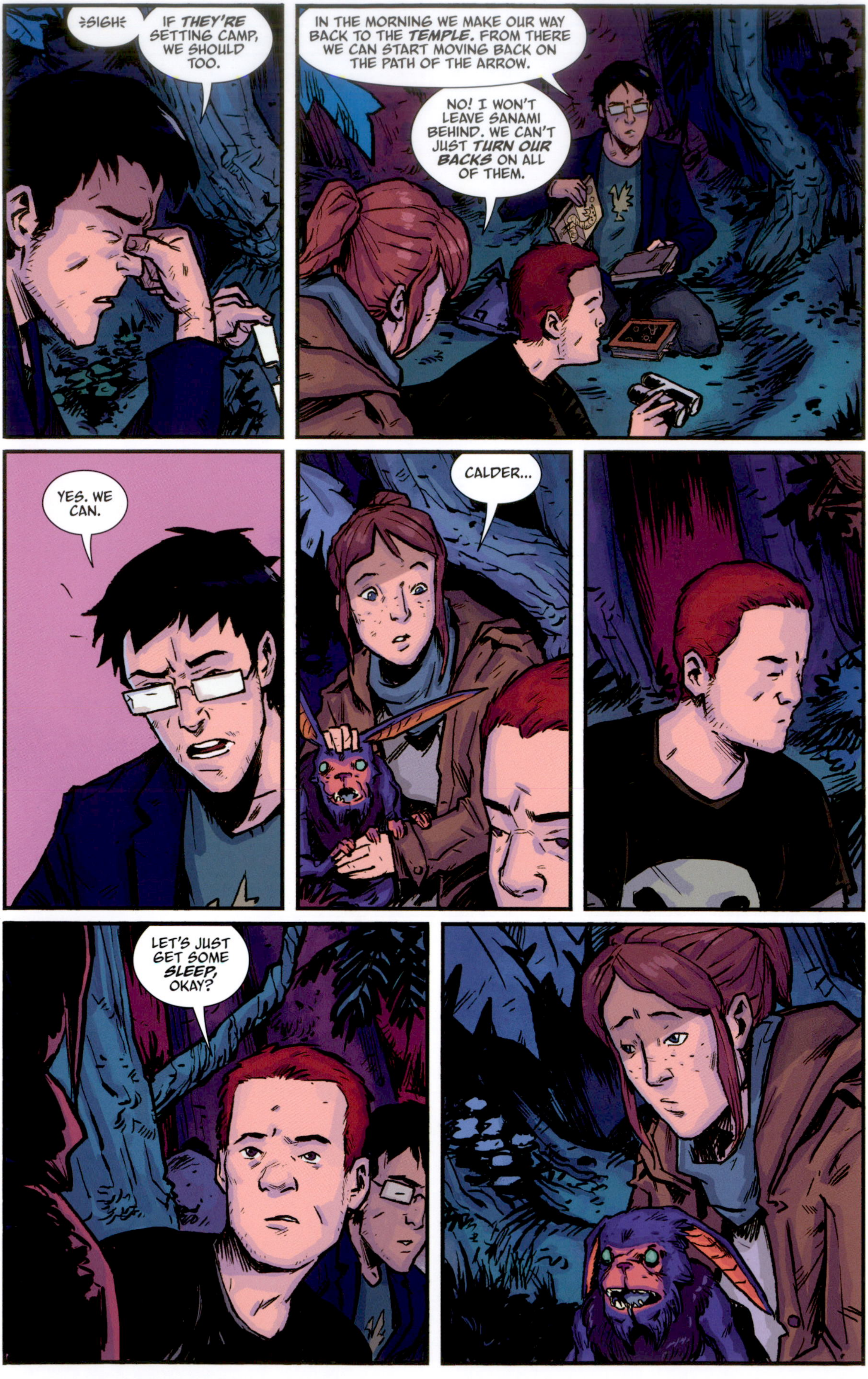

≷SIGH≶
IF *THEY'RE* SETTING CAMP, WE SHOULD TOO.
IN THE MORNING WE MAKE OUR WAY BACK TO THE *TEMPLE.* FROM THERE WE CAN START MOVING BACK ON THE PATH OF THE ARROW.
NO! I WON'T LEAVE SANAMI BEHIND. WE CAN'T JUST *TURN OUR BACKS* ON ALL OF THEM.
YES. WE CAN.
CALDER...
LET'S JUST GET SOME *SLEEP,* OKAY?

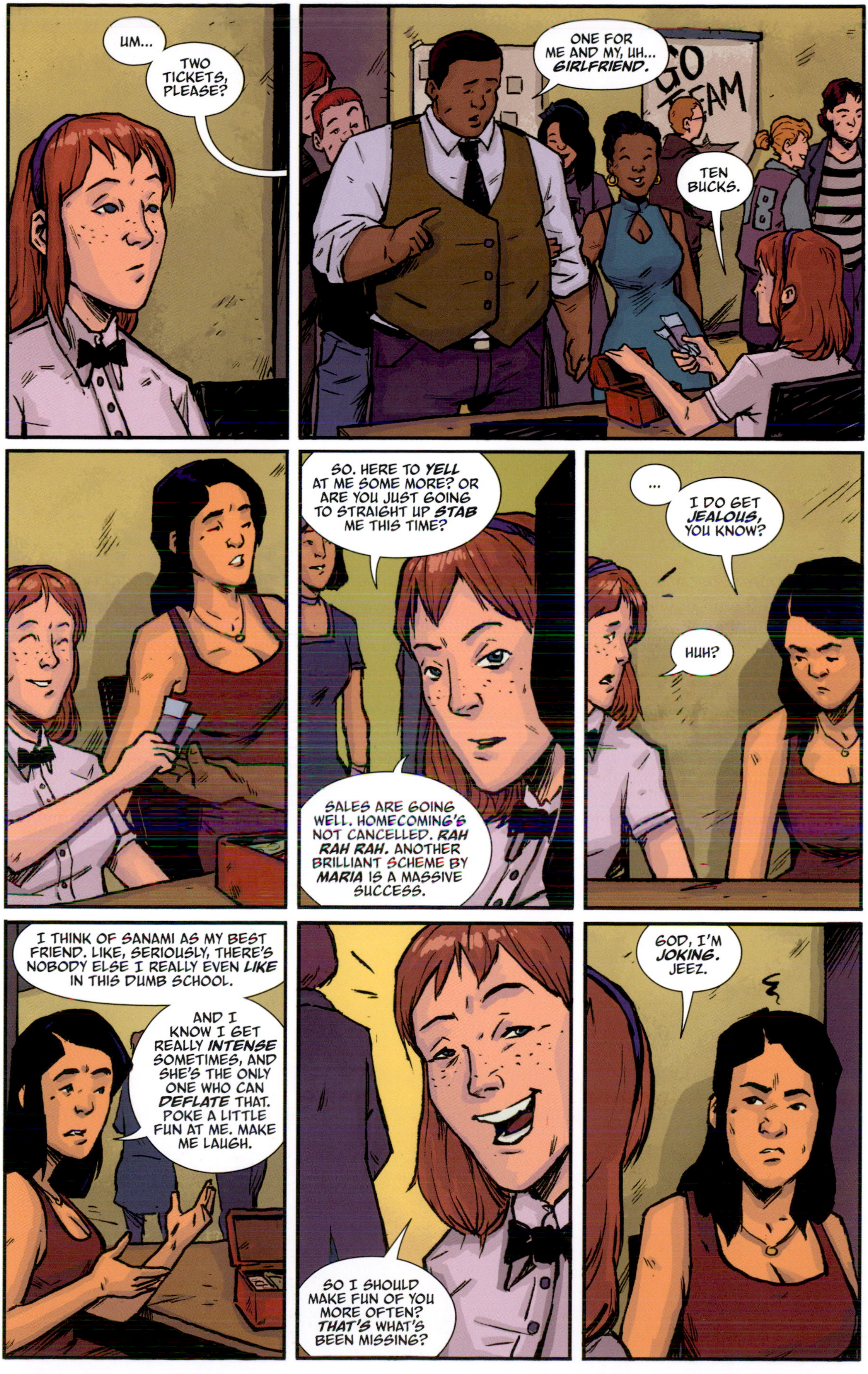
UM...
TWO TICKETS, PLEASE?
ONE FOR ME AND MY, UH... GIRLFRIEND.
GO TEAM
TEN BUCKS.
SO. HERE TO YELL AT ME SOME MORE? OR ARE YOU JUST GOING TO STRAIGHT UP STAB ME THIS TIME?
SALES ARE GOING WELL. HOMECOMING'S NOT CANCELLED. RAH RAH RAH. ANOTHER BRILLIANT SCHEME BY MARIA IS A MASSIVE SUCCESS.
...
I DO GET JEALOUS, YOU KNOW?
HUH?
I THINK OF SANAMI AS MY BEST FRIEND. LIKE, SERIOUSLY, THERE'S NOBODY ELSE I REALLY EVEN LIKE IN THIS DUMB SCHOOL.
AND I KNOW I GET REALLY INTENSE SOMETIMES, AND SHE'S THE ONLY ONE WHO CAN DEFLATE THAT. POKE A LITTLE FUN AT ME. MAKE ME LAUGH.
SO I SHOULD MAKE FUN OF YOU MORE OFTEN? THAT'S WHAT'S BEEN MISSING?
GOD, I'M JOKING. JEEZ.

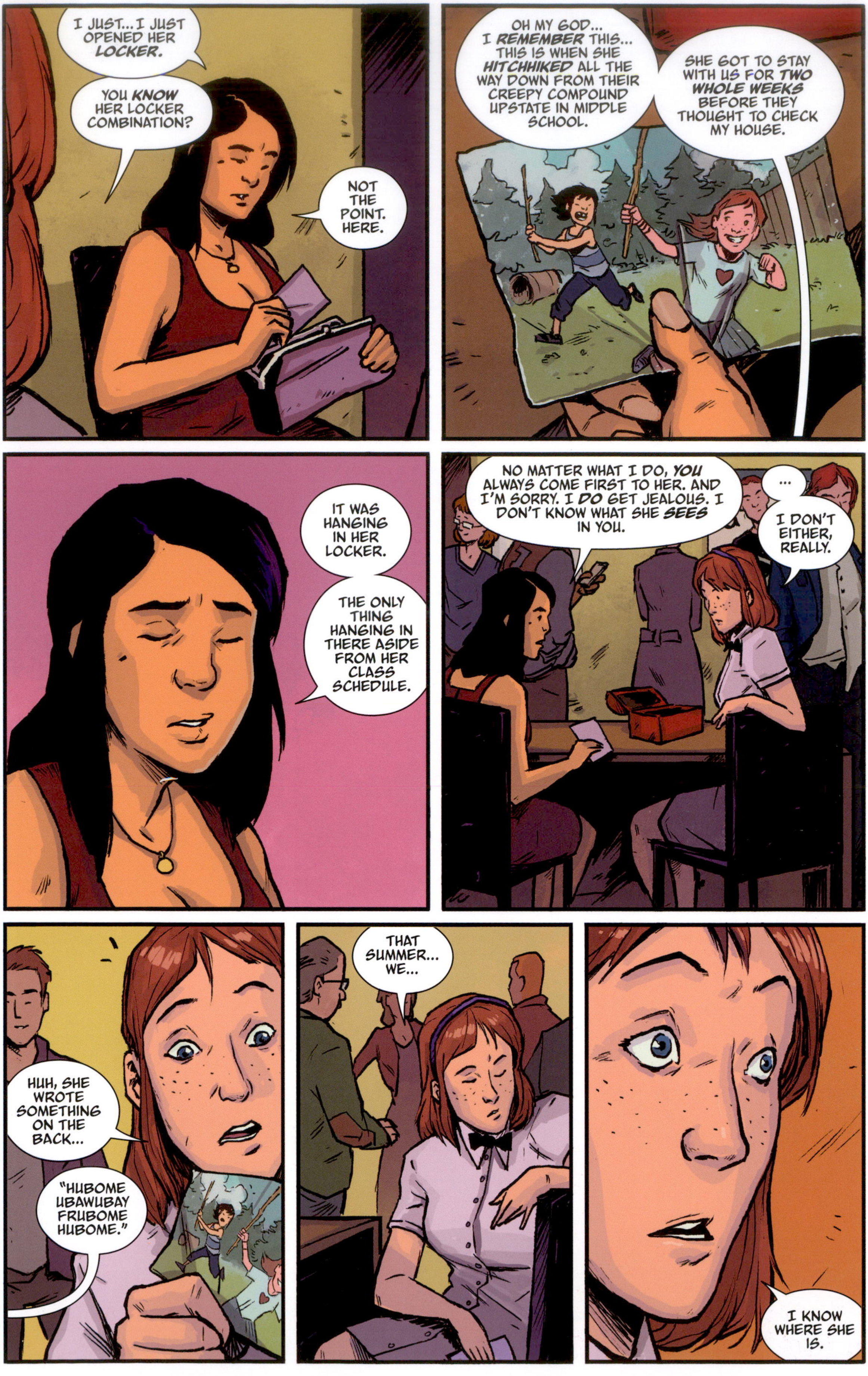
I JUST... I JUST OPENED HER LOCKER.
YOU KNOW HER LOCKER COMBINATION?
NOT THE POINT. HERE.
OH MY GOD... I REMEMBER THIS... THIS IS WHEN SHE HITCHHIKED ALL THE WAY DOWN FROM THEIR CREEPY COMPOUND UPSTATE IN MIDDLE SCHOOL.
SHE GOT TO STAY WITH US FOR TWO WHOLE WEEKS BEFORE THEY THOUGHT TO CHECK MY HOUSE.
IT WAS HANGING IN HER LOCKER.
THE ONLY THING HANGING IN THERE ASIDE FROM HER CLASS SCHEDULE.
NO MATTER WHAT I DO, YOU ALWAYS COME FIRST TO HER. AND I'M SORRY. I DO GET JEALOUS. I DON'T KNOW WHAT SHE SEES IN YOU.
...
I DON'T EITHER, REALLY.
HUH, SHE WROTE SOMETHING ON THE BACK...
"HUBOME UBAWUBAY FRUBOME HUBOME."
THAT SUMMER... WE...
I KNOW WHERE SHE IS.

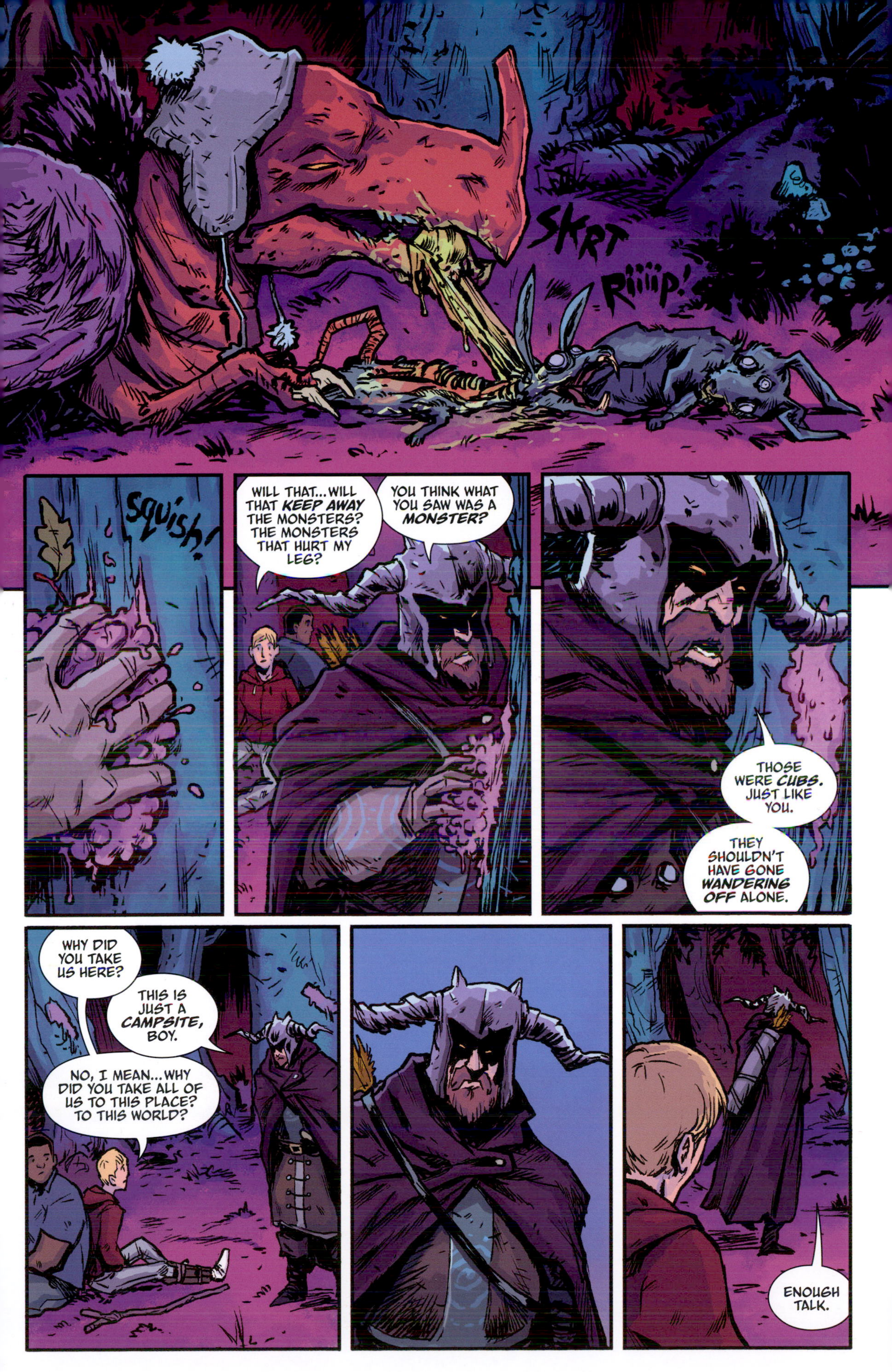
SKRT
Riiiip!
squish!
WILL THAT...WILL THAT KEEP AWAY THE MONSTERS? THE MONSTERS THAT HURT MY LEG?
YOU THINK WHAT YOU SAW WAS A MONSTER?
THOSE WERE CUBS. JUST LIKE YOU.
THEY SHOULDN'T HAVE GONE WANDERING OFF ALONE.
WHY DID YOU TAKE US HERE?
THIS IS JUST A CAMPSITE, BOY.
NO, I MEAN...WHY DID YOU TAKE ALL OF US TO THIS PLACE? TO THIS WORLD?
ENOUGH TALK.

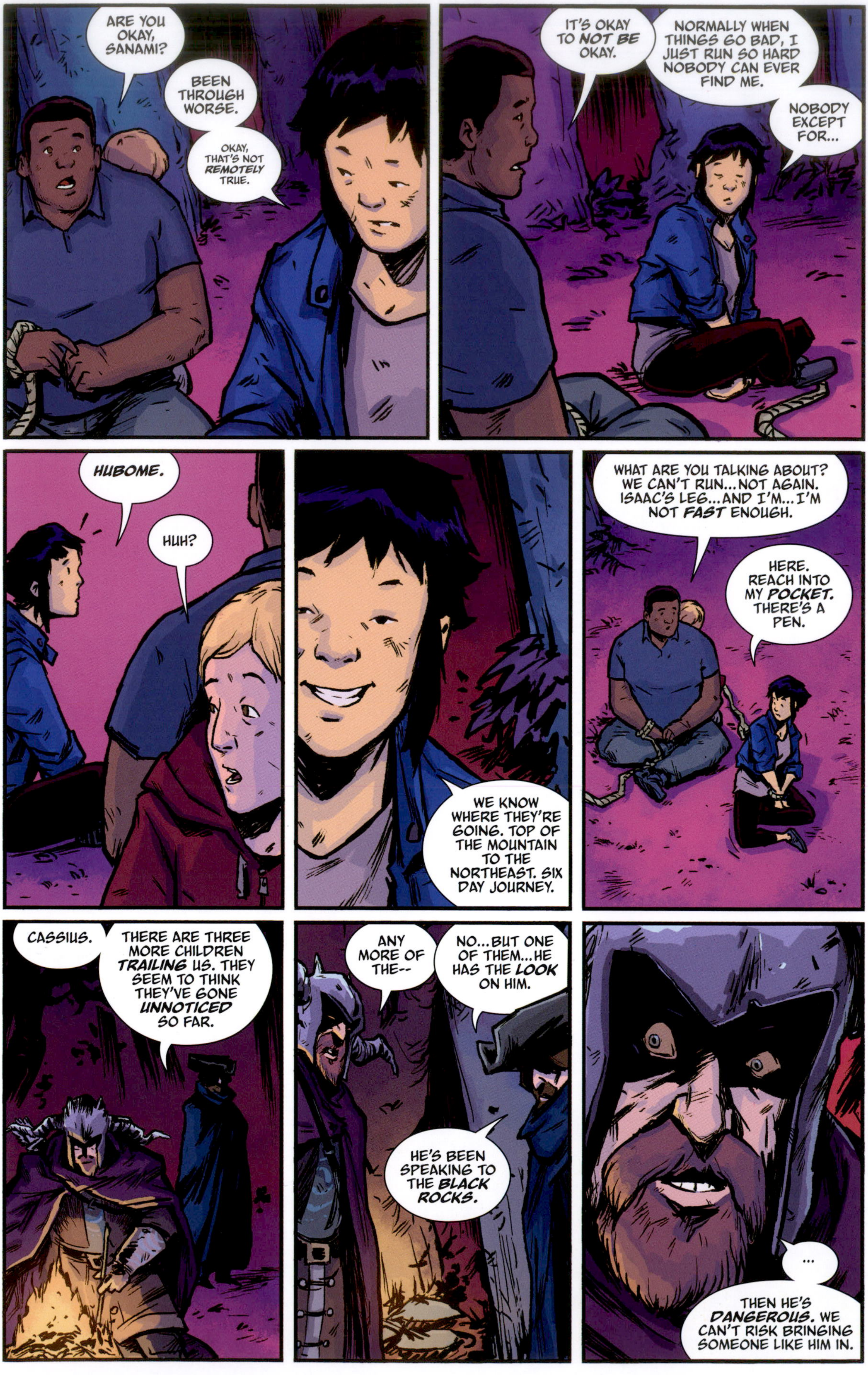
ARE YOU OKAY, SANAMI?
BEEN THROUGH WORSE.
OKAY, THAT'S NOT REMOTELY TRUE.
IT'S OKAY TO NOT BE OKAY.
NORMALLY WHEN THINGS GO BAD, I JUST RUN SO HARD NOBODY CAN EVER FIND ME.
NOBODY EXCEPT FOR...
HUBOME.
HUH?
WE KNOW WHERE THEY'RE GOING. TOP OF THE MOUNTAIN TO THE NORTHEAST. SIX DAY JOURNEY.
WHAT ARE YOU TALKING ABOUT? WE CAN'T RUN...NOT AGAIN. ISAAC'S LEG...AND I'M...I'M NOT FAST ENOUGH.
HERE. REACH INTO MY POCKET. THERE'S A PEN.
CASSIUS.
THERE ARE THREE MORE CHILDREN TRAILING US. THEY SEEM TO THINK THEY'VE GONE UNNOTICED SO FAR.
ANY MORE OF THE--
NO...BUT ONE OF THEM...HE HAS THE LOOK ON HIM.
HE'S BEEN SPEAKING TO THE BLACK ROCKS.
...
THEN HE'S DANGEROUS. WE CAN'T RISK BRINGING SOMEONE LIKE HIM IN.

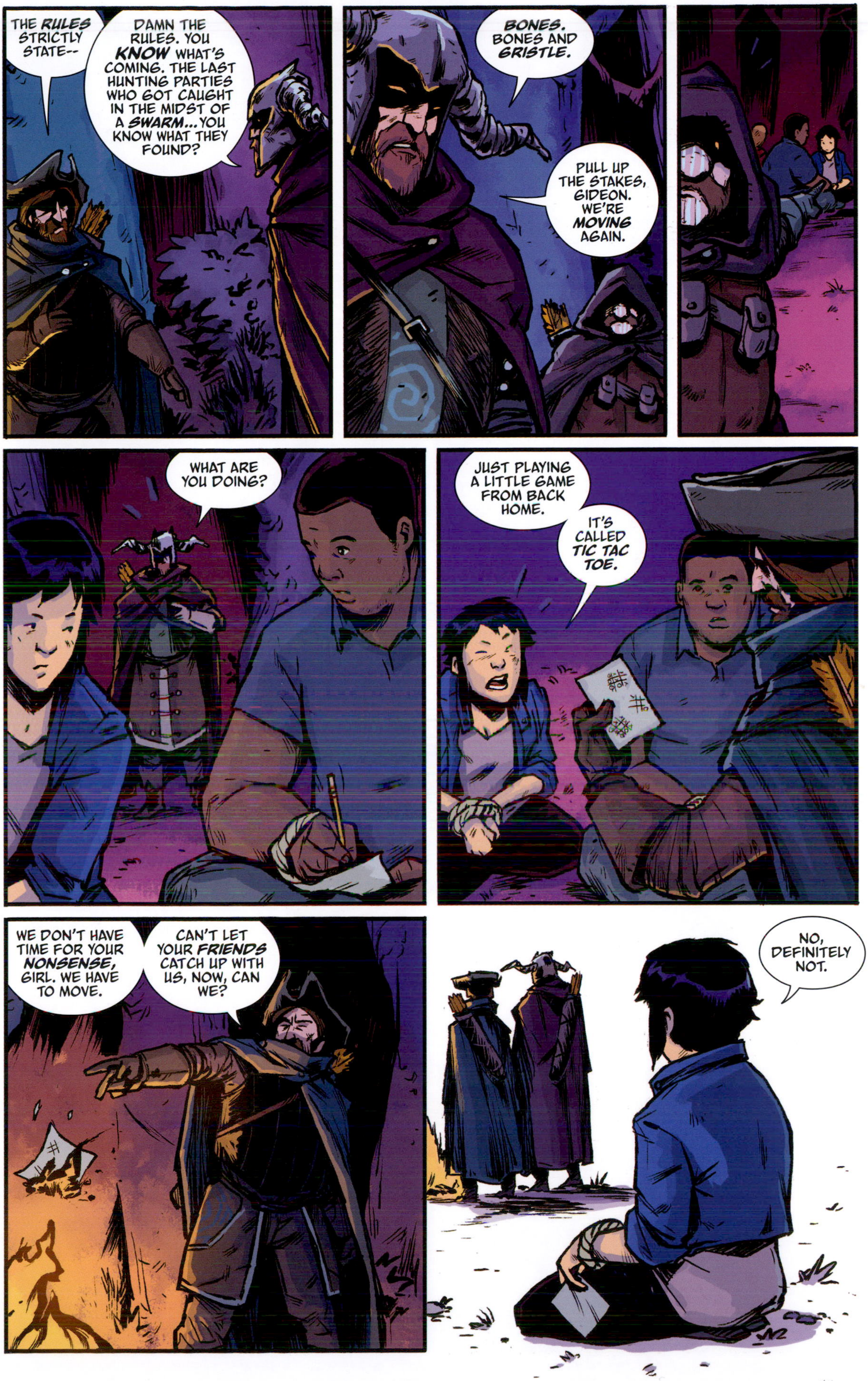
THE RULES STRICTLY STATE--
DAMN THE RULES. YOU KNOW WHAT'S COMING. THE LAST HUNTING PARTIES WHO GOT CAUGHT IN THE MIDST OF A SWARM... YOU KNOW WHAT THEY FOUND?
BONES. BONES AND GRISTLE.
PULL UP THE STAKES, GIDEON. WE'RE MOVING AGAIN.
WHAT ARE YOU DOING?
JUST PLAYING A LITTLE GAME FROM BACK HOME.
IT'S CALLED TIC TAC TOE.
WE DON'T HAVE TIME FOR YOUR NONSENSE, GIRL. WE HAVE TO MOVE.
CAN'T LET YOUR FRIENDS CATCH UP WITH US, NOW, CAN WE?
NO, DEFINITELY NOT.

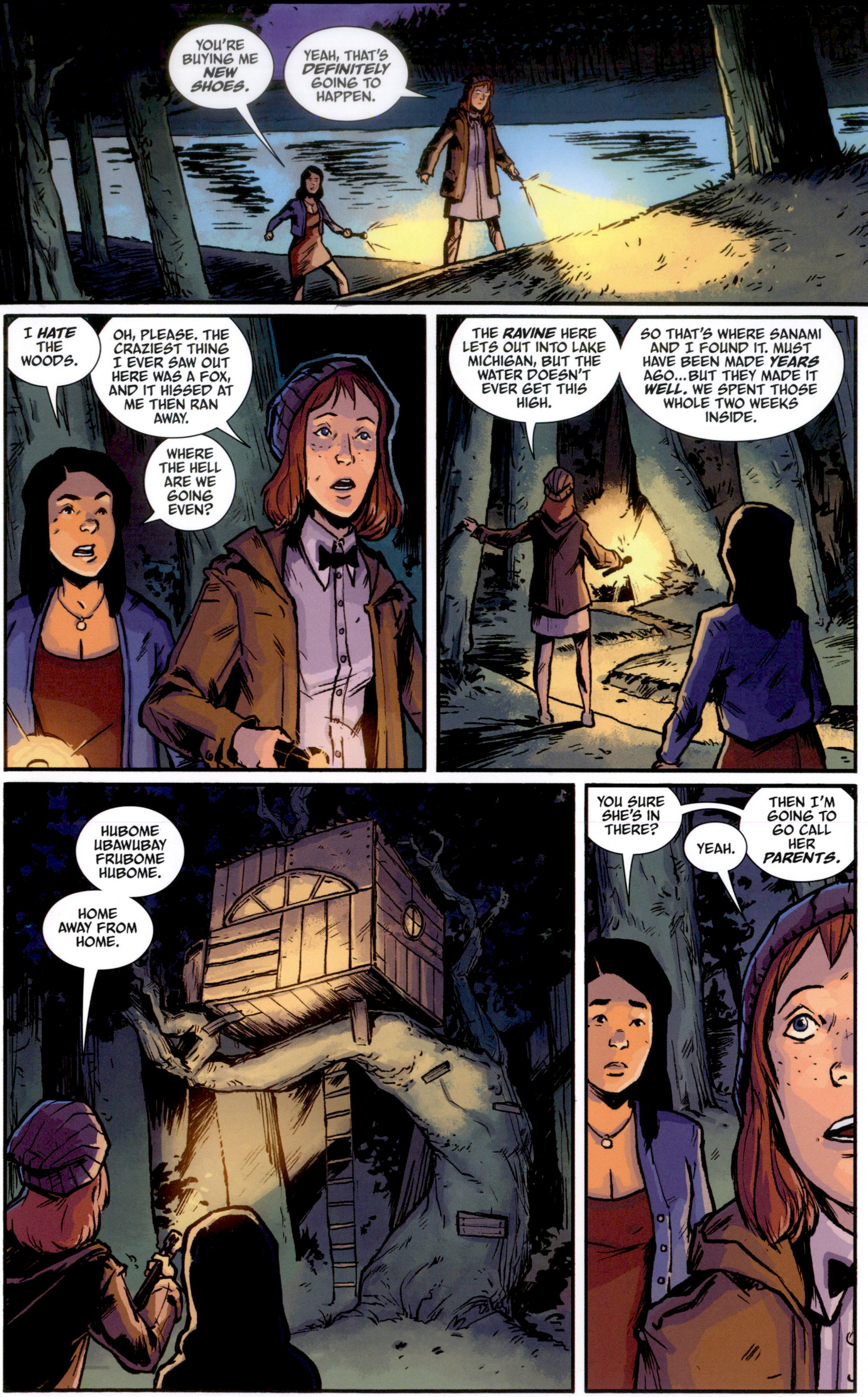
YOU'RE BUYING ME NEW SHOES.
YEAH, THAT'S DEFINITELY GOING TO HAPPEN.
I HATE THE WOODS.
OH, PLEASE. THE CRAZIEST THING I EVER SAW OUT HERE WAS A FOX, AND IT HISSED AT ME THEN RAN AWAY.
WHERE THE HELL ARE WE GOING EVEN?
THE RAVINE HERE LETS OUT INTO LAKE MICHIGAN, BUT THE WATER DOESN'T EVER GET THIS HIGH.
SO THAT'S WHERE SANAMI AND I FOUND IT. MUST HAVE BEEN MADE YEARS AGO...BUT THEY MADE IT WELL. WE SPENT THOSE WHOLE TWO WEEKS INSIDE.
HUBOME UBAWUBAY FRUBOME HUBOME.
HOME AWAY FROM HOME.
YOU SURE SHE'S IN THERE?
YEAH.
THEN I'M GOING TO GO CALL HER PARENTS.

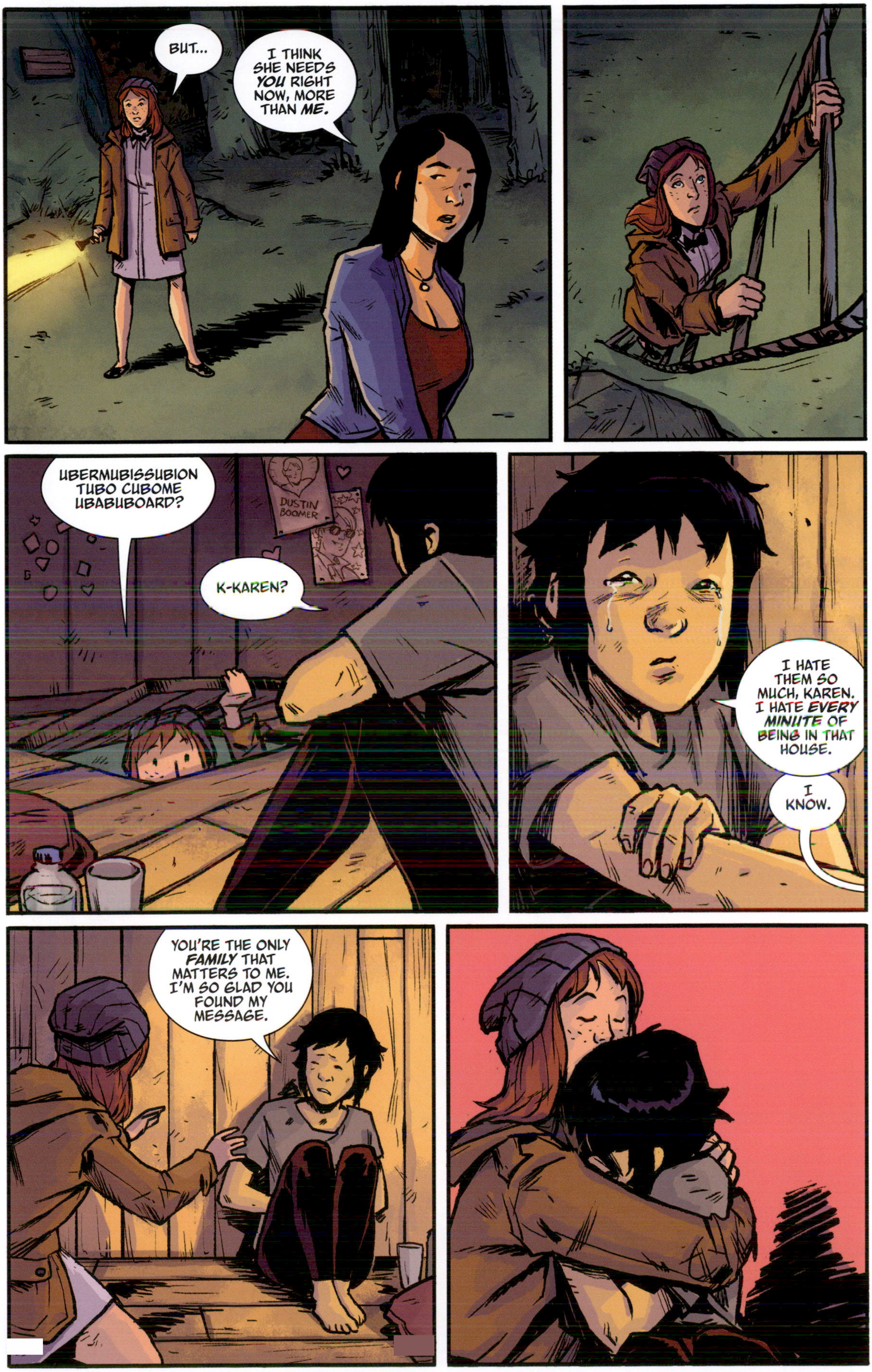
BUT...
I THINK SHE NEEDS YOU RIGHT NOW, MORE THAN ME.
UBERMUBISSUBION TUBO CUBOME UBABUBOARD?
DUSTIN BOOMER
K-KAREN?
I HATE THEM SO MUCH, KAREN. I HATE EVERY MINUTE OF BEING IN THAT HOUSE.
I KNOW.
YOU'RE THE ONLY FAMILY THAT MATTERS TO ME. I'M SO GLAD YOU FOUND MY MESSAGE.

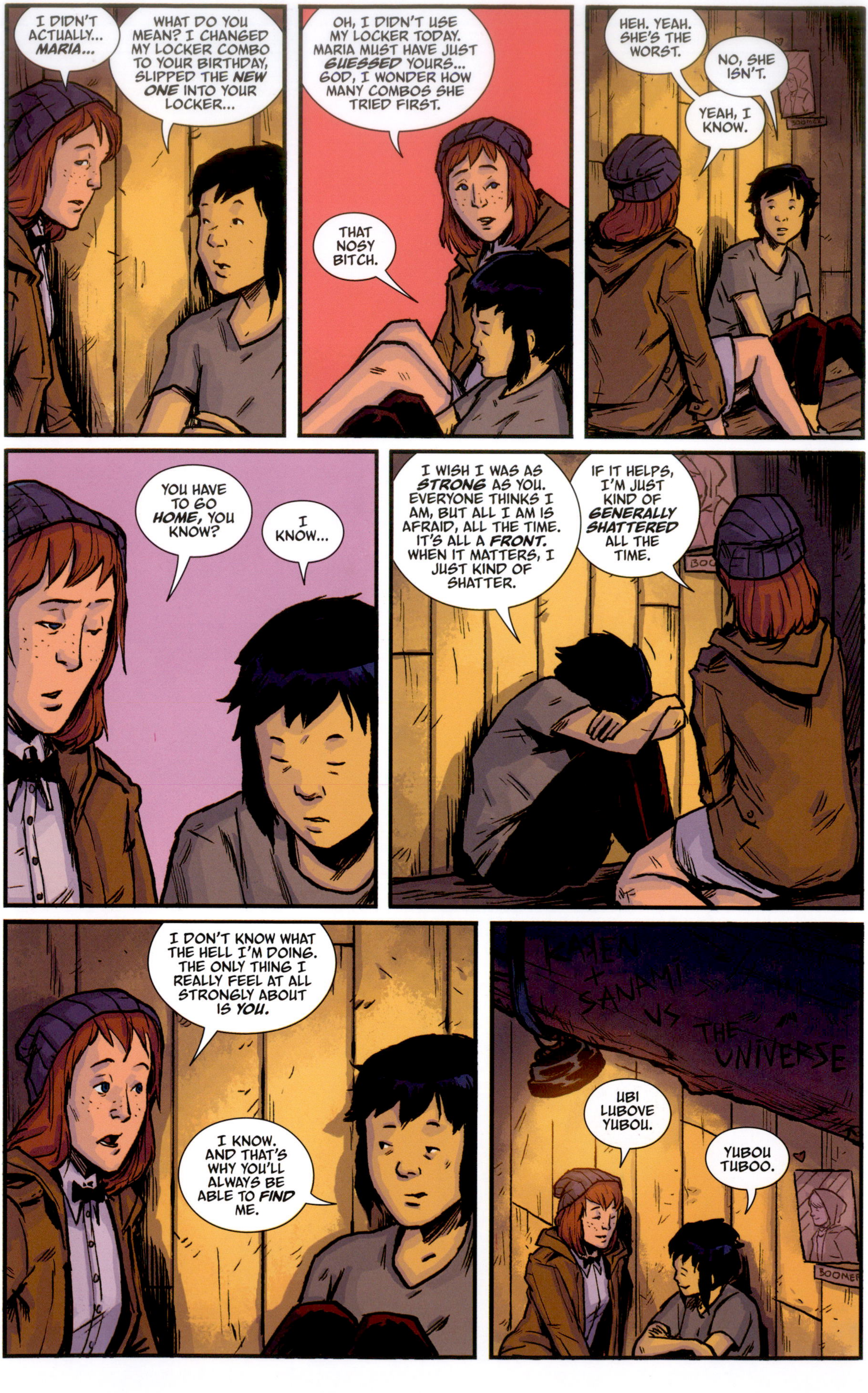
I DIDN'T ACTUALLY... MARIA...
WHAT DO YOU MEAN? I CHANGED MY LOCKER COMBO TO YOUR BIRTHDAY, SLIPPED THE NEW ONE INTO YOUR LOCKER...
OH, I DIDN'T USE MY LOCKER TODAY. MARIA MUST HAVE JUST GUESSED YOURS... GOD, I WONDER HOW MANY COMBOS SHE TRIED FIRST.
THAT NOSY BITCH.
HEH. YEAH. SHE'S THE WORST.
NO, SHE ISN'T.
YEAH, I KNOW.
YOU HAVE TO GO HOME, YOU KNOW?
I KNOW...
I WISH I WAS AS STRONG AS YOU. EVERYONE THINKS I AM, BUT ALL I AM IS AFRAID, ALL THE TIME. IT'S ALL A FRONT. WHEN IT MATTERS, I JUST KIND OF SHATTER.
IF IT HELPS, I'M JUST KIND OF GENERALLY SHATTERED ALL THE TIME.
I DON'T KNOW WHAT THE HELL I'M DOING. THE ONLY THING I REALLY FEEL AT ALL STRONGLY ABOUT IS YOU.
I KNOW. AND THAT'S WHY YOU'LL ALWAYS BE ABLE TO FIND ME.
KAREN + SANAMI VS THE UNIVERSE
UBI LUBOVE YUBOU.
YUBOU TUBOO.
BOOMER

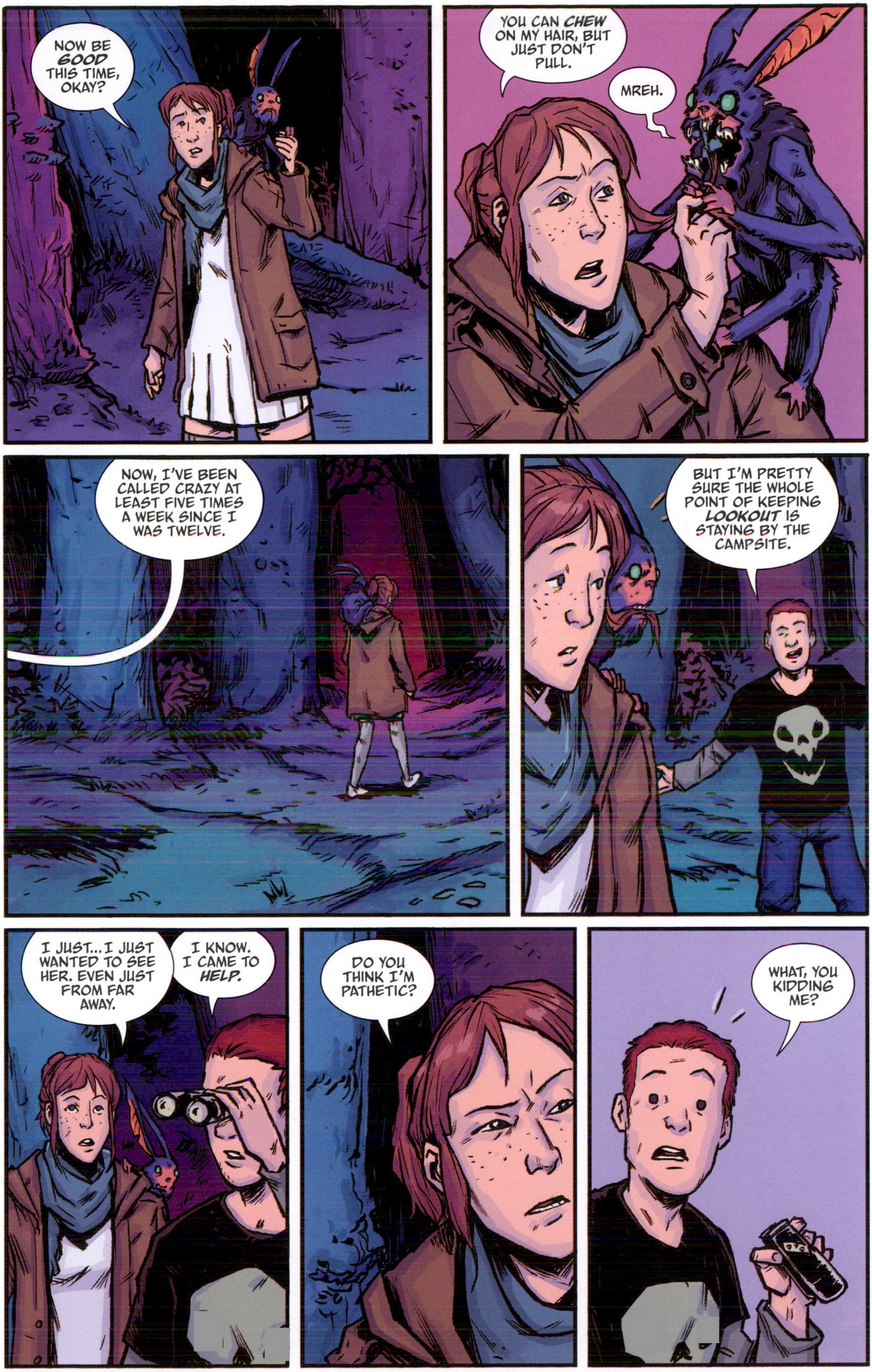
NOW BE GOOD THIS TIME, OKAY?
YOU CAN CHEW ON MY HAIR, BUT JUST DON'T PULL.
MREH.
NOW, I'VE BEEN CALLED CRAZY AT LEAST FIVE TIMES A WEEK SINCE I WAS TWELVE.
BUT I'M PRETTY SURE THE WHOLE POINT OF KEEPING LOOKOUT IS STAYING BY THE CAMPSITE.
I JUST... I JUST WANTED TO SEE HER. EVEN JUST FROM FAR AWAY.
I KNOW. I CAME TO HELP.
DO YOU THINK I'M PATHETIC?
WHAT, YOU KIDDING ME?

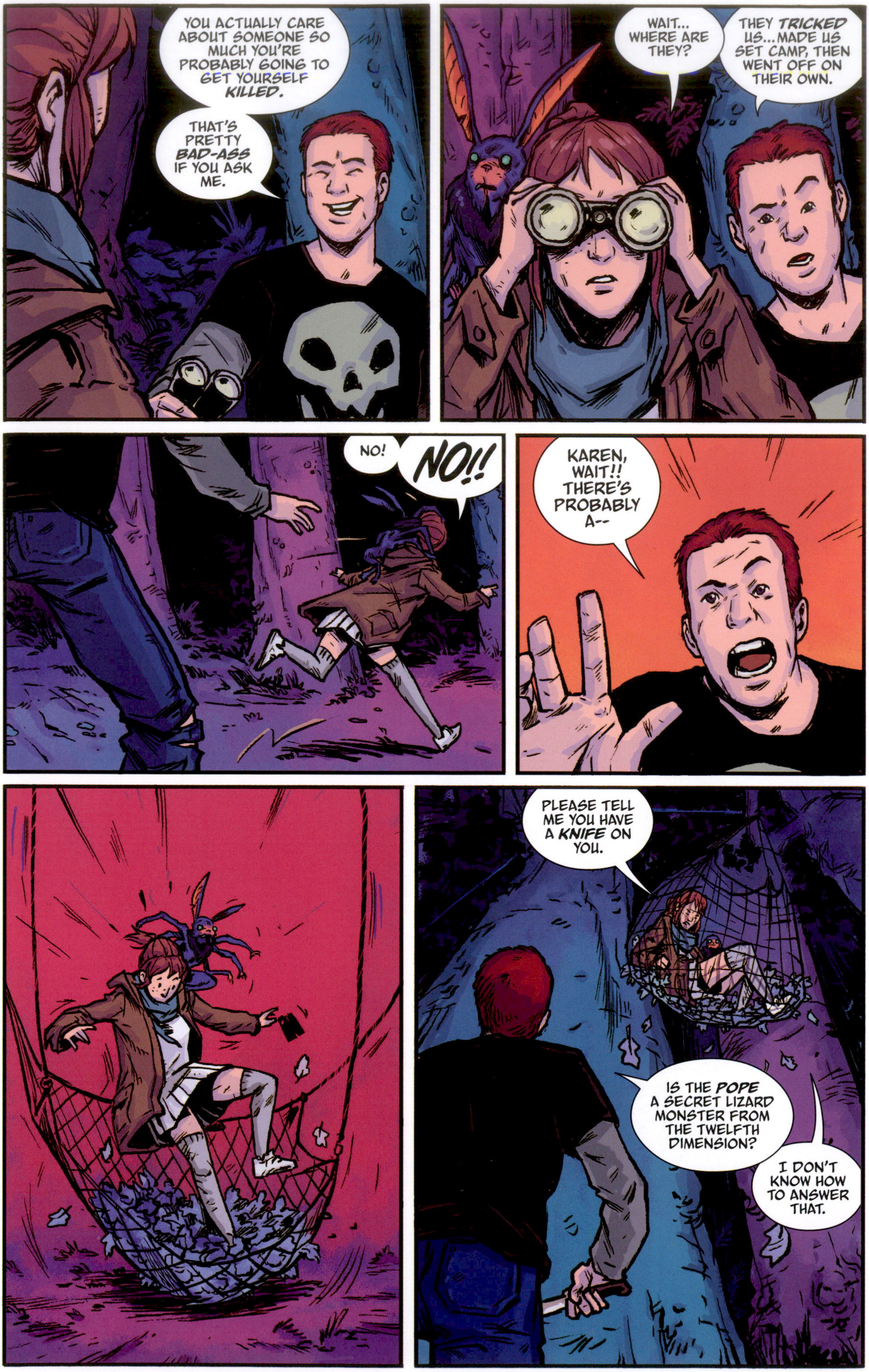
YOU ACTUALLY CARE ABOUT SOMEONE SO MUCH YOU'RE PROBABLY GOING TO GET YOURSELF KILLED.
THAT'S PRETTY BAD-ASS IF YOU ASK ME.
WAIT... WHERE ARE THEY?
THEY TRICKED US...MADE US SET CAMP, THEN WENT OFF ON THEIR OWN.
NO!
NO!!
KAREN, WAIT!! THERE'S PROBABLY A--
PLEASE TELL ME YOU HAVE A KNIFE ON YOU.
IS THE POPE A SECRET LIZARD MONSTER FROM THE TWELFTH DIMENSION?
I DON'T KNOW HOW TO ANSWER THAT.

I SAW A SPECIAL ON IT ON THE *HISTORY CHANNEL.*

OF COURSE YOU DID.

JUST *WATCH OUT.* THERE'S ANOTHER TRAP RIGHT BEHIND YOU...

DAMMIT!

HEY... IT'LL BE OKAY...

I MEAN... THEY'RE NOT *DEAD* OR ANYTHING.

HEY, COME ON.

WHAT THE--

WHAT DO YOU HAVE THERE...

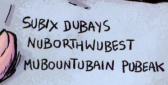

SUBIX DUBAYS NUBORTHWUBEST MUBOUNTUBAIN PUBEAK

UBI NUBEED YUBOU TUBO FUBIND MUBE UBAGUBAIN.

WHAT IS IT?

DIRECTIONS... WHERE THEY'RE GOING...

SO, WHAT DIFFERENCE DOES THAT MAKE?

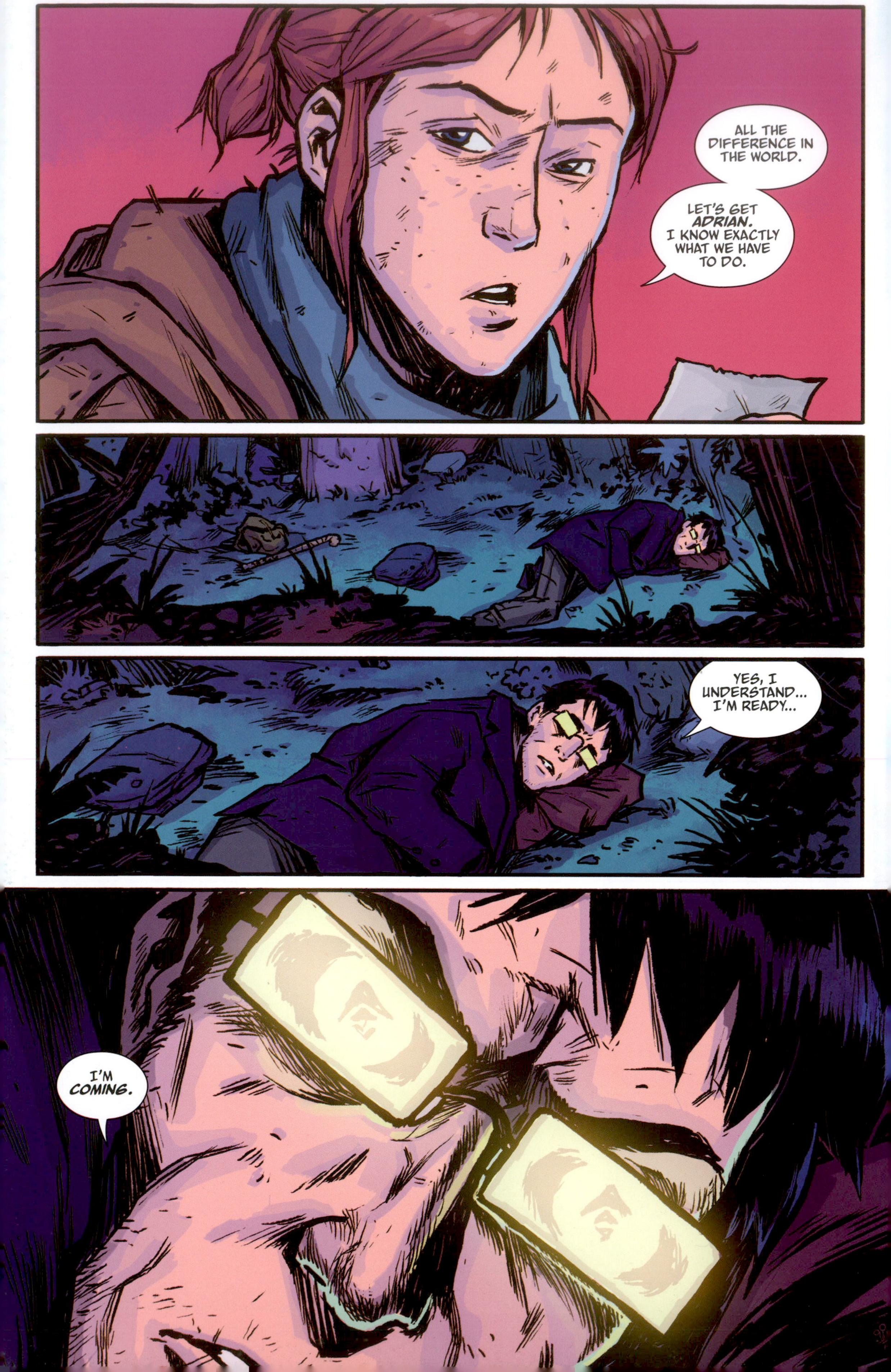
ALL THE DIFFERENCE IN THE WORLD.
LET'S GET ADRIAN. I KNOW EXACTLY WHAT WE HAVE TO DO.
YES, I UNDERSTAND... I'M READY...
I'M COMING.

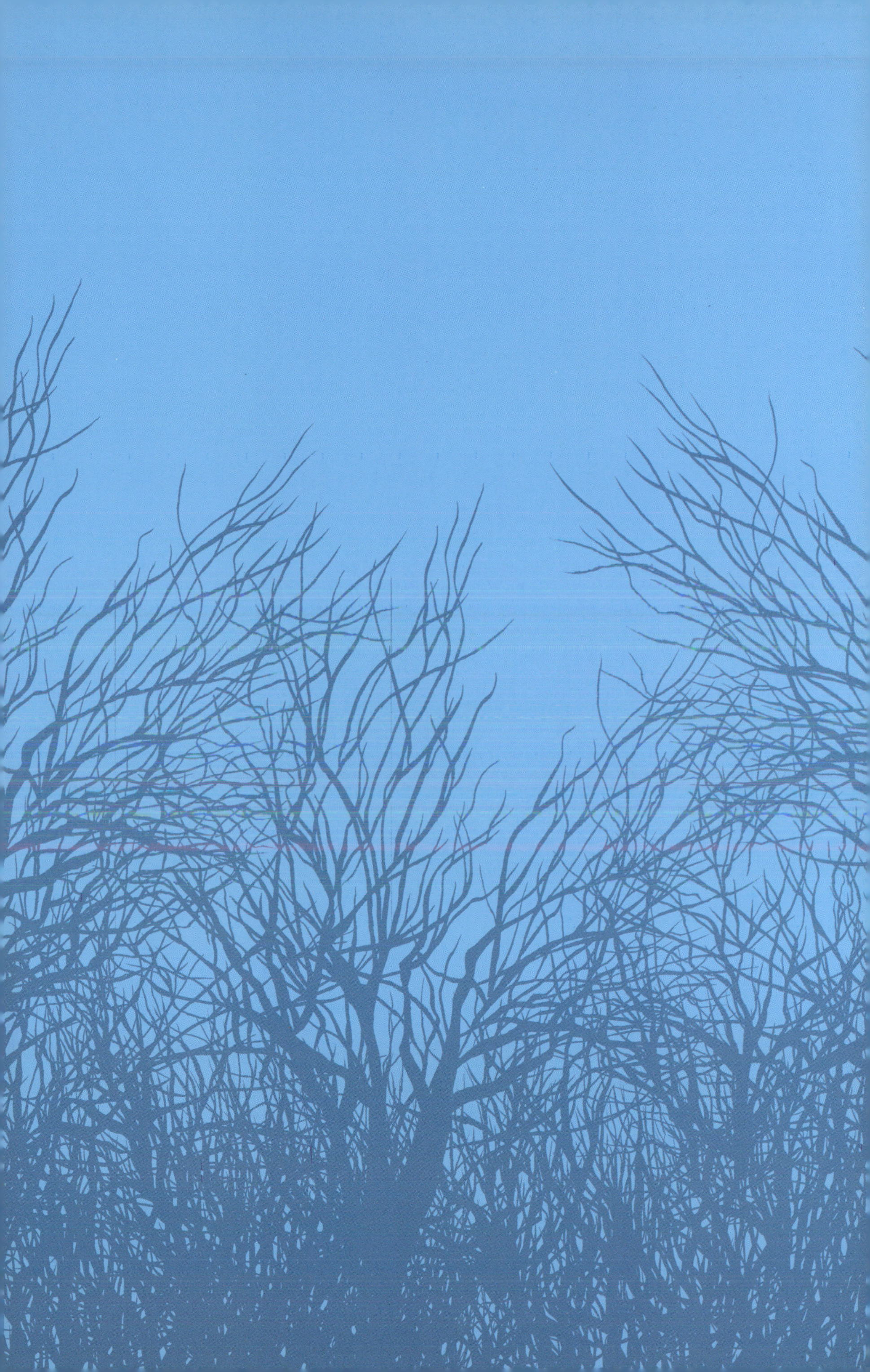

CHAPTER
SIX

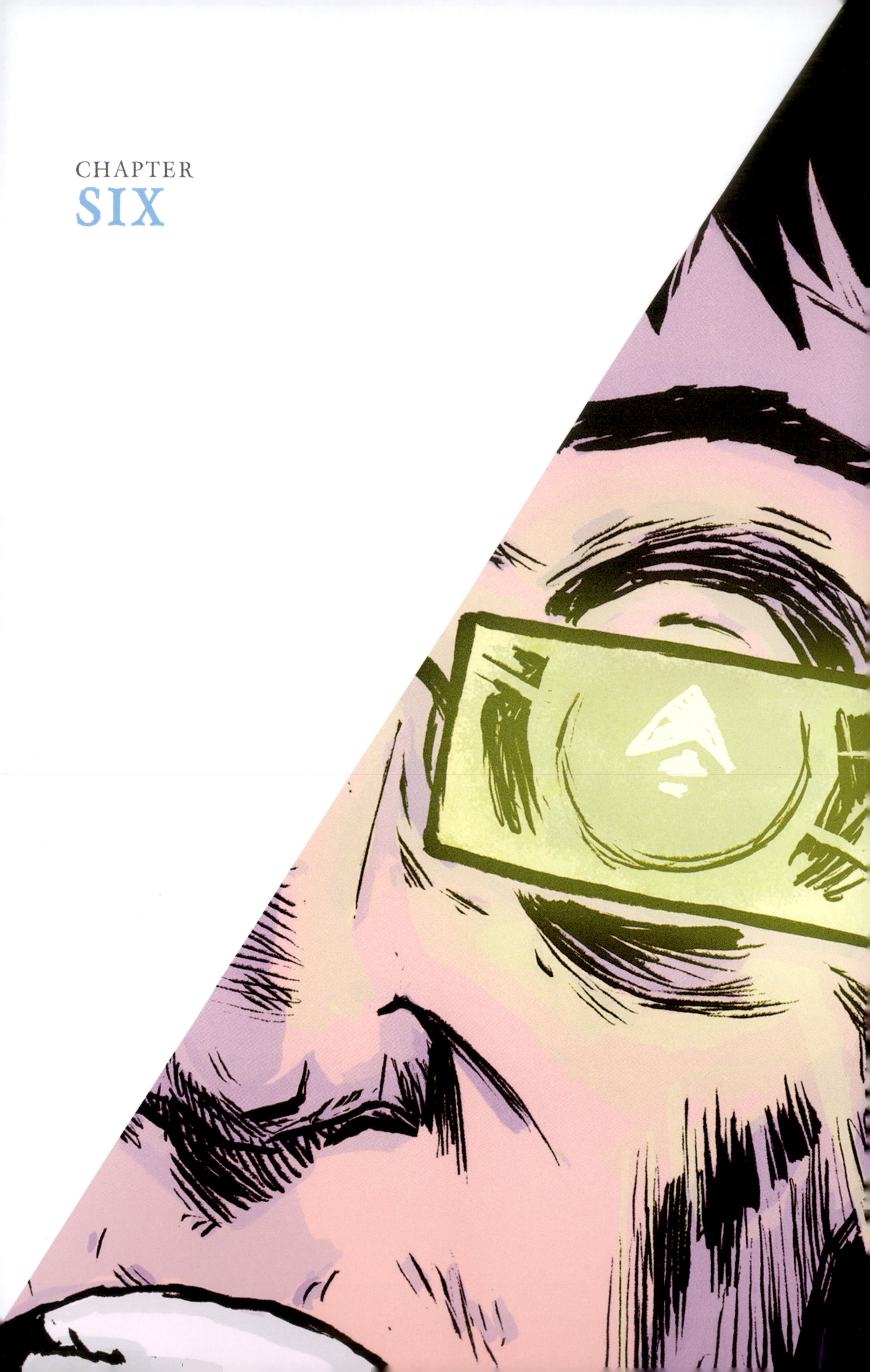

ONE YEAR AGO.

THEY THOUGHT HE WAS CRAZY. LIKE *FULL-ON* CRAZY.

AND HELL, MAYBE HE *WAS*.

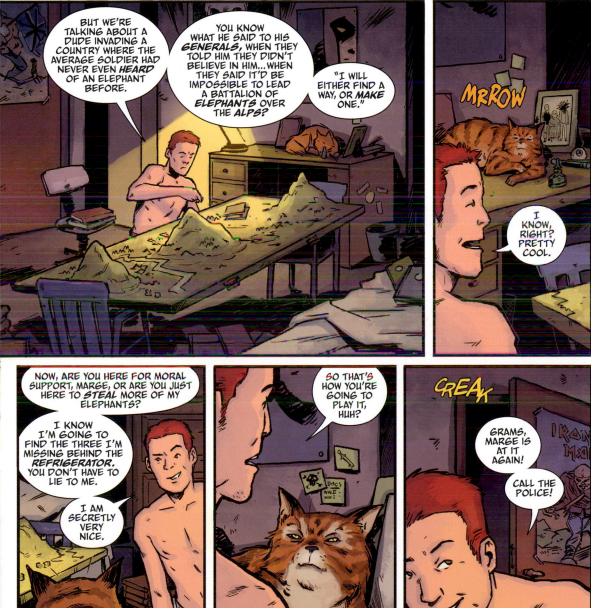

BUT WE'RE TALKING ABOUT A *DUDE* INVADING A COUNTRY WHERE THE AVERAGE SOLDIER HAD NEVER EVEN *HEARD* OF AN ELEPHANT BEFORE.

YOU KNOW WHAT HE SAID TO HIS *GENERALS*, WHEN THEY TOLD HIM THEY DIDN'T BELIEVE IN HIM...WHEN THEY SAID IT'D BE IMPOSSIBLE TO LEAD A BATTALION OF *ELEPHANTS* OVER THE *ALPS*?

"I WILL EITHER FIND A WAY, OR *MAKE* ONE."

MRROW

I KNOW, RIGHT? PRETTY COOL.

NOW, ARE YOU HERE FOR MORAL SUPPORT, MARGE, OR ARE YOU JUST HERE TO *STEAL* MORE OF MY ELEPHANTS?

I KNOW I'M GOING TO FIND THE THREE I'M MISSING BEHIND THE *REFRIGERATOR*. YOU DON'T HAVE TO LIE TO ME.

I AM SECRETLY VERY NICE.

SO THAT'S HOW YOU'RE GOING TO PLAY IT, HUH?

CREAK

GRAMS, MARGE IS AT IT AGAIN!

CALL THE POLICE!

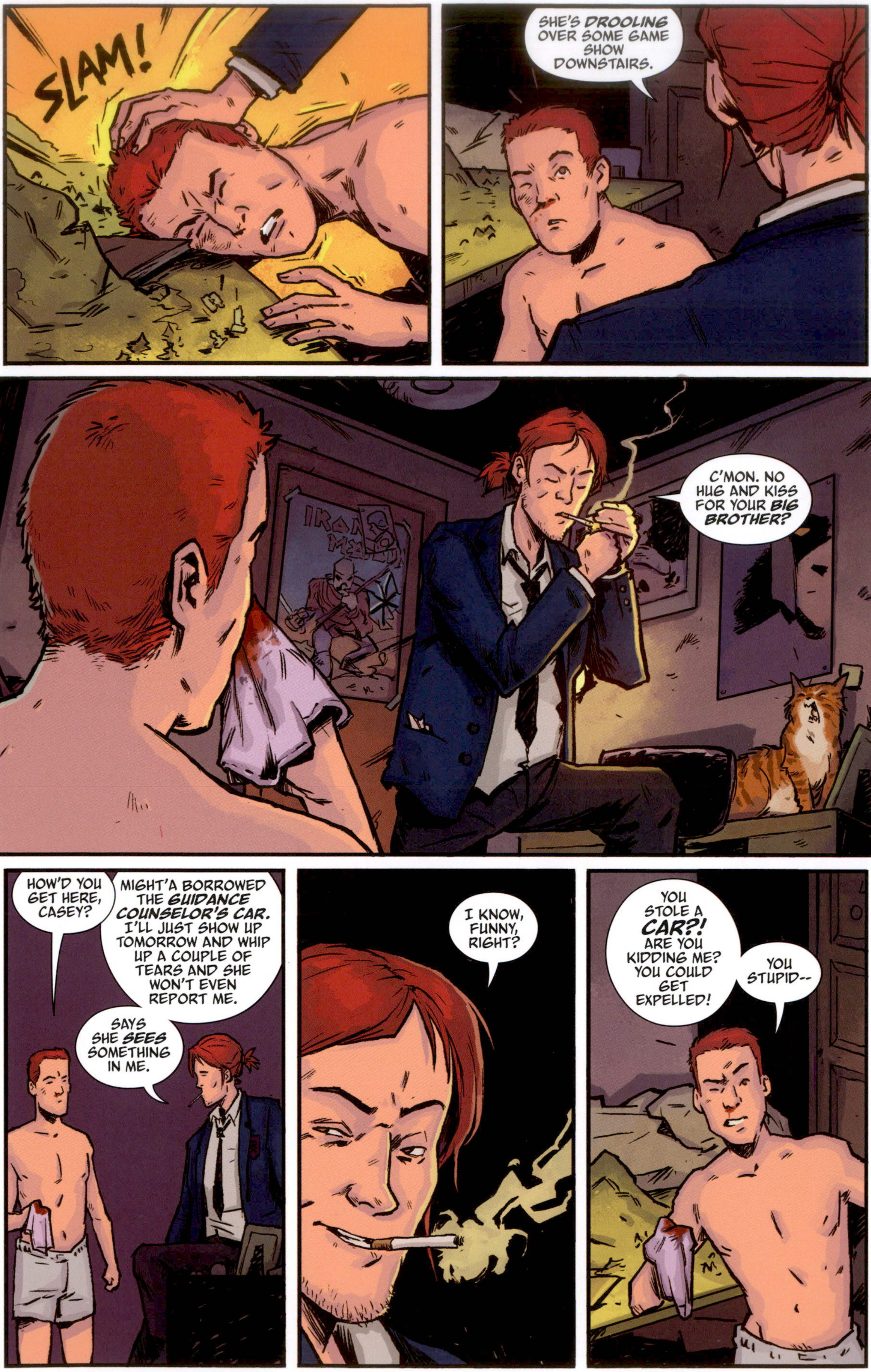
SLAM!
SHE'S DROOLING OVER SOME GAME SHOW DOWNSTAIRS.
C'MON. NO HUG AND KISS FOR YOUR BIG BROTHER?
HOW'D YOU GET HERE, CASEY?
MIGHT'A BORROWED THE GUIDANCE COUNSELOR'S CAR. I'LL JUST SHOW UP TOMORROW AND WHIP UP A COUPLE OF TEARS AND SHE WON'T EVEN REPORT ME.
SAYS SHE SEES SOMETHING IN ME.
I KNOW, FUNNY, RIGHT?
YOU STOLE A CAR?! ARE YOU KIDDING ME? YOU COULD GET EXPELLED!
YOU STUPID--

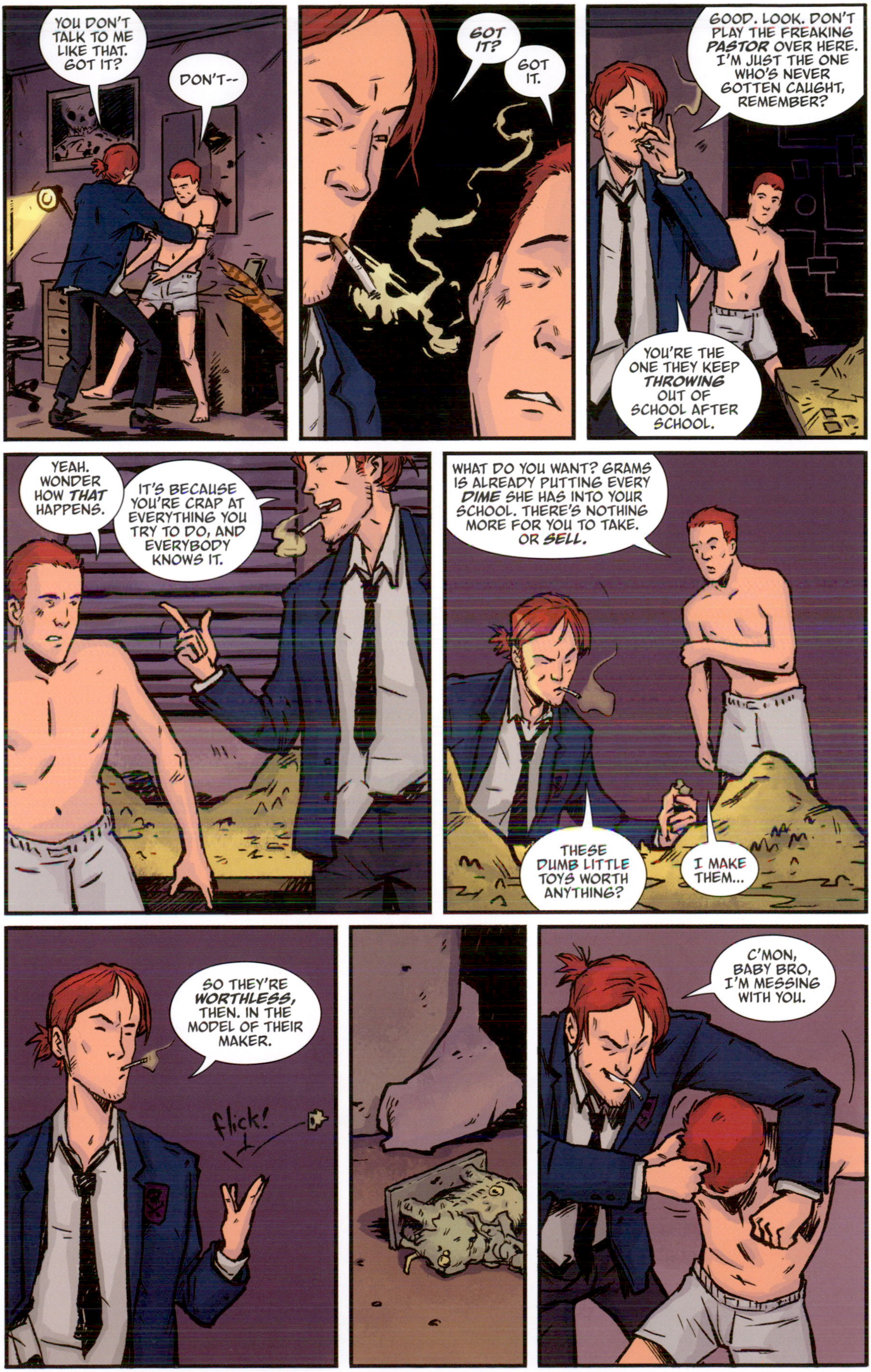
YOU DON'T TALK TO ME LIKE THAT. GOT IT?
DON'T--
GOT IT?
GOT IT.
GOOD. LOOK. DON'T PLAY THE FREAKING PASTOR OVER HERE. I'M JUST THE ONE WHO'S NEVER GOTTEN CAUGHT, REMEMBER?
YOU'RE THE ONE THEY KEEP THROWING OUT OF SCHOOL AFTER SCHOOL.
YEAH. WONDER HOW THAT HAPPENS.
IT'S BECAUSE YOU'RE CRAP AT EVERYTHING YOU TRY TO DO, AND EVERYBODY KNOWS IT.
WHAT DO YOU WANT? GRAMS IS ALREADY PUTTING EVERY DIME SHE HAS INTO YOUR SCHOOL. THERE'S NOTHING MORE FOR YOU TO TAKE. OR SELL.
THESE DUMB LITTLE TOYS WORTH ANYTHING?
I MAKE THEM...
SO THEY'RE WORTHLESS, THEN. IN THE MODEL OF THEIR MAKER.
flick!
C'MON, BABY BRO, I'M MESSING WITH YOU.

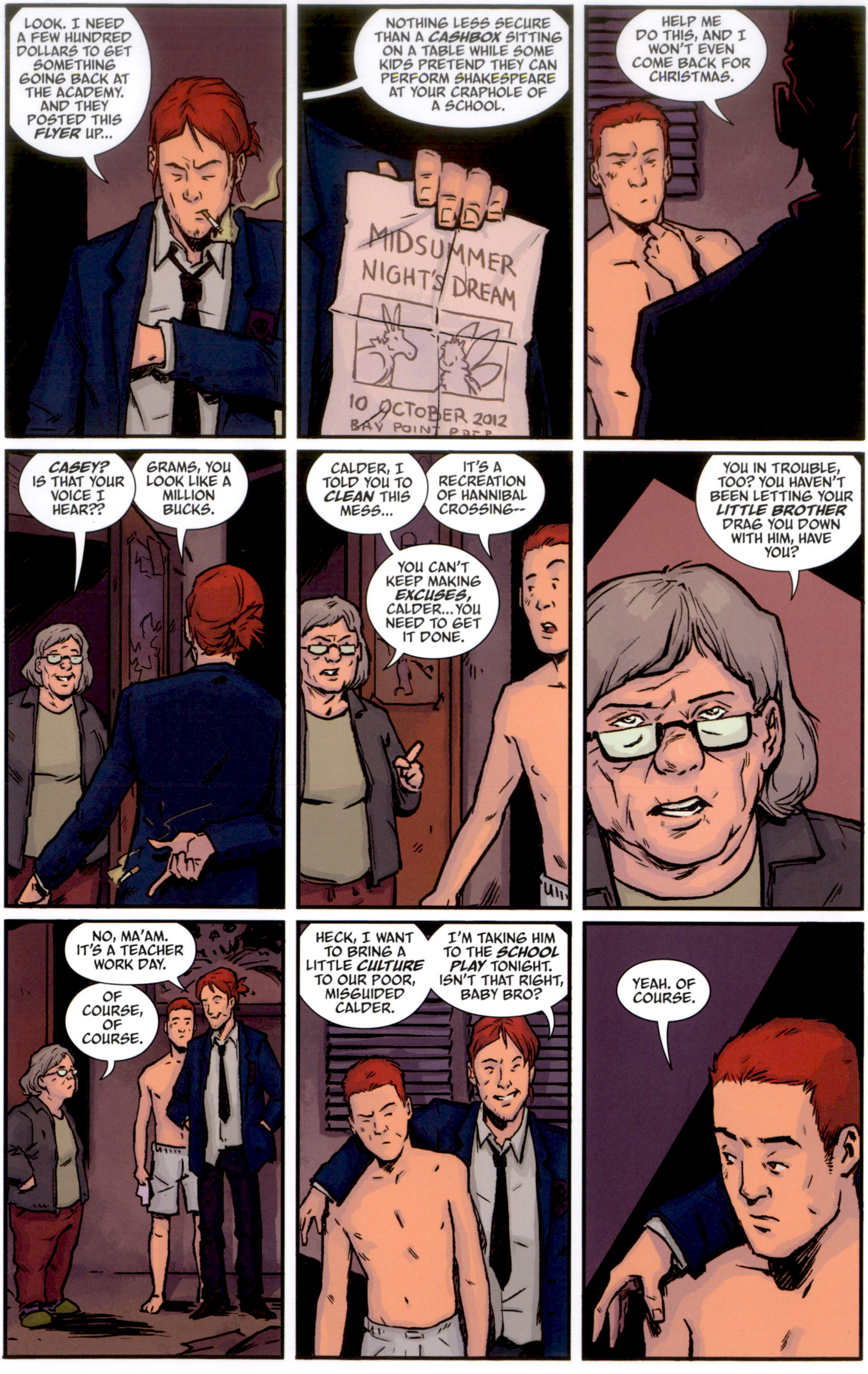
LOOK. I NEED A FEW HUNDRED DOLLARS TO GET SOMETHING GOING BACK AT THE ACADEMY. AND THEY POSTED THIS FLYER UP...
NOTHING LESS SECURE THAN A CASHBOX SITTING ON A TABLE WHILE SOME KIDS PRETEND THEY CAN PERFORM SHAKESPEARE AT YOUR CRAPHOLE OF A SCHOOL.
MIDSUMMER NIGHT'S DREAM
10 OCTOBER 2012
HELP ME DO THIS, AND I WON'T EVEN COME BACK FOR CHRISTMAS.
CASEY? IS THAT YOUR VOICE I HEAR??
GRAMS, YOU LOOK LIKE A MILLION BUCKS.
CALDER, I TOLD YOU TO CLEAN THIS MESS...
IT'S A RECREATION OF HANNIBAL CROSSING--
YOU CAN'T KEEP MAKING EXCUSES, CALDER... YOU NEED TO GET IT DONE.
YOU IN TROUBLE, TOO? YOU HAVEN'T BEEN LETTING YOUR LITTLE BROTHER DRAG YOU DOWN WITH HIM, HAVE YOU?
NO, MA'AM. IT'S A TEACHER WORK DAY.
OF COURSE, OF COURSE.
HECK, I WANT TO BRING A LITTLE CULTURE TO OUR POOR, MISGUIDED CALDER.
I'M TAKING HIM TO THE SCHOOL PLAY TONIGHT. ISN'T THAT RIGHT, BABY BRO?
YEAH. OF COURSE.

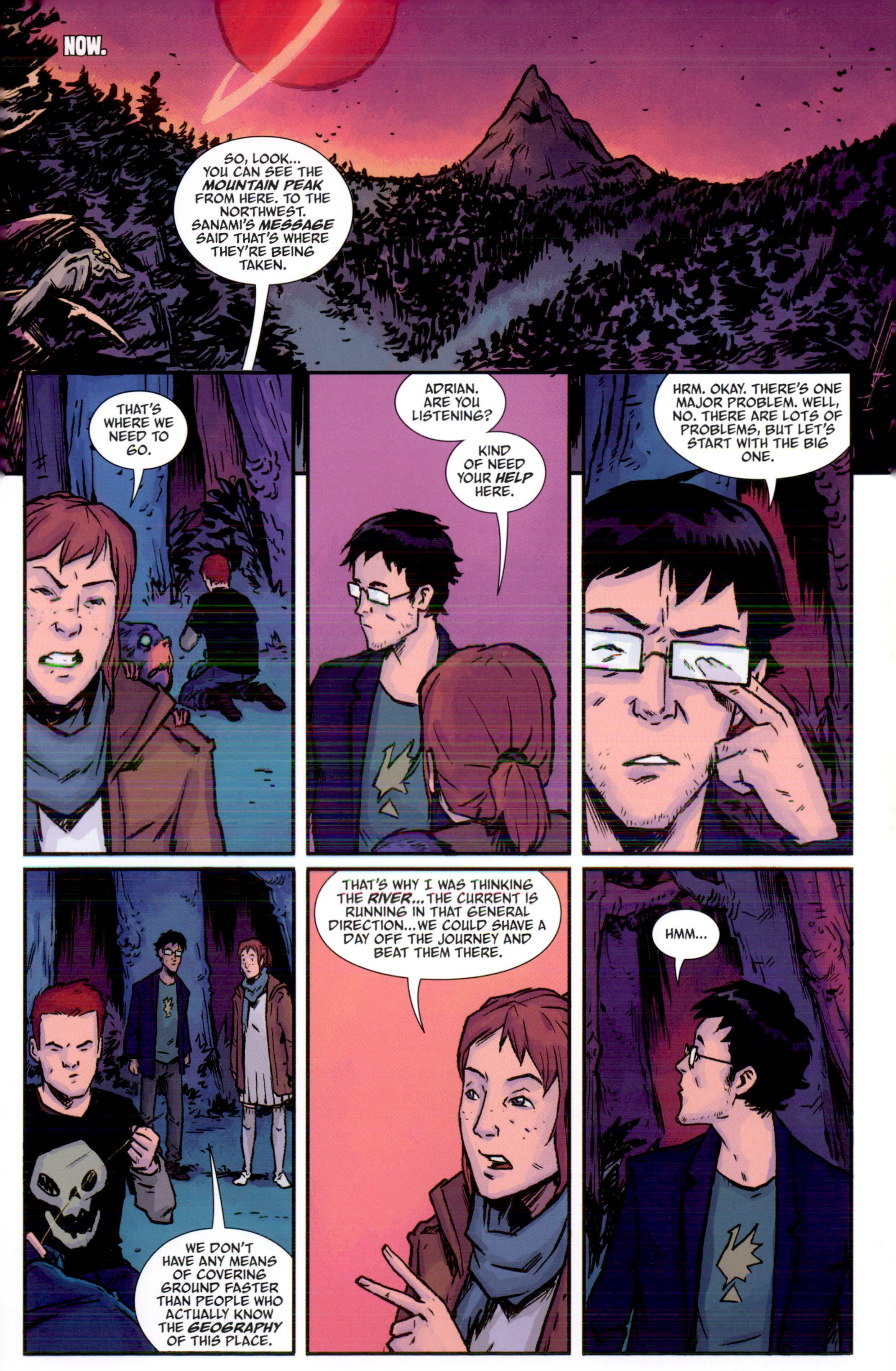
NOW.
SO, LOOK... YOU CAN SEE THE MOUNTAIN PEAK FROM HERE. TO THE NORTHWEST. SANAMI'S MESSAGE SAID THAT'S WHERE THEY'RE BEING TAKEN.
THAT'S WHERE WE NEED TO GO.
ADRIAN. ARE YOU LISTENING?
KIND OF NEED YOUR HELP HERE.
HRM. OKAY. THERE'S ONE MAJOR PROBLEM. WELL, NO. THERE ARE LOTS OF PROBLEMS, BUT LET'S START WITH THE BIG ONE.
WE DON'T HAVE ANY MEANS OF COVERING GROUND FASTER THAN PEOPLE WHO ACTUALLY KNOW THE GEOGRAPHY OF THIS PLACE.
THAT'S WHY I WAS THINKING THE RIVER... THE CURRENT IS RUNNING IN THAT GENERAL DIRECTION... WE COULD SHAVE A DAY OFF THE JOURNEY AND BEAT THEM THERE.
HMM...

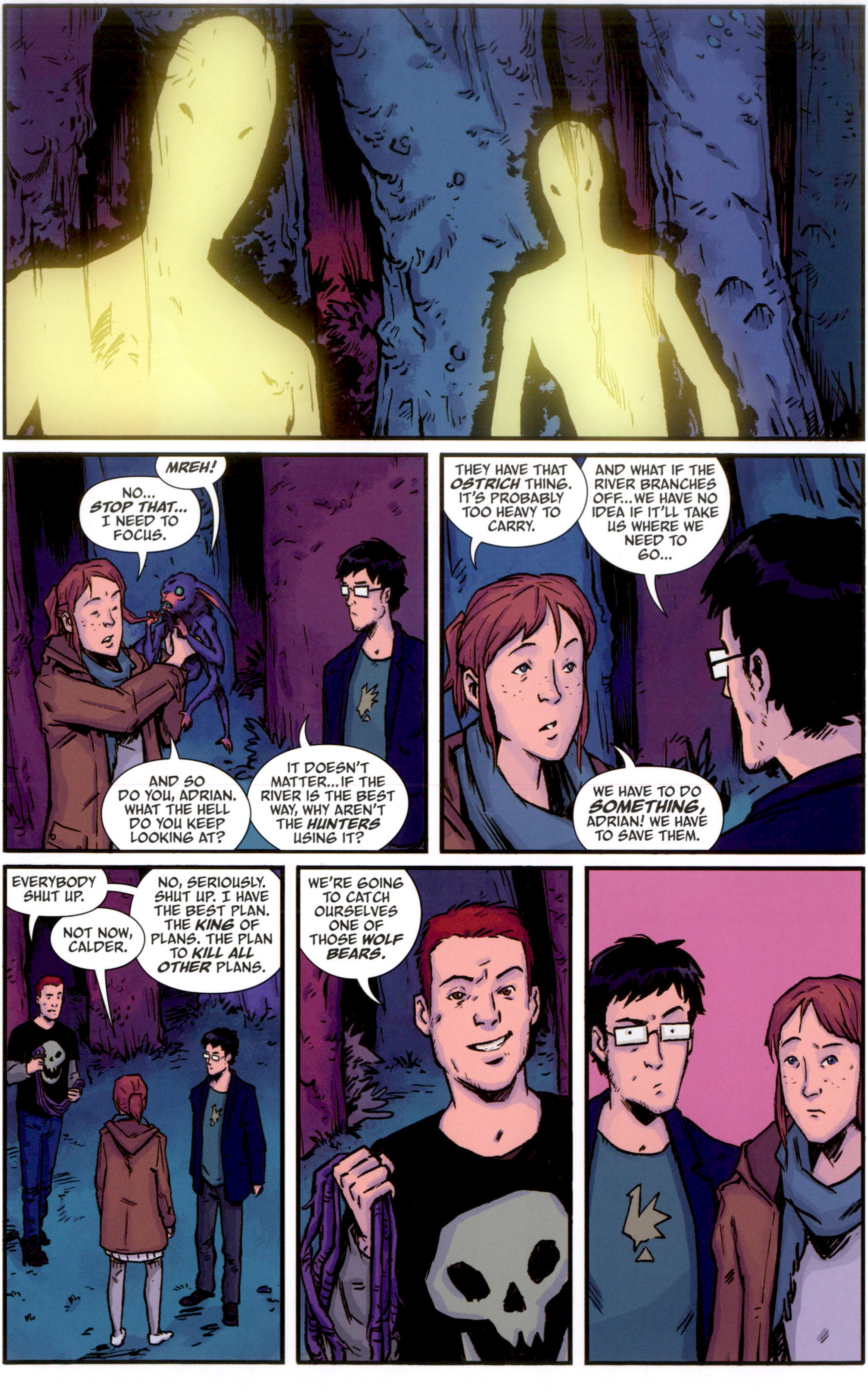
MREH!
NO... STOP THAT... I NEED TO FOCUS.
AND SO DO YOU, ADRIAN. WHAT THE HELL DO YOU KEEP LOOKING AT?
IT DOESN'T MATTER... IF THE RIVER IS THE BEST WAY, WHY AREN'T THE HUNTERS USING IT?
THEY HAVE THAT OSTRICH THING. IT'S PROBABLY TOO HEAVY TO CARRY.
AND WHAT IF THE RIVER BRANCHES OFF... WE HAVE NO IDEA IF IT'LL TAKE US WHERE WE NEED TO GO...
WE HAVE TO DO SOMETHING, ADRIAN! WE HAVE TO SAVE THEM.
EVERYBODY SHUT UP.
NOT NOW, CALDER.
NO, SERIOUSLY. SHUT UP. I HAVE THE BEST PLAN. THE KING OF PLANS. THE PLAN TO KILL ALL OTHER PLANS.
WE'RE GOING TO CATCH OURSELVES ONE OF THOSE WOLF BEARS.

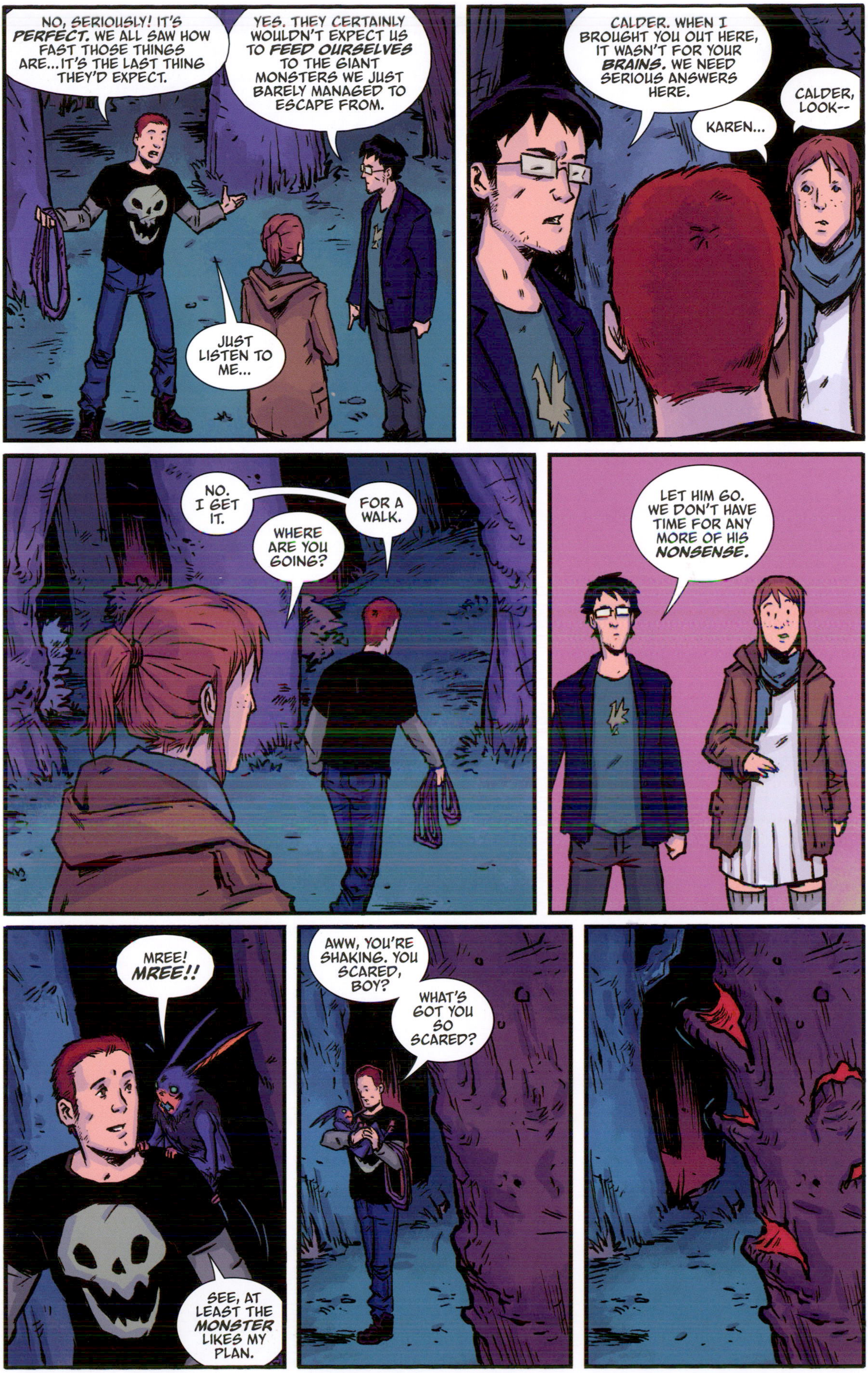
NO, SERIOUSLY! IT'S PERFECT. WE ALL SAW HOW FAST THOSE THINGS ARE...IT'S THE LAST THING THEY'D EXPECT.
YES. THEY CERTAINLY WOULDN'T EXPECT US TO FEED OURSELVES TO THE GIANT MONSTERS WE JUST BARELY MANAGED TO ESCAPE FROM.
JUST LISTEN TO ME...
CALDER. WHEN I BROUGHT YOU OUT HERE, IT WASN'T FOR YOUR BRAINS. WE NEED SERIOUS ANSWERS HERE.
KAREN...
CALDER, LOOK--
NO. I GET IT.
FOR A WALK.
WHERE ARE YOU GOING?
LET HIM GO. WE DON'T HAVE TIME FOR ANY MORE OF HIS NONSENSE.
MREE! MREE!!
SEE, AT LEAST THE MONSTER LIKES MY PLAN.
AWW, YOU'RE SHAKING. YOU SCARED, BOY?
WHAT'S GOT YOU SO SCARED?

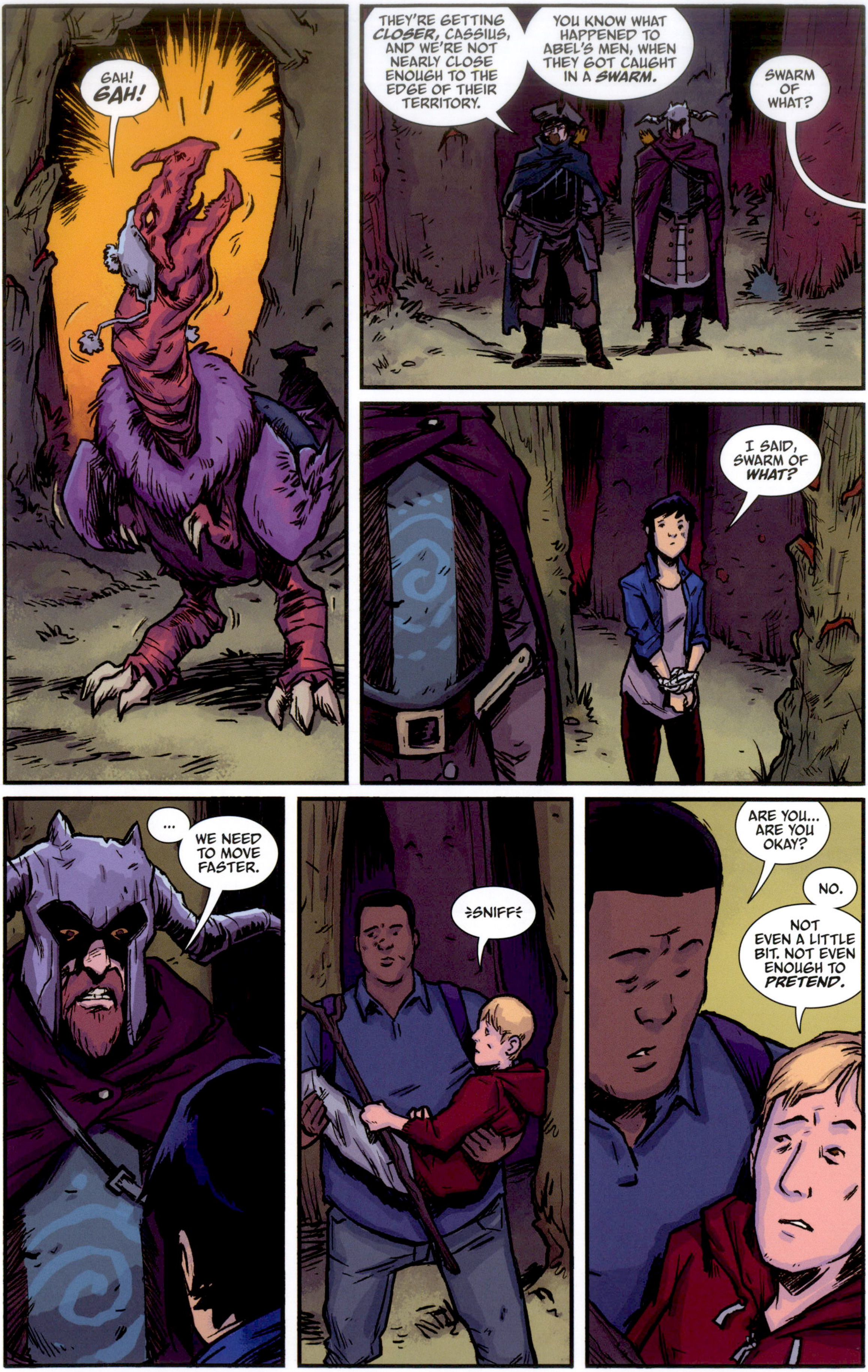
GAH! GAH!
THEY'RE GETTING CLOSER, CASSIUS, AND WE'RE NOT NEARLY CLOSE ENOUGH TO THE EDGE OF THEIR TERRITORY.
YOU KNOW WHAT HAPPENED TO ABEL'S MEN, WHEN THEY GOT CAUGHT IN A SWARM.
SWARM OF WHAT?
I SAID, SWARM OF WHAT?
...
WE NEED TO MOVE FASTER.
SNIFF
ARE YOU... ARE YOU OKAY?
NO.
NOT EVEN A LITTLE BIT. NOT EVEN ENOUGH TO PRETEND.

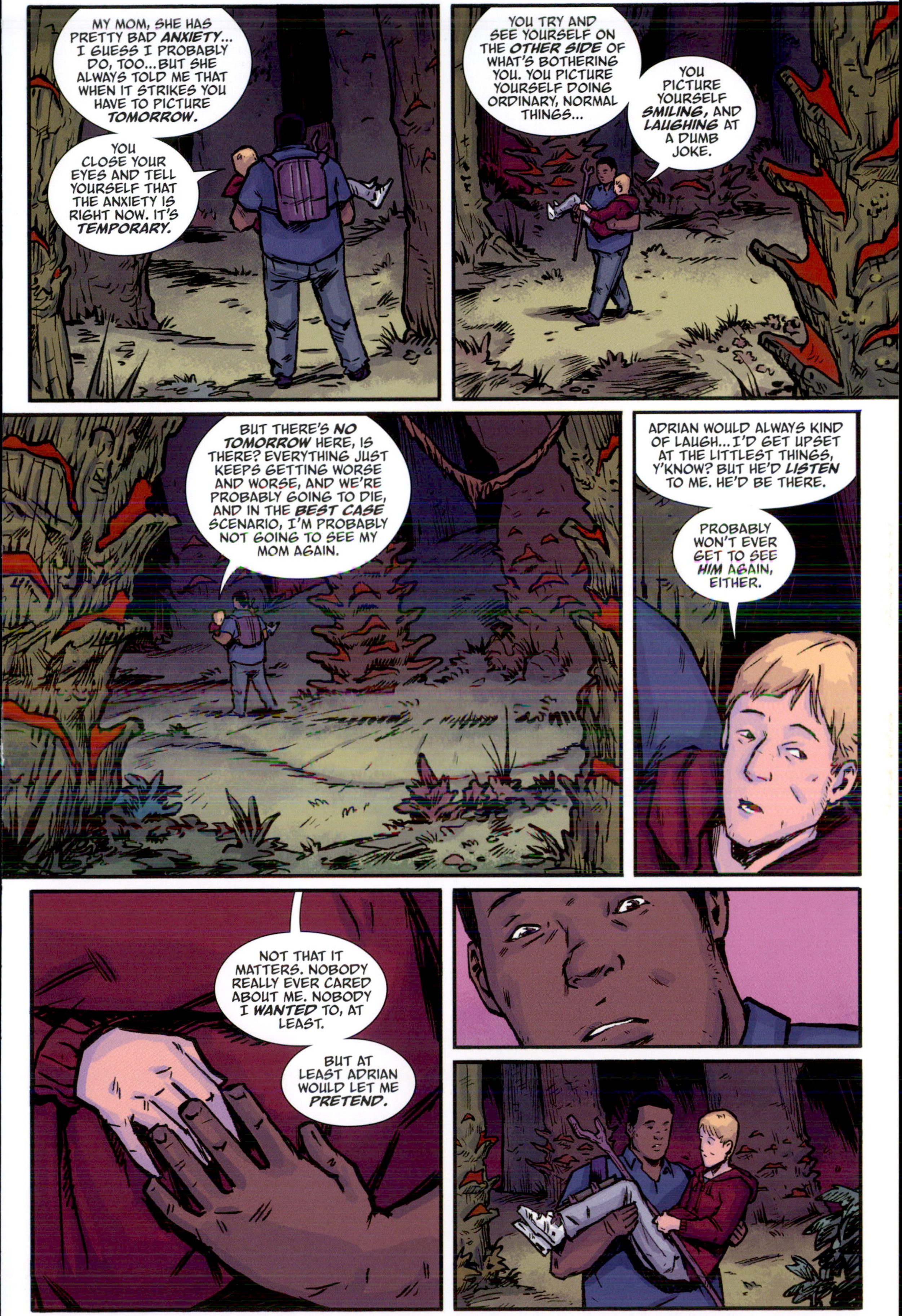
MY MOM, SHE HAS PRETTY BAD ANXIETY... I GUESS I PROBABLY DO, TOO...BUT SHE ALWAYS TOLD ME THAT WHEN IT STRIKES YOU HAVE TO PICTURE TOMORROW.
YOU CLOSE YOUR EYES AND TELL YOURSELF THAT THE ANXIETY IS RIGHT NOW. IT'S TEMPORARY.
YOU TRY AND SEE YOURSELF ON THE OTHER SIDE OF WHAT'S BOTHERING YOU. YOU PICTURE YOURSELF DOING ORDINARY, NORMAL THINGS...
YOU PICTURE YOURSELF SMILING, AND LAUGHING AT A DUMB JOKE.
BUT THERE'S NO TOMORROW HERE, IS THERE? EVERYTHING JUST KEEPS GETTING WORSE AND WORSE, AND WE'RE PROBABLY GOING TO DIE, AND IN THE BEST CASE SCENARIO, I'M PROBABLY NOT GOING TO SEE MY MOM AGAIN.
ADRIAN WOULD ALWAYS KIND OF LAUGH...I'D GET UPSET AT THE LITTLEST THINGS, Y'KNOW? BUT HE'D LISTEN TO ME. HE'D BE THERE.
PROBABLY WON'T EVER GET TO SEE HIM AGAIN, EITHER.
NOT THAT IT MATTERS. NOBODY REALLY EVER CARED ABOUT ME. NOBODY I WANTED TO, AT LEAST.
BUT AT LEAST ADRIAN WOULD LET ME PRETEND.

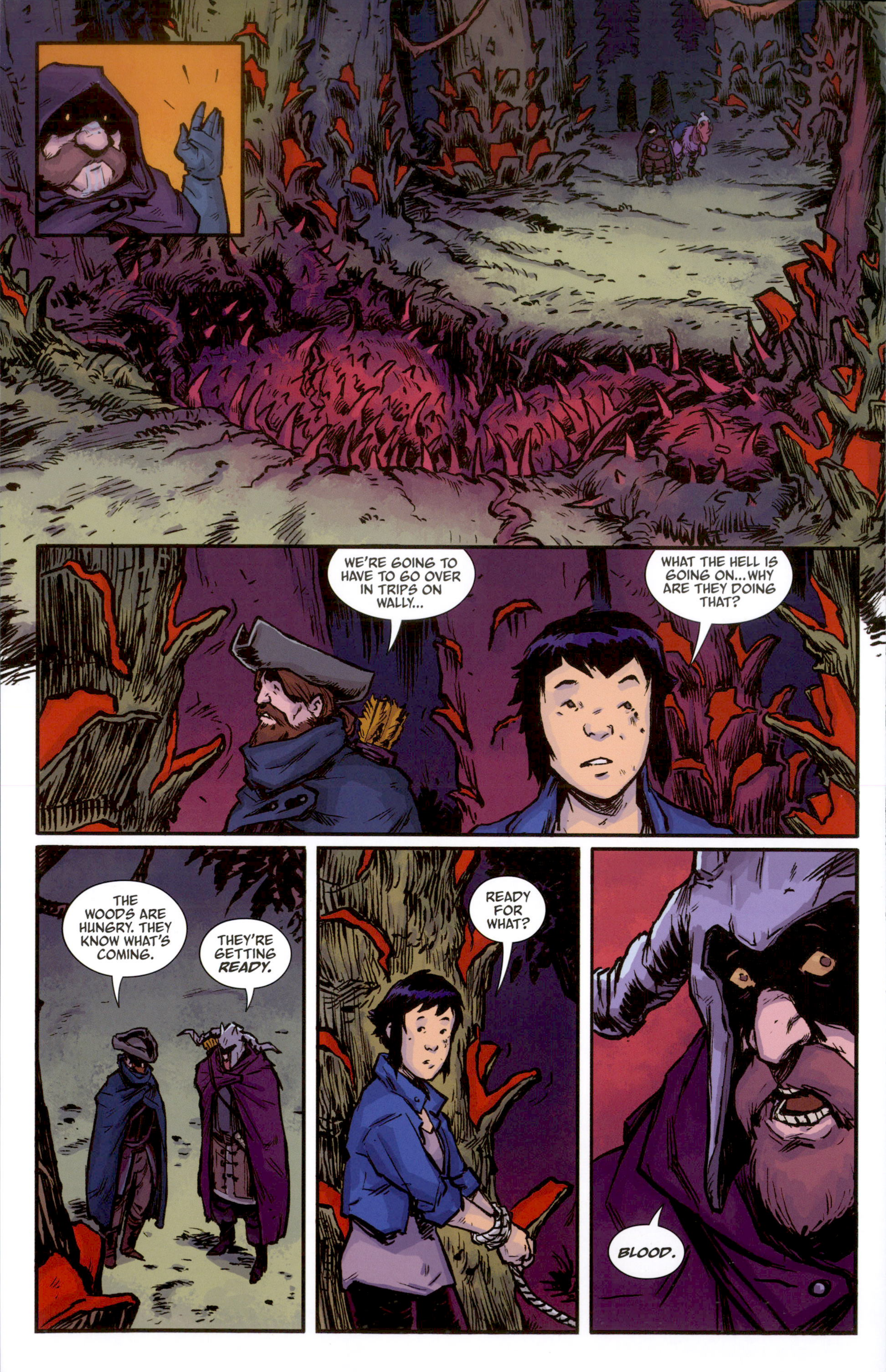
WE'RE GOING TO HAVE TO GO OVER IN TRIPS ON WALLY...
WHAT THE HELL IS GOING ON...WHY ARE THEY DOING THAT?
THE WOODS ARE HUNGRY. THEY KNOW WHAT'S COMING.
THEY'RE GETTING *READY.*
READY FOR WHAT?
BLOOD.

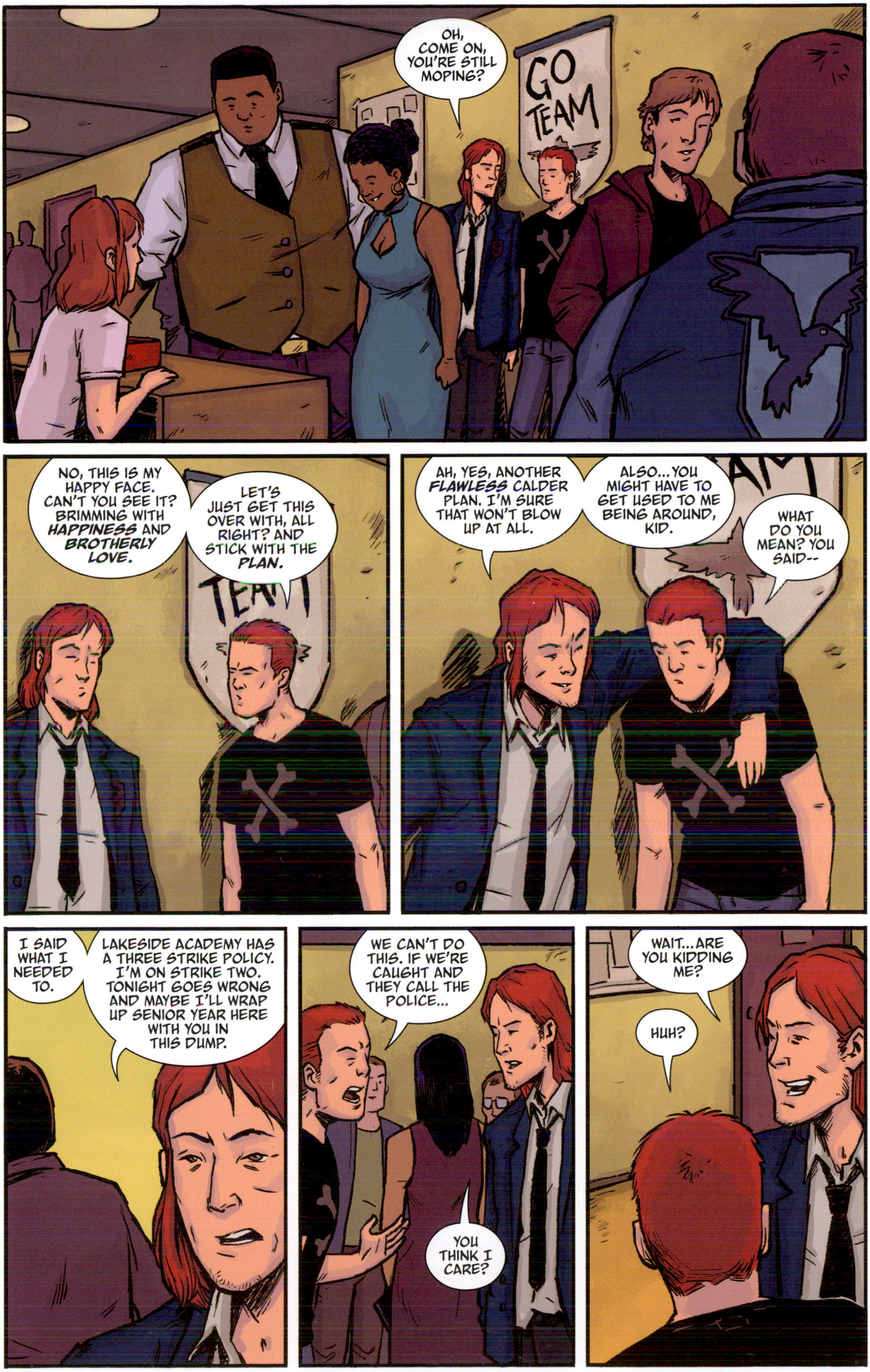
OH, COME ON, YOU'RE STILL MOPING?
NO, THIS IS MY HAPPY FACE. CAN'T YOU SEE IT? BRIMMING WITH HAPPINESS AND BROTHERLY LOVE.
LET'S JUST GET THIS OVER WITH, ALL RIGHT? AND STICK WITH THE PLAN.
GO TEAM
AH, YES, ANOTHER FLAWLESS CALDER PLAN. I'M SURE THAT WON'T BLOW UP AT ALL.
ALSO...YOU MIGHT HAVE TO GET USED TO ME BEING AROUND, KID.
WHAT DO YOU MEAN? YOU SAID--
I SAID WHAT I NEEDED TO.
LAKESIDE ACADEMY HAS A THREE STRIKE POLICY. I'M ON STRIKE TWO. TONIGHT GOES WRONG AND MAYBE I'LL WRAP UP SENIOR YEAR HERE WITH YOU IN THIS DUMP.
WE CAN'T DO THIS. IF WE'RE CAUGHT AND THEY CALL THE POLICE...
YOU THINK I CARE?
WAIT...ARE YOU KIDDING ME?
HUH?

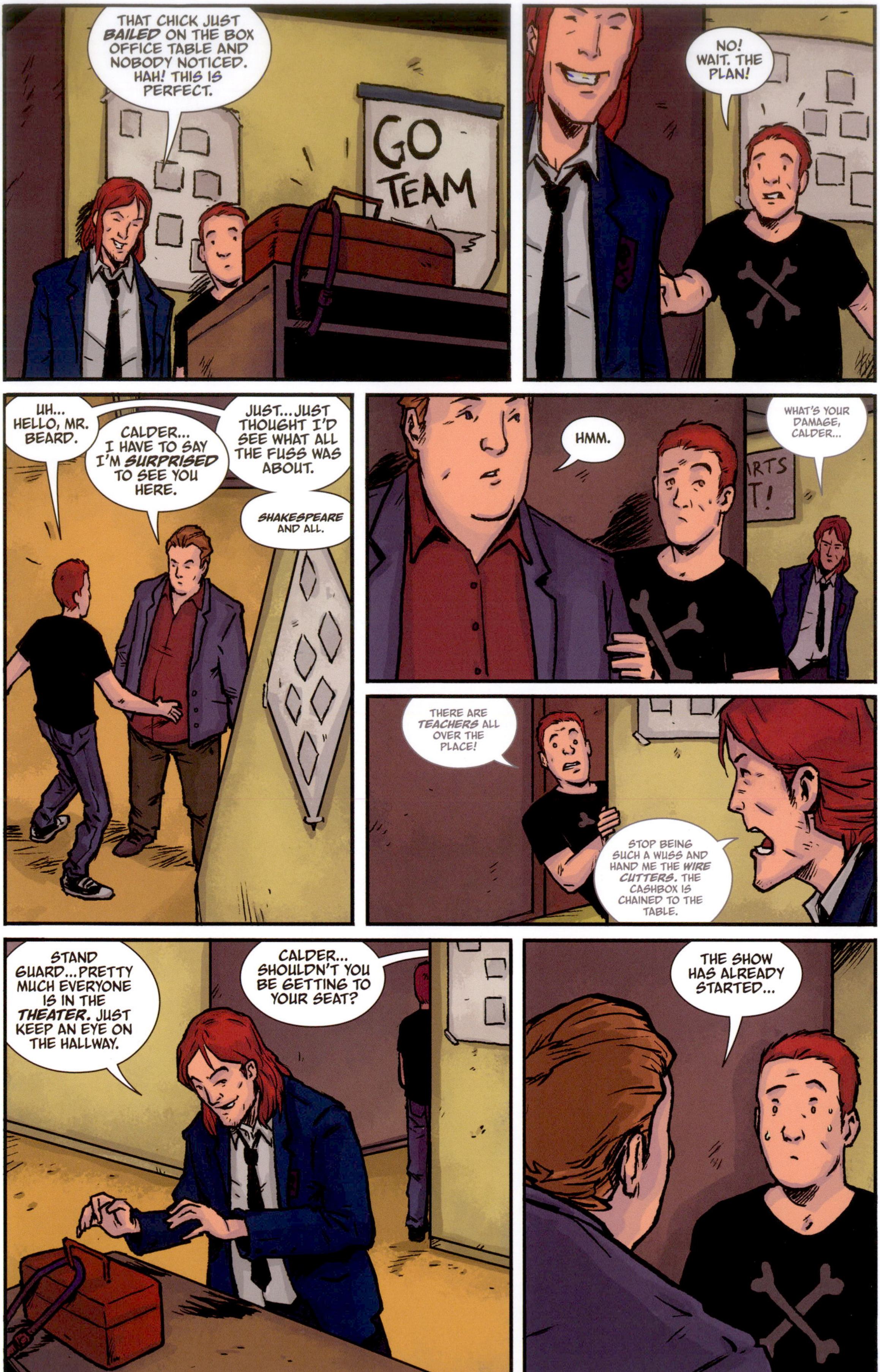
THAT CHICK JUST BAILED ON THE BOX OFFICE TABLE AND NOBODY NOTICED. HAH! THIS IS PERFECT.
GO TEAM
NO! WAIT. THE PLAN!
UH... HELLO, MR. BEARD.
CALDER... I HAVE TO SAY I'M SURPRISED TO SEE YOU HERE.
JUST...JUST THOUGHT I'D SEE WHAT ALL THE FUSS WAS ABOUT.
SHAKESPEARE AND ALL.
HMM.
WHAT'S YOUR DAMAGE, CALDER...
THERE ARE TEACHERS ALL OVER THE PLACE!
STOP BEING SUCH A WUSS AND HAND ME THE WIRE CUTTERS. THE CASHBOX IS CHAINED TO THE TABLE.
STAND GUARD...PRETTY MUCH EVERYONE IS IN THE THEATER. JUST KEEP AN EYE ON THE HALLWAY.
CALDER... SHOULDN'T YOU BE GETTING TO YOUR SEAT?
THE SHOW HAS ALREADY STARTED...

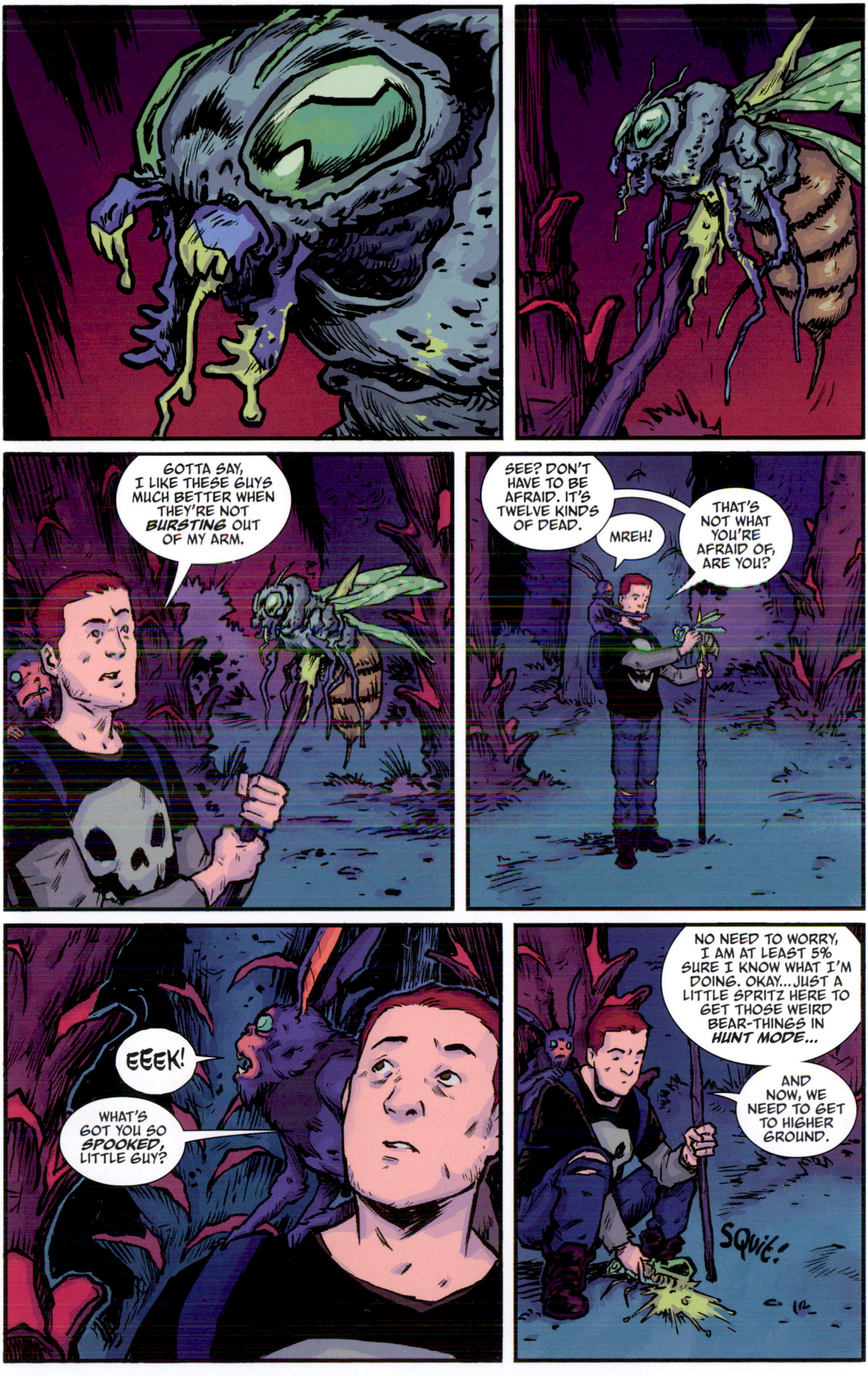
GOTTA SAY, I LIKE THESE GUYS MUCH BETTER WHEN THEY'RE NOT BURSTING OUT OF MY ARM.
SEE? DON'T HAVE TO BE AFRAID. IT'S TWELVE KINDS OF DEAD.
MREH!
THAT'S NOT WHAT YOU'RE AFRAID OF, ARE YOU?
EEEK!
WHAT'S GOT YOU SO SPOOKED, LITTLE GUY?
NO NEED TO WORRY, I AM AT LEAST 5% SURE I KNOW WHAT I'M DOING. OKAY... JUST A LITTLE SPRITZ HERE TO GET THOSE WEIRD BEAR-THINGS IN HUNT MODE...
AND NOW, WE NEED TO GET TO HIGHER GROUND.
SQUIT!

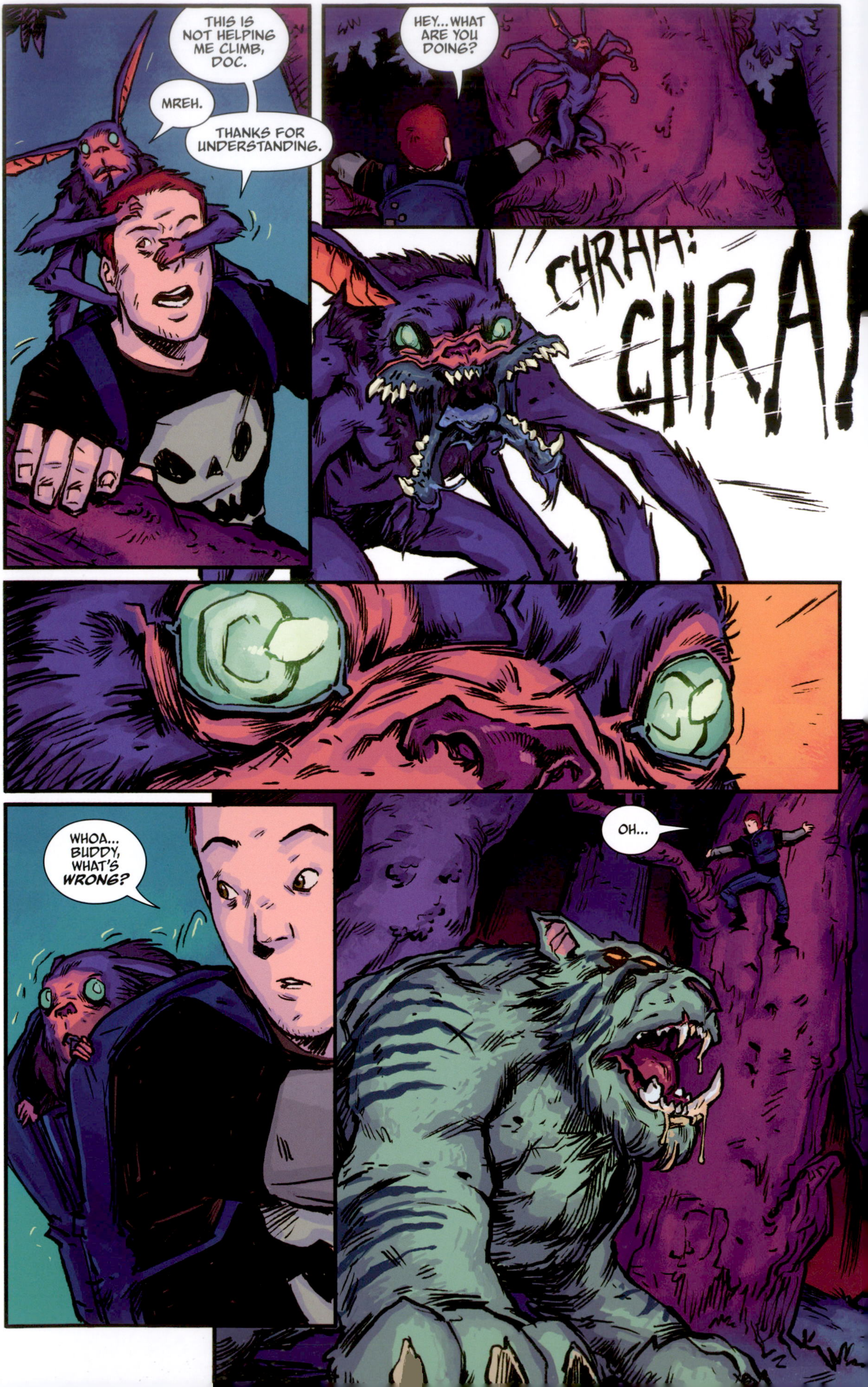
THIS IS NOT HELPING ME CLIMB, DOC.
MREH.
THANKS FOR UNDERSTANDING.
HEY... WHAT ARE YOU DOING?
CHRAA!
CHRA
WHOA... BUDDY, WHAT'S *WRONG*?
OH...

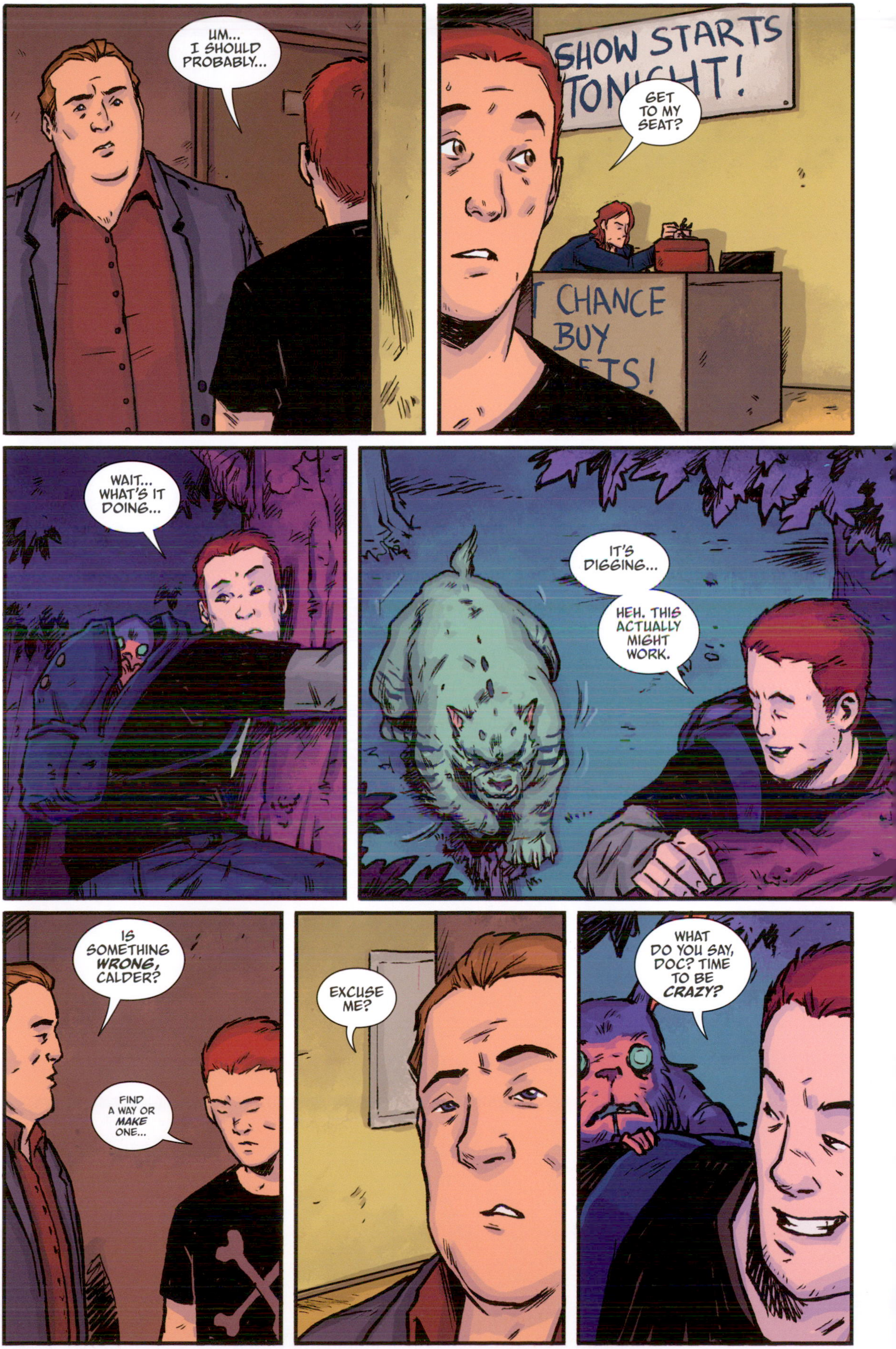
UM... I SHOULD PROBABLY...
SHOW STARTS TONIGHT!
GET TO MY SEAT?
CHANCE BUY
WAIT... WHAT'S IT DOING...
IT'S DIGGING...
HEH. THIS ACTUALLY MIGHT WORK.
IS SOMETHING *WRONG*, CALDER?
FIND A WAY OR *MAKE* ONE...
EXCUSE ME?
WHAT DO YOU SAY, DOC? TIME TO BE *CRAZY?*

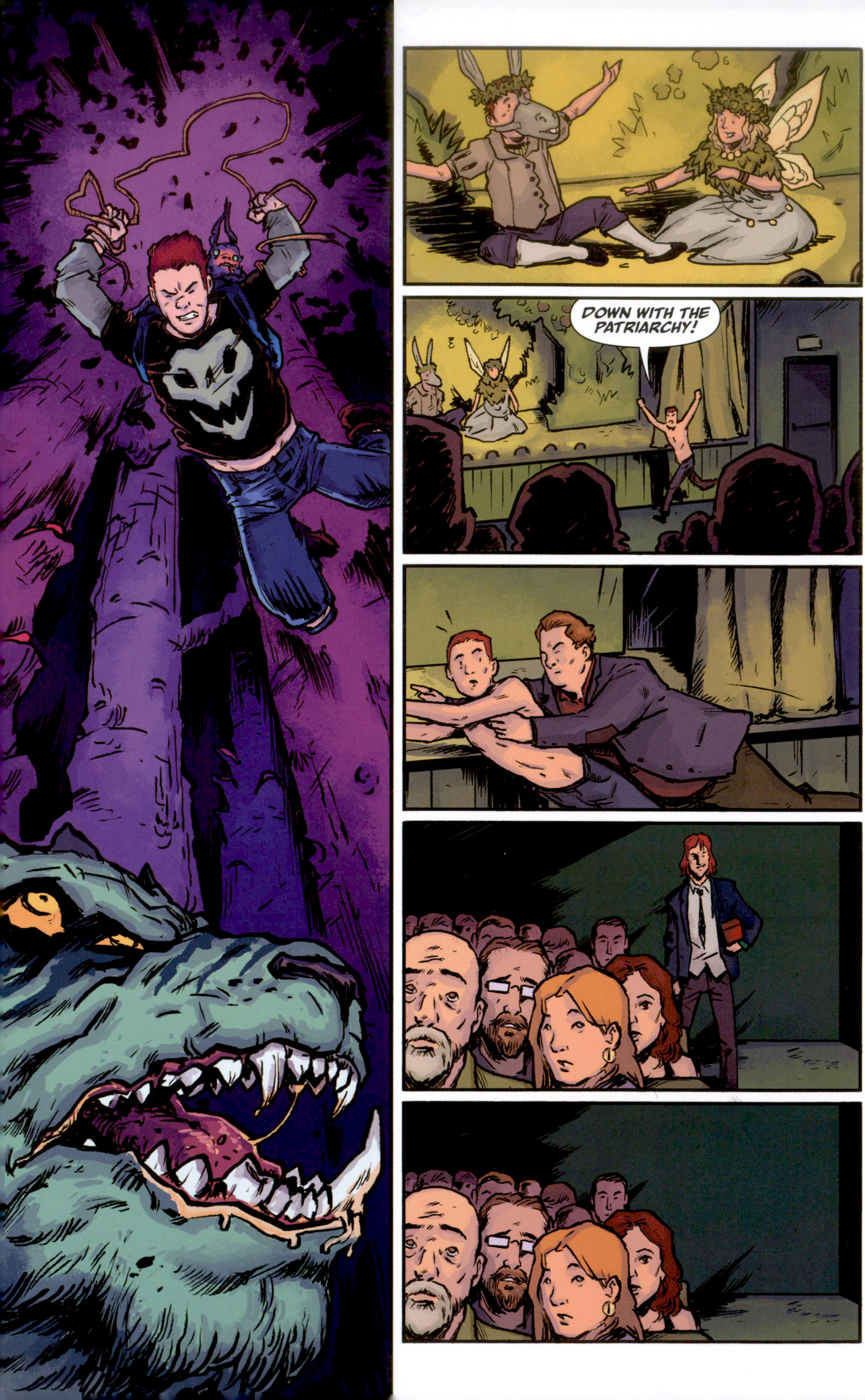
DOWN WITH THE PATRIARCHY!

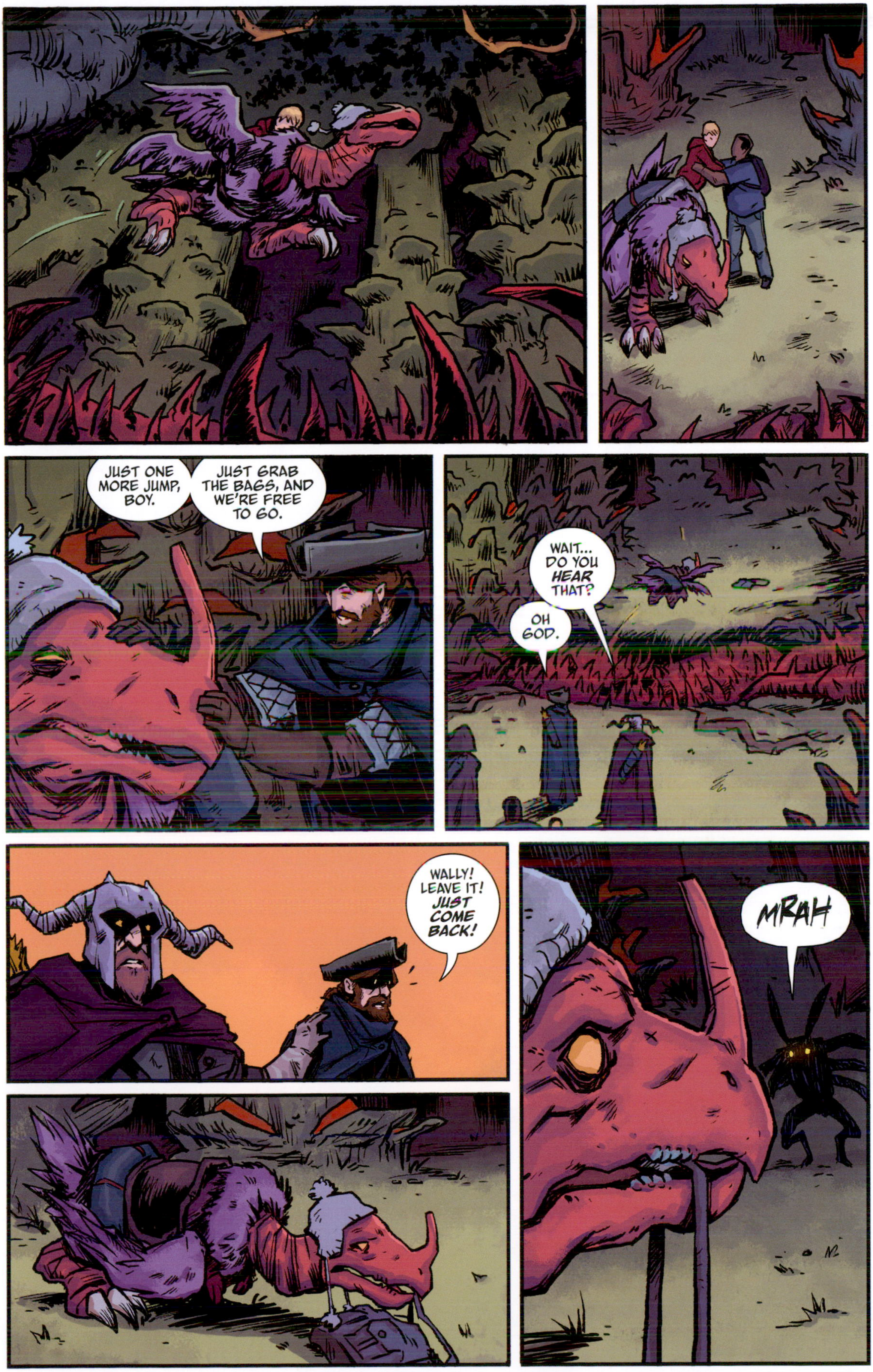

JUST ONE MORE JUMP, BOY.
JUST GRAB THE BAGS, AND WE'RE FREE TO GO.
WAIT... DO YOU HEAR THAT?
OH GOD.
WALLY! LEAVE IT! JUST COME BACK!
MRAH

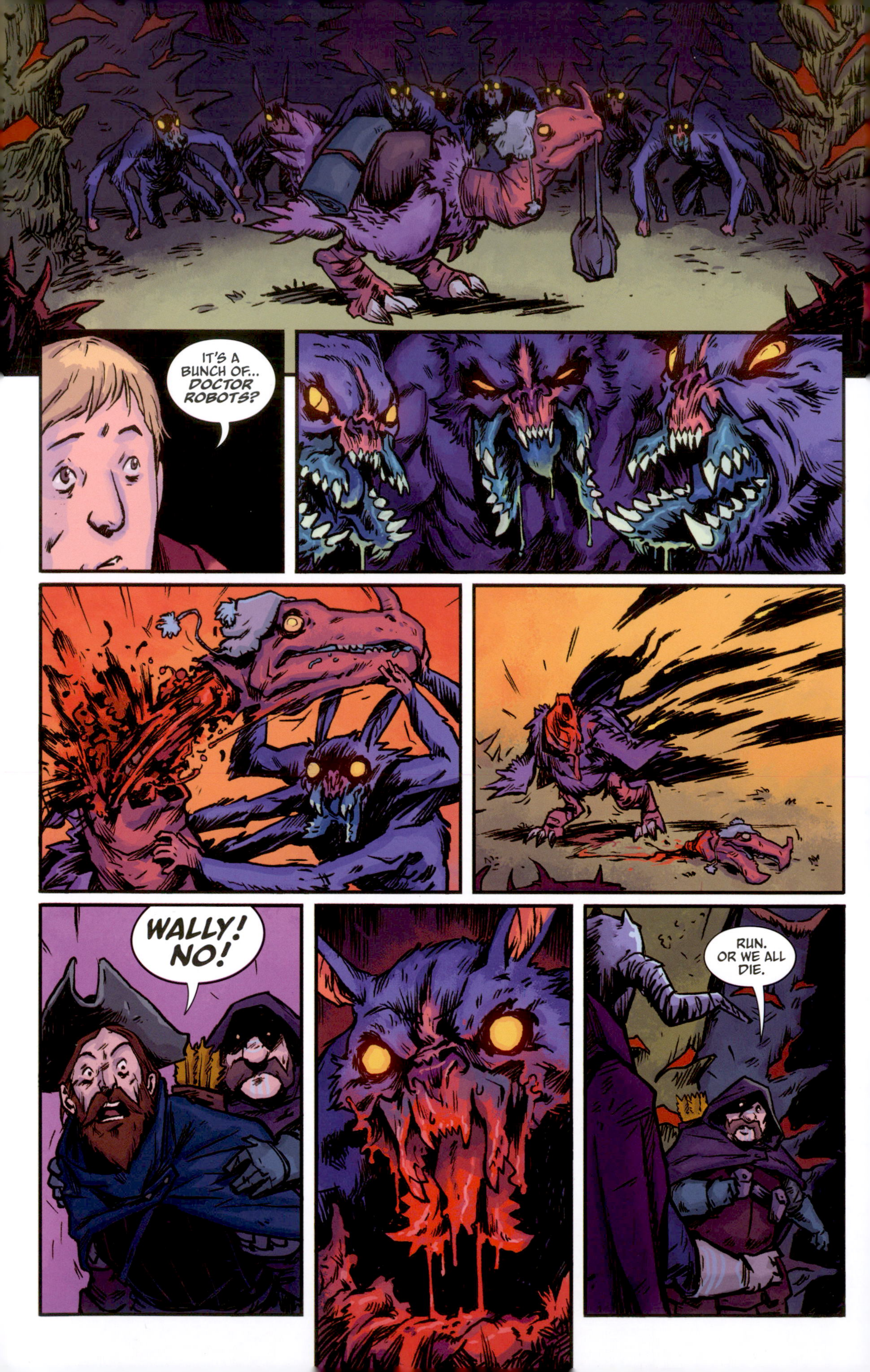
IT'S A BUNCH OF... DOCTOR ROBOTS?
WALLY! NO!
RUN. OR WE ALL DIE.

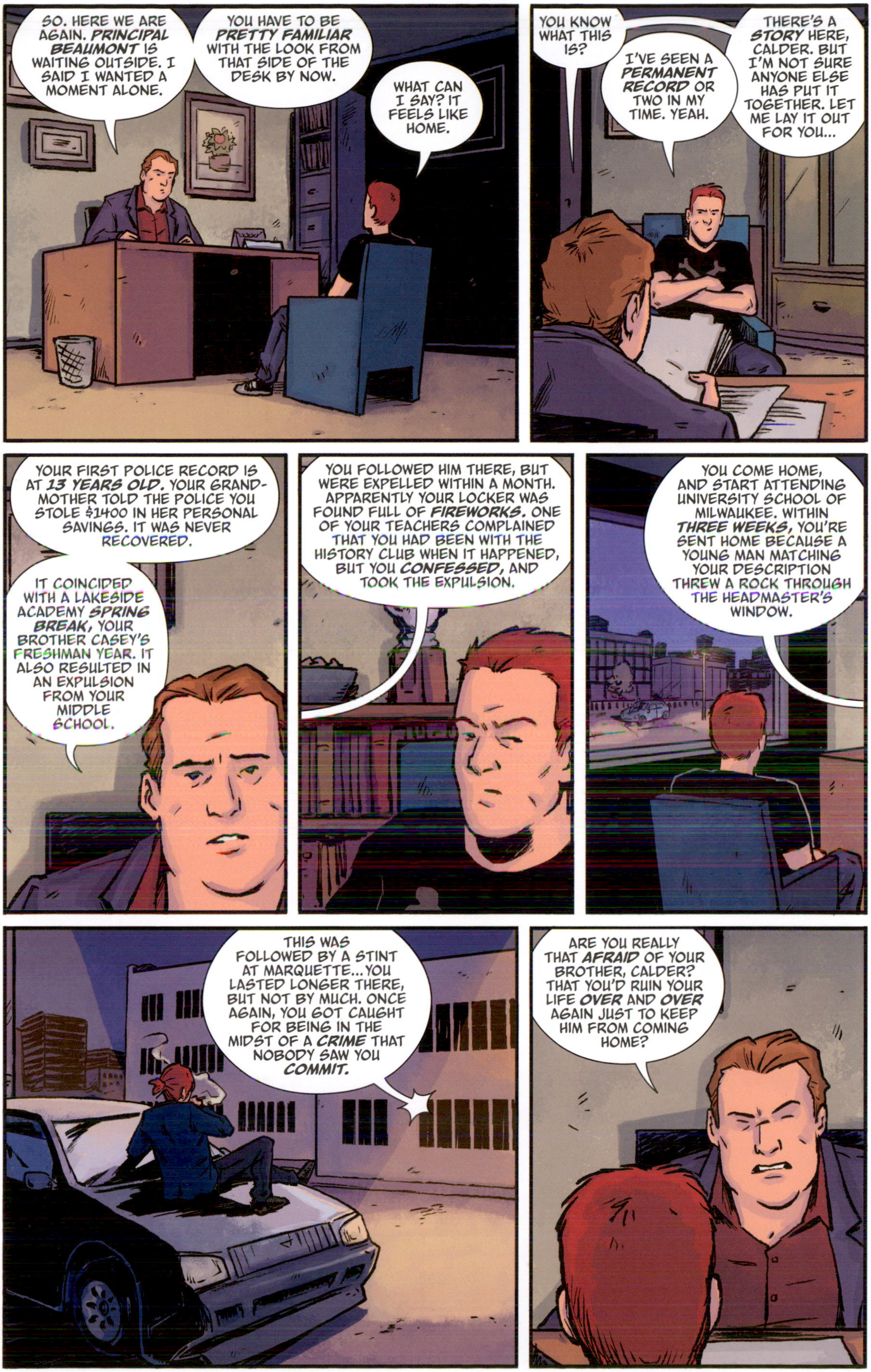
SO. HERE WE ARE AGAIN. PRINCIPAL BEAUMONT IS WAITING OUTSIDE. I SAID I WANTED A MOMENT ALONE.
YOU HAVE TO BE PRETTY FAMILIAR WITH THE LOOK FROM THAT SIDE OF THE DESK BY NOW.
WHAT CAN I SAY? IT FEELS LIKE HOME.
YOU KNOW WHAT THIS IS?
I'VE SEEN A PERMANENT RECORD OR TWO IN MY TIME. YEAH.
THERE'S A STORY HERE, CALDER. BUT I'M NOT SURE ANYONE ELSE HAS PUT IT TOGETHER. LET ME LAY IT OUT FOR YOU...
YOUR FIRST POLICE RECORD IS AT 13 YEARS OLD. YOUR GRAND-MOTHER TOLD THE POLICE YOU STOLE $1400 IN HER PERSONAL SAVINGS. IT WAS NEVER RECOVERED.
IT COINCIDED WITH A LAKESIDE ACADEMY SPRING BREAK, YOUR BROTHER CASEY'S FRESHMAN YEAR. IT ALSO RESULTED IN AN EXPULSION FROM YOUR MIDDLE SCHOOL.
YOU FOLLOWED HIM THERE, BUT WERE EXPELLED WITHIN A MONTH. APPARENTLY YOUR LOCKER WAS FOUND FULL OF FIREWORKS. ONE OF YOUR TEACHERS COMPLAINED THAT YOU HAD BEEN WITH THE HISTORY CLUB WHEN IT HAPPENED, BUT YOU CONFESSED, AND TOOK THE EXPULSION.
YOU COME HOME, AND START ATTENDING UNIVERSITY SCHOOL OF MILWAUKEE. WITHIN THREE WEEKS, YOU'RE SENT HOME BECAUSE A YOUNG MAN MATCHING YOUR DESCRIPTION THREW A ROCK THROUGH THE HEADMASTER'S WINDOW.
THIS WAS FOLLOWED BY A STINT AT MARQUETTE...YOU LASTED LONGER THERE, BUT NOT BY MUCH. ONCE AGAIN, YOU GOT CAUGHT FOR BEING IN THE MIDST OF A CRIME THAT NOBODY SAW YOU COMMIT.
ARE YOU REALLY THAT AFRAID OF YOUR BROTHER, CALDER? THAT YOU'D RUIN YOUR LIFE OVER AND OVER AGAIN JUST TO KEEP HIM FROM COMING HOME?

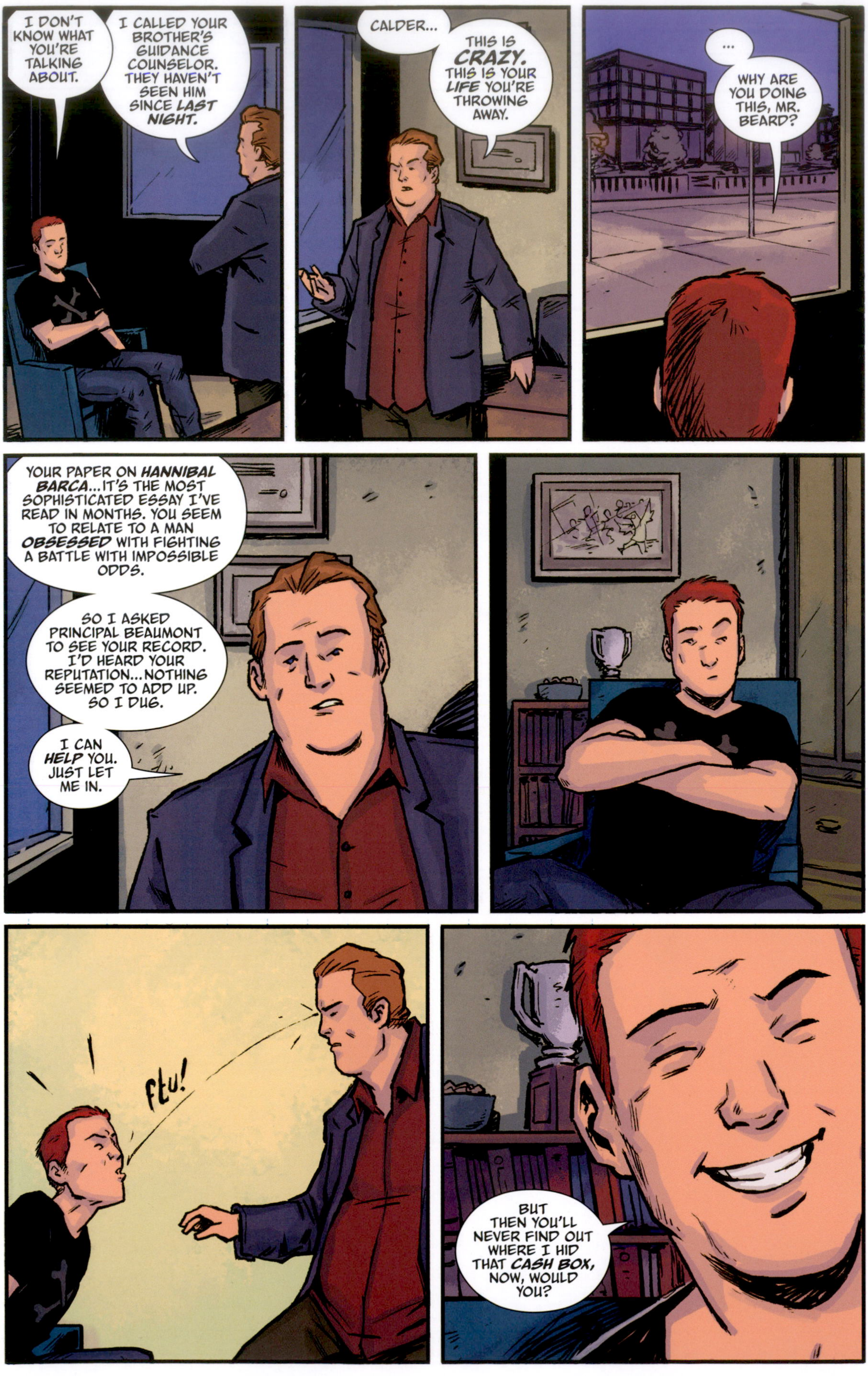
I DON'T KNOW WHAT YOU'RE TALKING ABOUT.
I CALLED YOUR BROTHER'S GUIDANCE COUNSELOR. THEY HAVEN'T SEEN HIM SINCE LAST NIGHT.
CALDER...
THIS IS CRAZY. THIS IS YOUR LIFE YOU'RE THROWING AWAY.
...
WHY ARE YOU DOING THIS, MR. BEARD?
YOUR PAPER ON HANNIBAL BARCA...IT'S THE MOST SOPHISTICATED ESSAY I'VE READ IN MONTHS. YOU SEEM TO RELATE TO A MAN OBSESSED WITH FIGHTING A BATTLE WITH IMPOSSIBLE ODDS.
SO I ASKED PRINCIPAL BEAUMONT TO SEE YOUR RECORD. I'D HEARD YOUR REPUTATION...NOTHING SEEMED TO ADD UP. SO I DUG.
I CAN HELP YOU. JUST LET ME IN.
ftu!
BUT THEN YOU'LL NEVER FIND OUT WHERE I HID THAT CASH BOX, NOW, WOULD YOU?

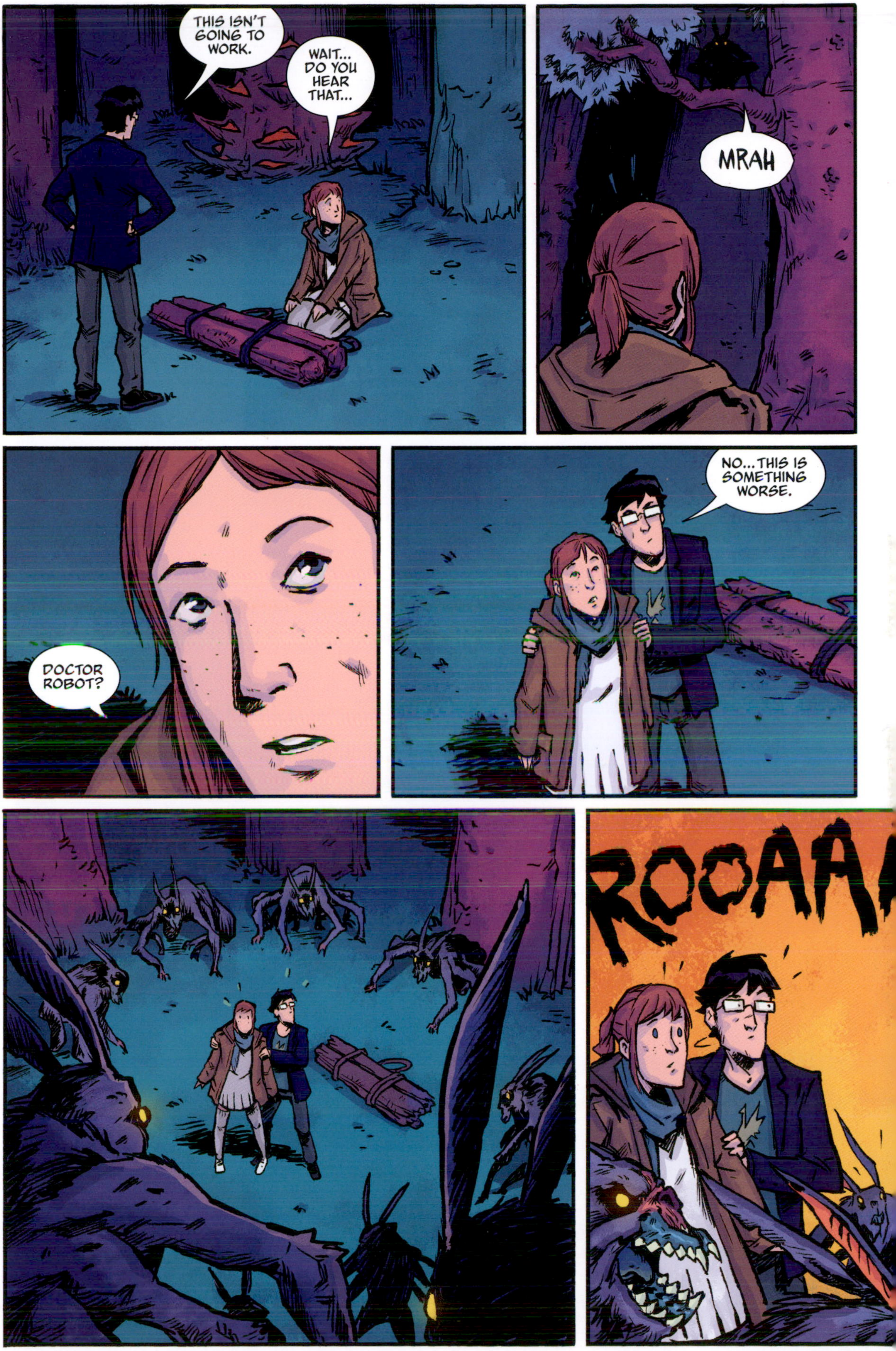
THIS ISN'T GOING TO WORK.
WAIT... DO YOU HEAR THAT...
MRAH
DOCTOR ROBOT?
NO... THIS IS SOMETHING WORSE.
ROOAA

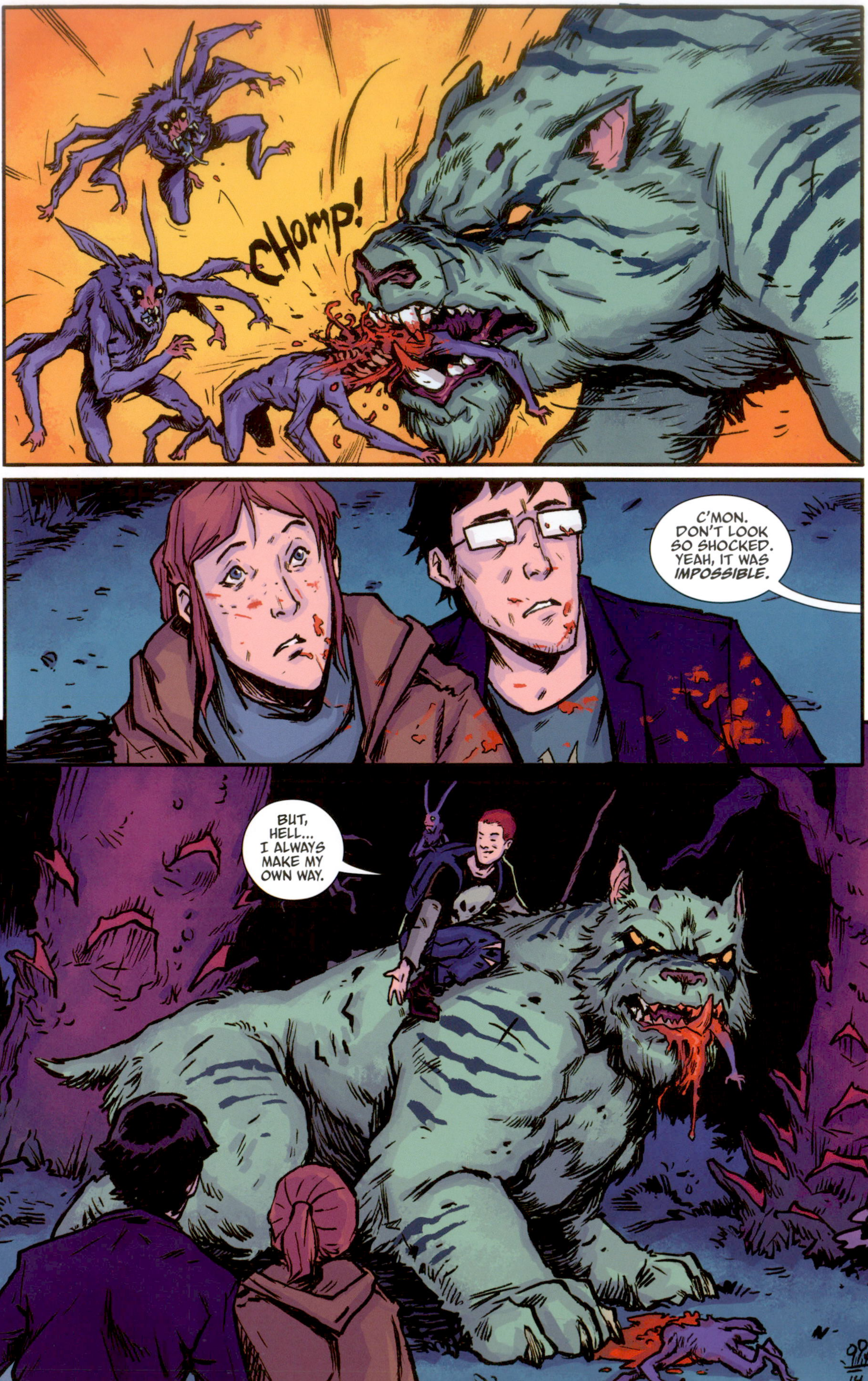
CHOMP!
C'MON. DON'T LOOK SO SHOCKED. YEAH, IT WAS IMPOSSIBLE.
BUT, HELL... I ALWAYS MAKE MY OWN WAY.

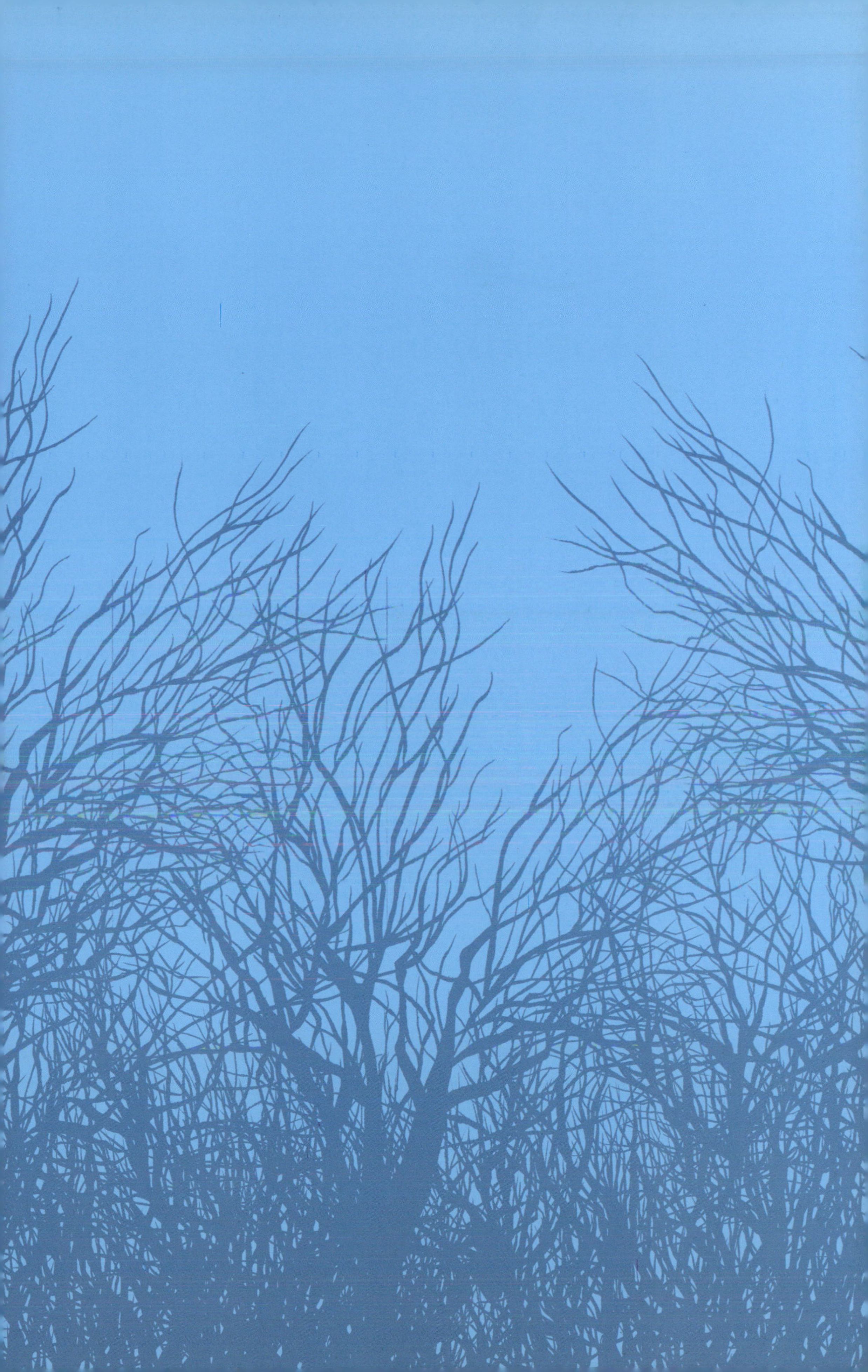

CHAPTER SEVEN

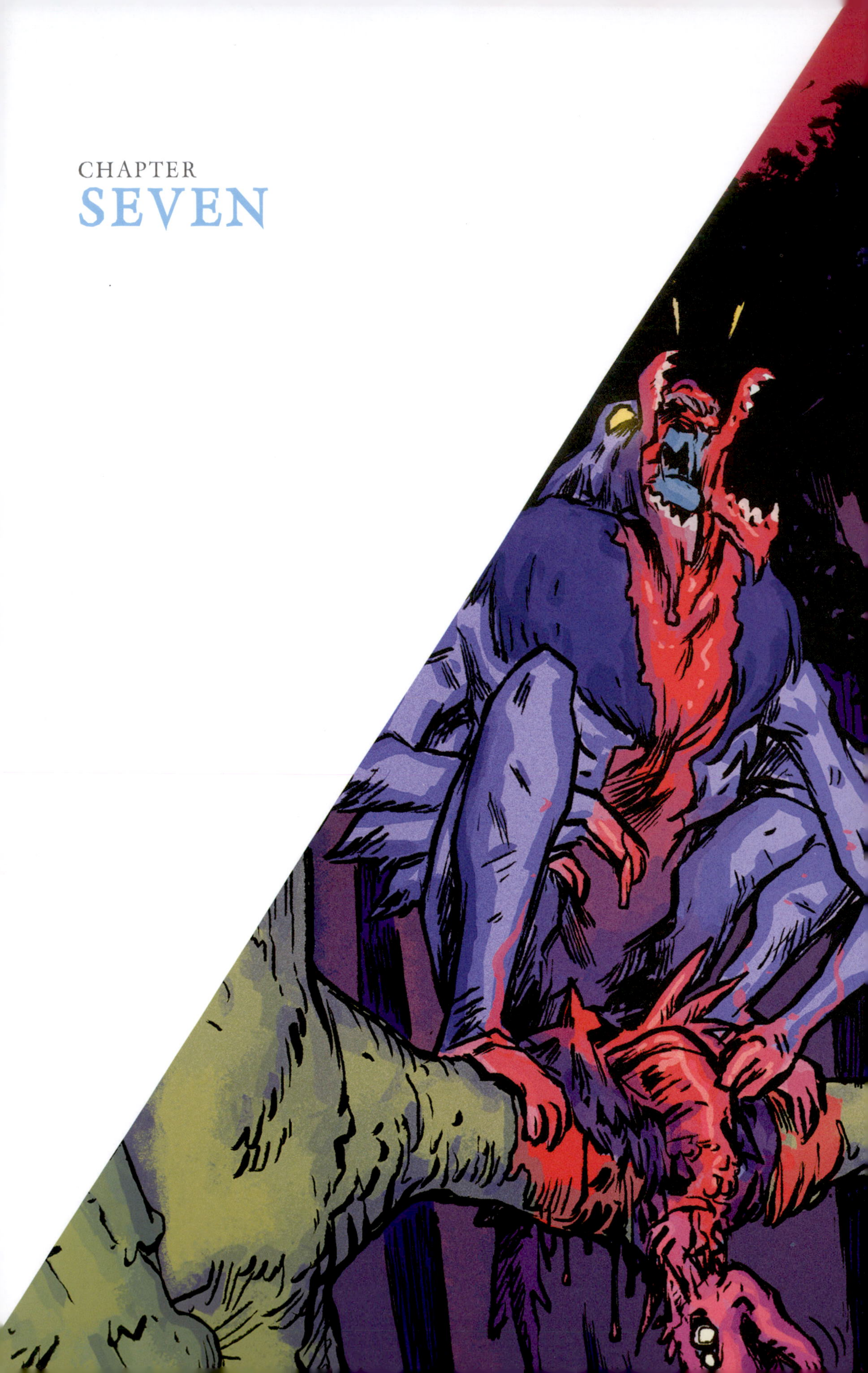

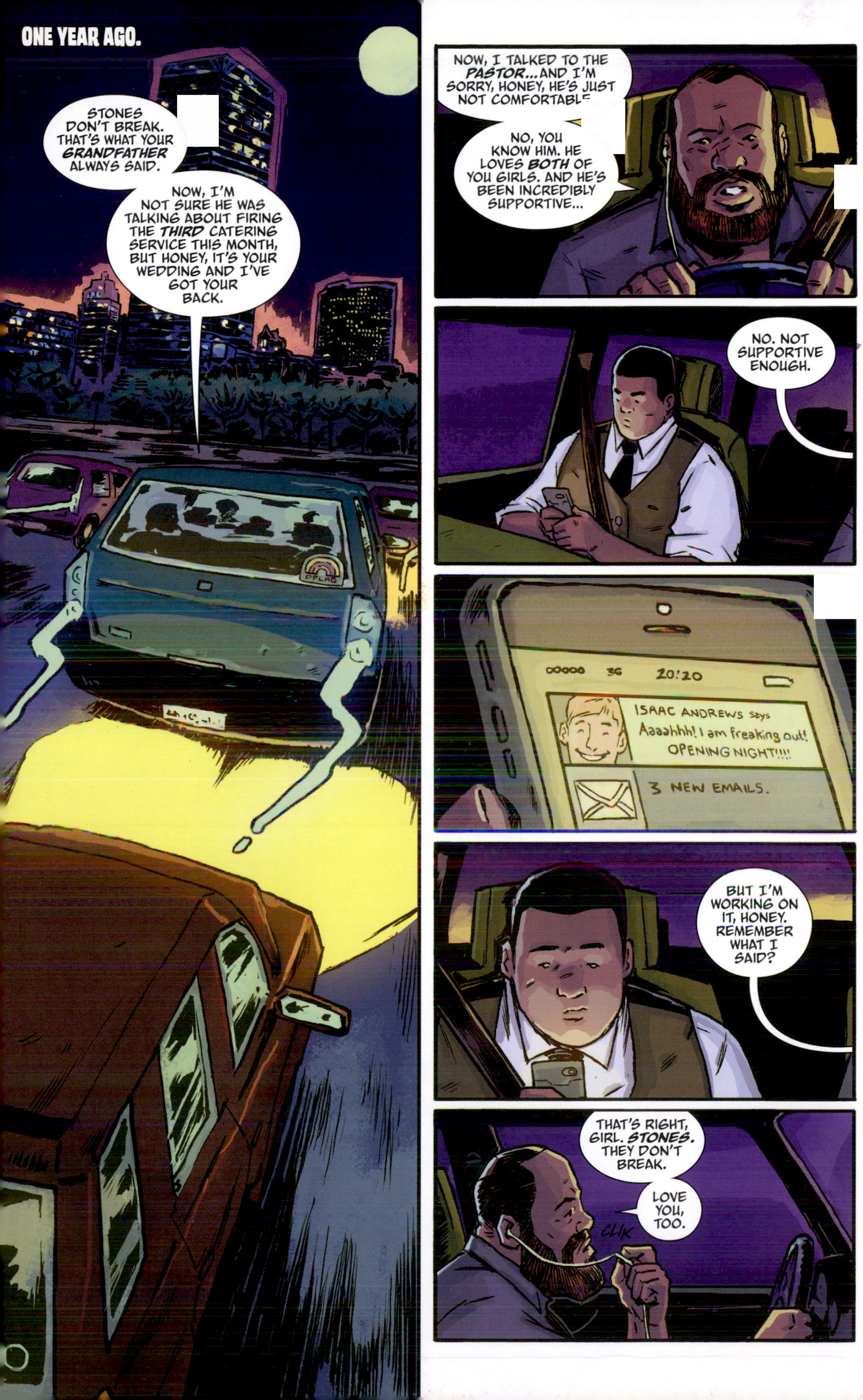

ONE YEAR AGO.
STONES DON'T BREAK. THAT'S WHAT YOUR GRANDFATHER ALWAYS SAID.
NOW, I'M NOT SURE HE WAS TALKING ABOUT FIRING THE THIRD CATERING SERVICE THIS MONTH, BUT HONEY, IT'S YOUR WEDDING AND I'VE GOT YOUR BACK.
PFLAG
NOW, I TALKED TO THE PASTOR... AND I'M SORRY, HONEY, HE'S JUST NOT COMFORTABL–
NO, YOU KNOW HIM. HE LOVES BOTH OF YOU GIRLS. AND HE'S BEEN INCREDIBLY SUPPORTIVE...
NO. NOT SUPPORTIVE ENOUGH.
3G 20:20
ISAAC ANDREWS says
Aaaahhh! I am freaking out! OPENING NIGHT!!!!
3 NEW EMAILS.
BUT I'M WORKING ON IT, HONEY. REMEMBER WHAT I SAID?
THAT'S RIGHT, GIRL. STONES. THEY DON'T BREAK.
LOVE YOU, TOO.
CLIK

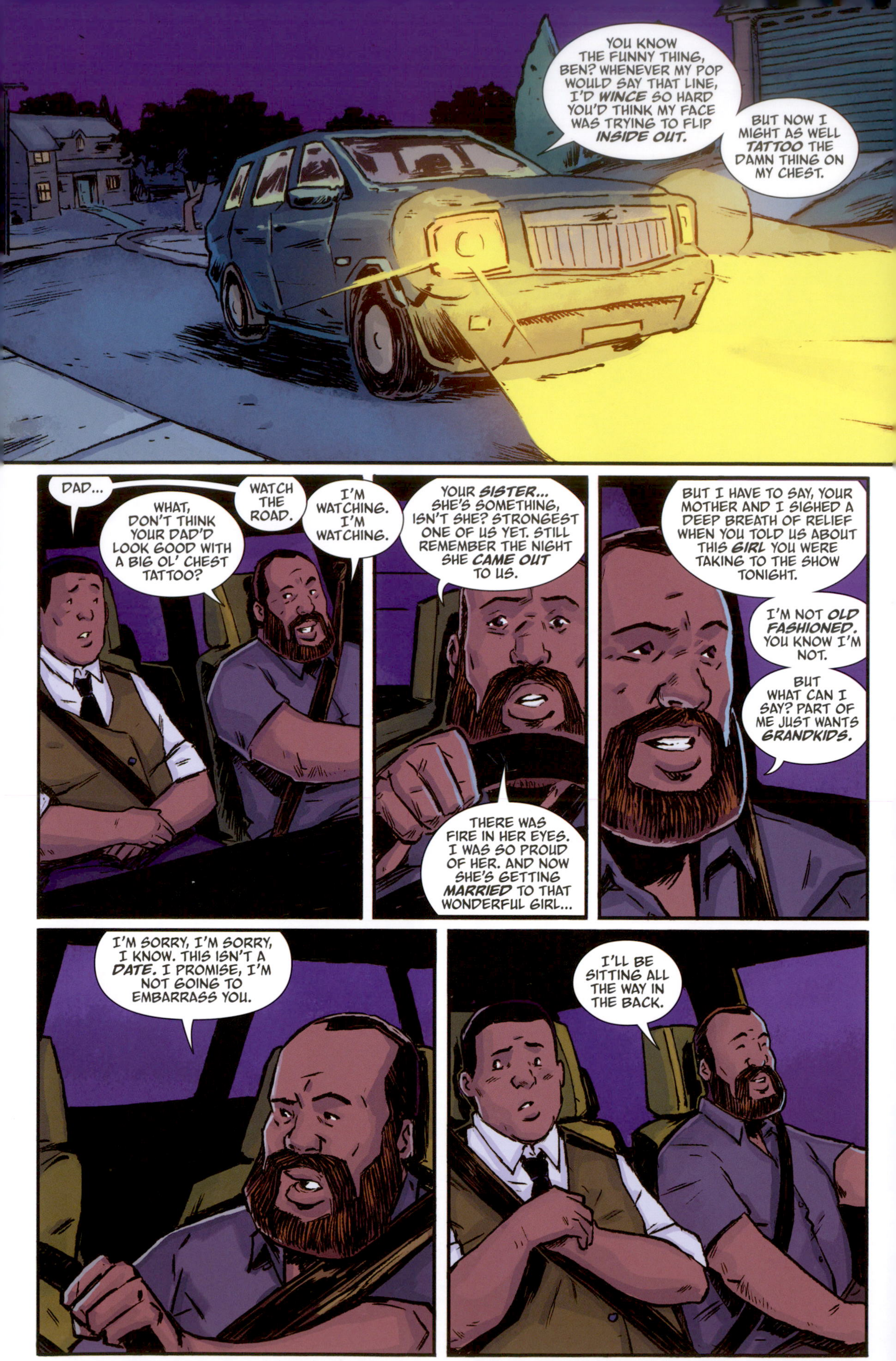
YOU KNOW THE FUNNY THING, BEN? WHENEVER MY POP WOULD SAY THAT LINE, I'D WINCE SO HARD YOU'D THINK MY FACE WAS TRYING TO FLIP INSIDE OUT.
BUT NOW I MIGHT AS WELL TATTOO THE DAMN THING ON MY CHEST.
DAD...
WHAT, DON'T THINK YOUR DAD'D LOOK GOOD WITH A BIG OL' CHEST TATTOO?
WATCH THE ROAD.
I'M WATCHING. I'M WATCHING.
YOUR SISTER... SHE'S SOMETHING, ISN'T SHE? STRONGEST ONE OF US YET. STILL REMEMBER THE NIGHT SHE CAME OUT TO US.
THERE WAS FIRE IN HER EYES. I WAS SO PROUD OF HER. AND NOW SHE'S GETTING MARRIED TO THAT WONDERFUL GIRL...
BUT I HAVE TO SAY, YOUR MOTHER AND I SIGHED A DEEP BREATH OF RELIEF WHEN YOU TOLD US ABOUT THIS GIRL YOU WERE TAKING TO THE SHOW TONIGHT.
I'M NOT OLD FASHIONED. YOU KNOW I'M NOT.
BUT WHAT CAN I SAY? PART OF ME JUST WANTS GRANDKIDS.
I'M SORRY, I'M SORRY, I KNOW. THIS ISN'T A DATE. I PROMISE, I'M NOT GOING TO EMBARRASS YOU.
I'LL BE SITTING ALL THE WAY IN THE BACK.

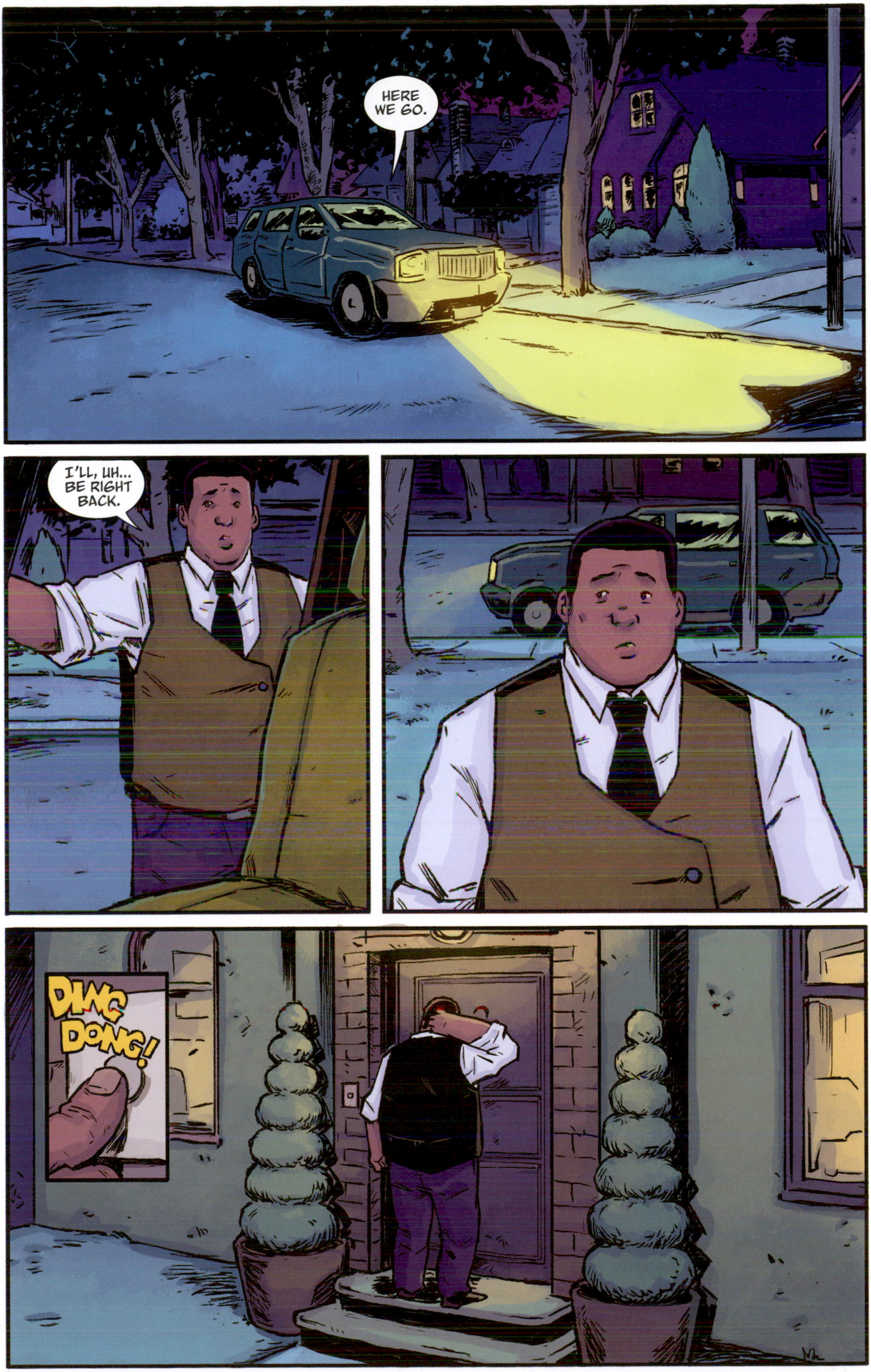
HERE WE GO.
I'LL, UH... BE RIGHT BACK.
DING DONG!

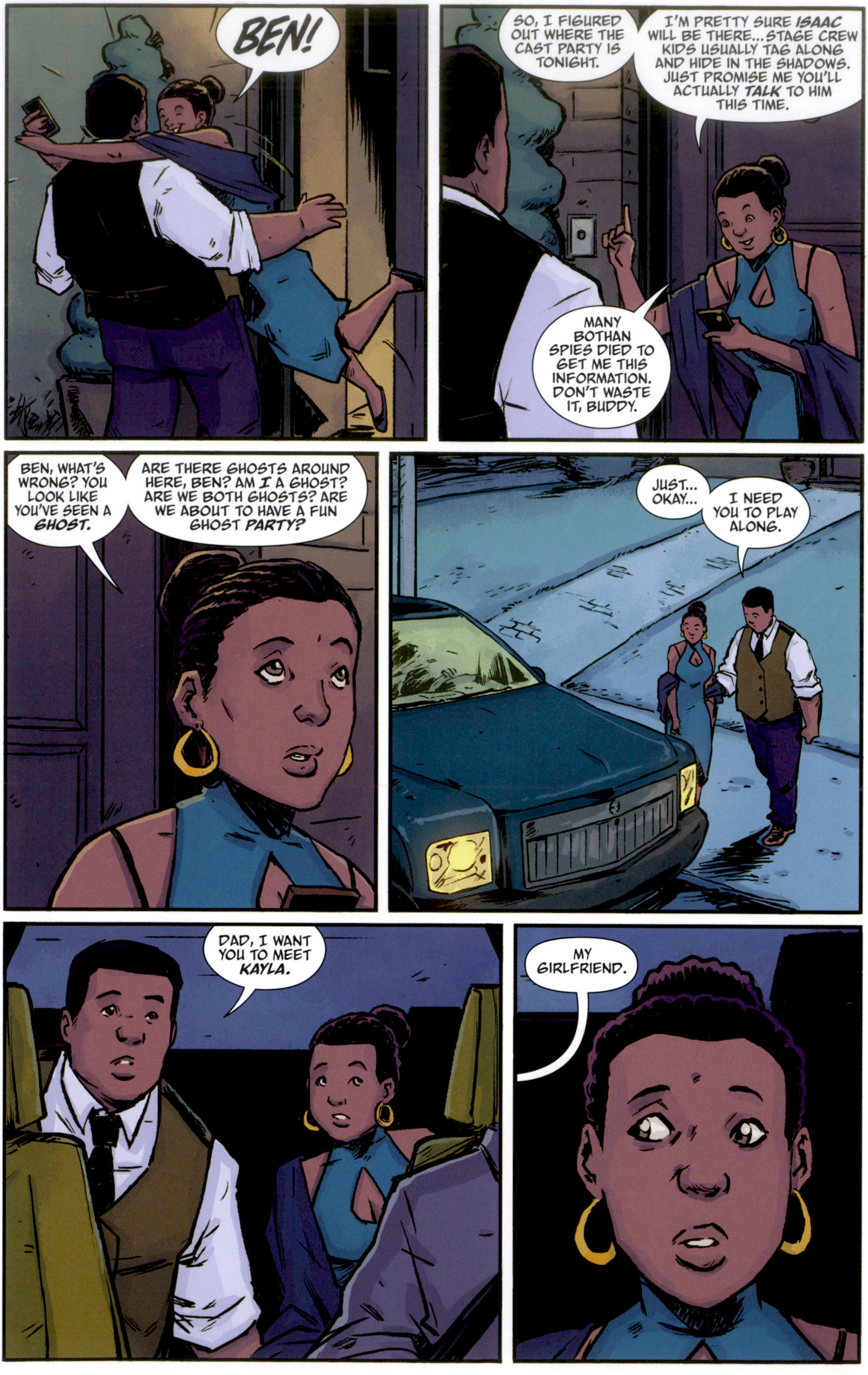
BEN!
SO, I FIGURED OUT WHERE THE CAST PARTY IS TONIGHT.
I'M PRETTY SURE ISAAC WILL BE THERE...STAGE CREW KIDS USUALLY TAG ALONG AND HIDE IN THE SHADOWS. JUST PROMISE ME YOU'LL ACTUALLY TALK TO HIM THIS TIME.
MANY BOTHAN SPIES DIED TO GET ME THIS INFORMATION. DON'T WASTE IT, BUDDY.
BEN, WHAT'S WRONG? YOU LOOK LIKE YOU'VE SEEN A GHOST.
ARE THERE GHOSTS AROUND HERE, BEN? AM I A GHOST? ARE WE BOTH GHOSTS? ARE WE ABOUT TO HAVE A FUN GHOST PARTY?
JUST... OKAY...
I NEED YOU TO PLAY ALONG.
DAD, I WANT YOU TO MEET KAYLA.
MY GIRLFRIEND.

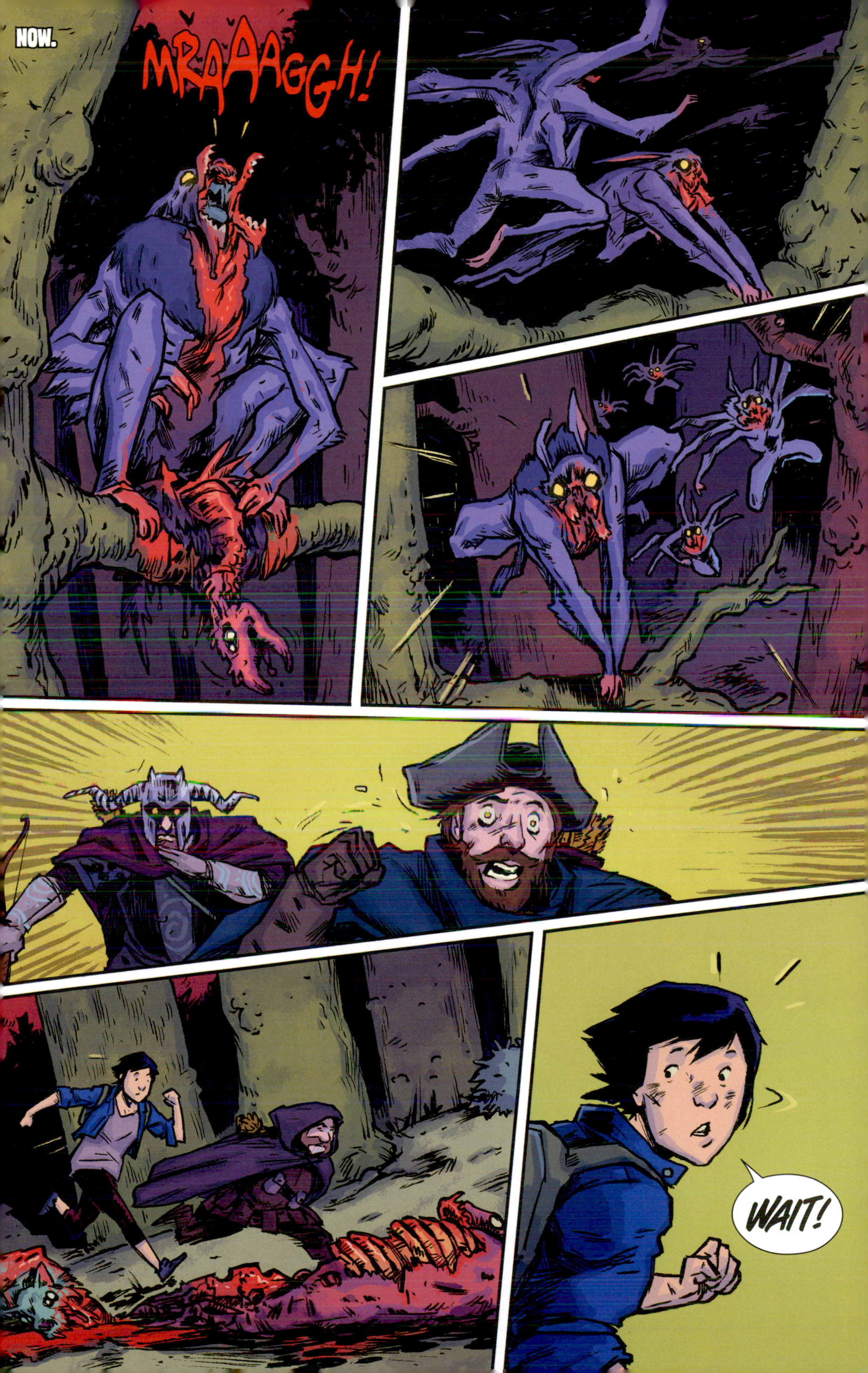
NOW.
MRAAAGGH!
WAIT!

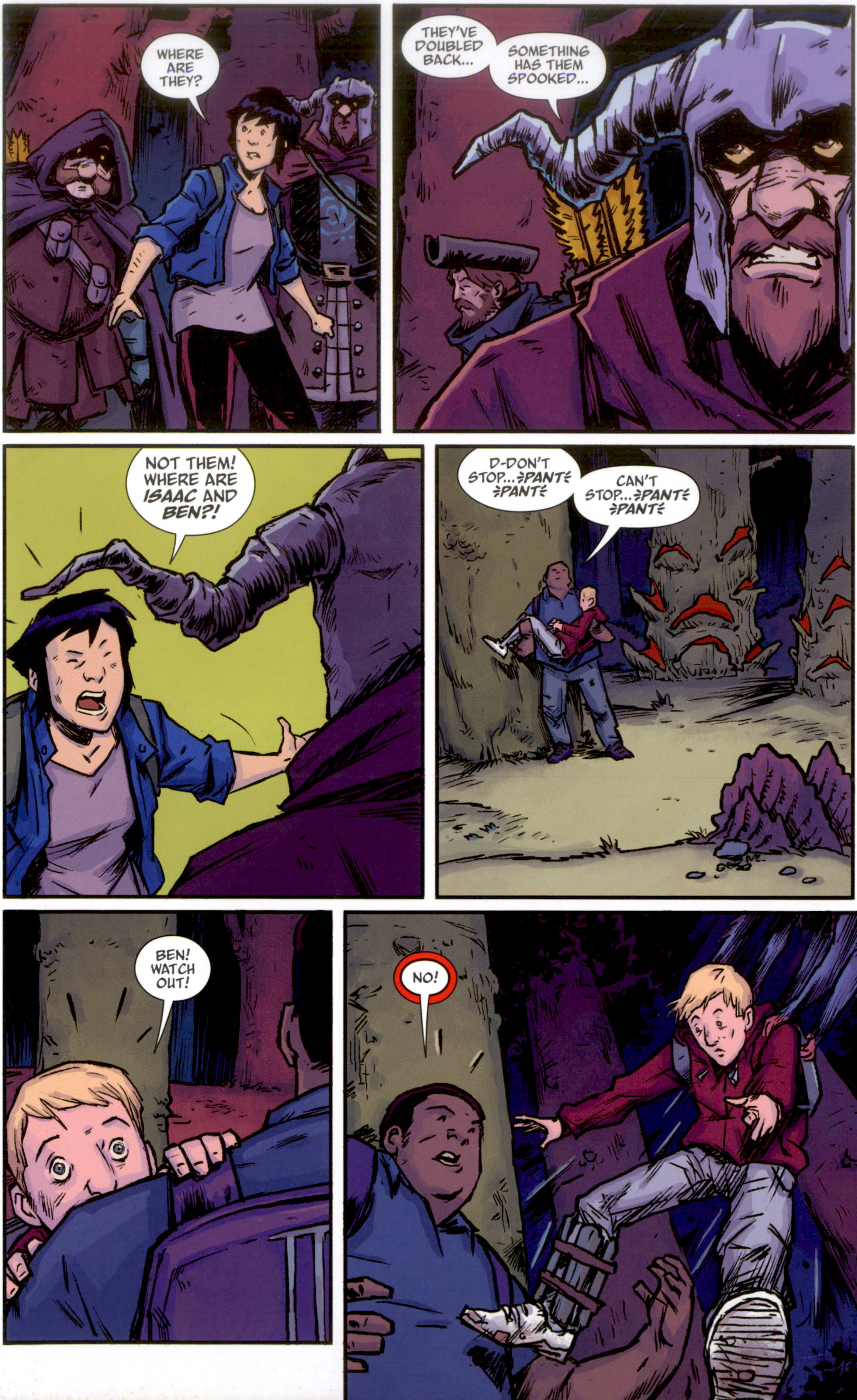
WHERE ARE THEY?
THEY'VE DOUBLED BACK...
SOMETHING HAS THEM SPOOKED...
NOT THEM! WHERE ARE ISAAC AND BEN?!
D-DON'T STOP... PANT PANT
CAN'T STOP... PANT PANT
BEN! WATCH OUT!
NO!

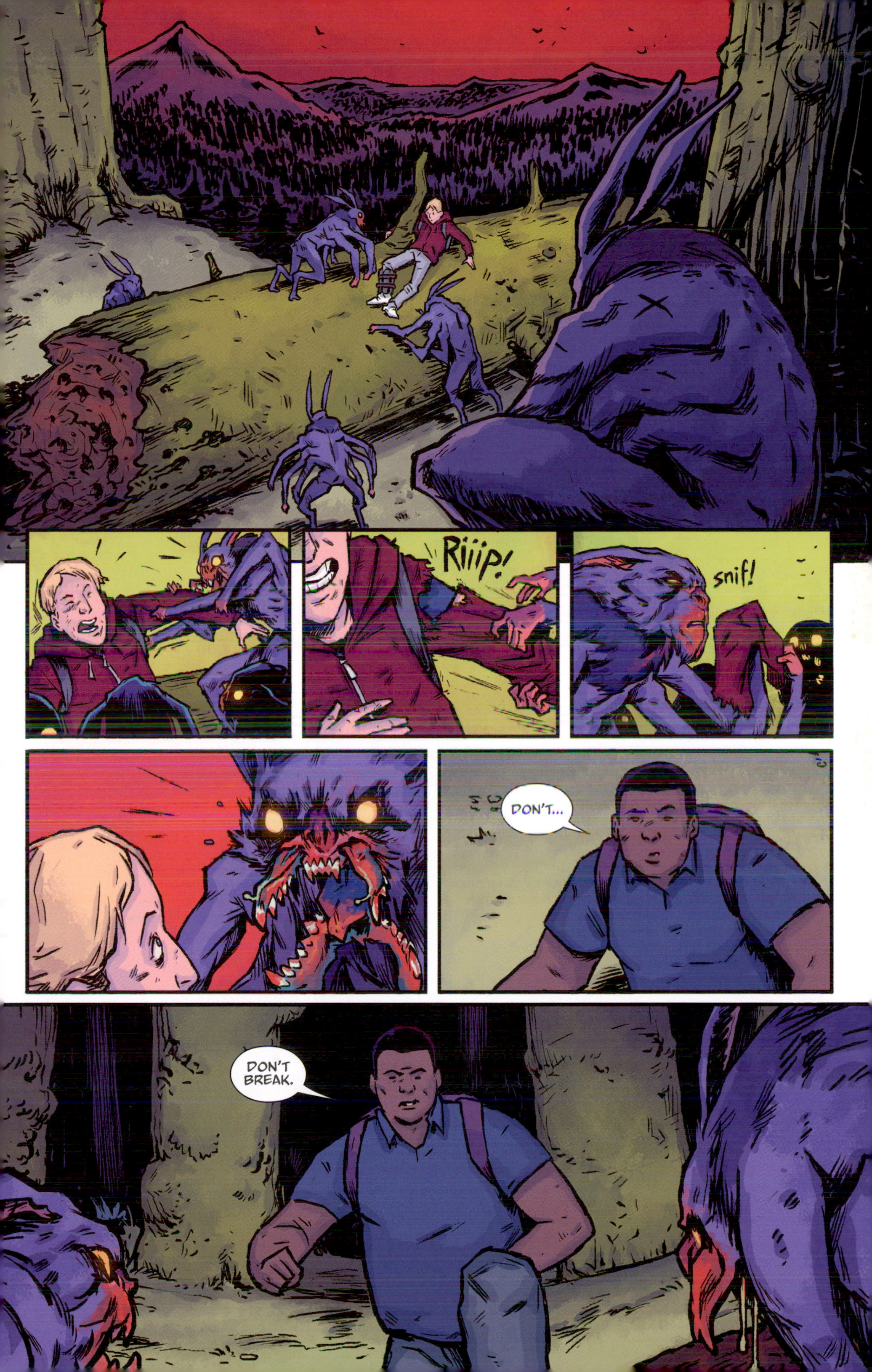
Riiip!
snif!
DON'T...
DON'T BREAK.

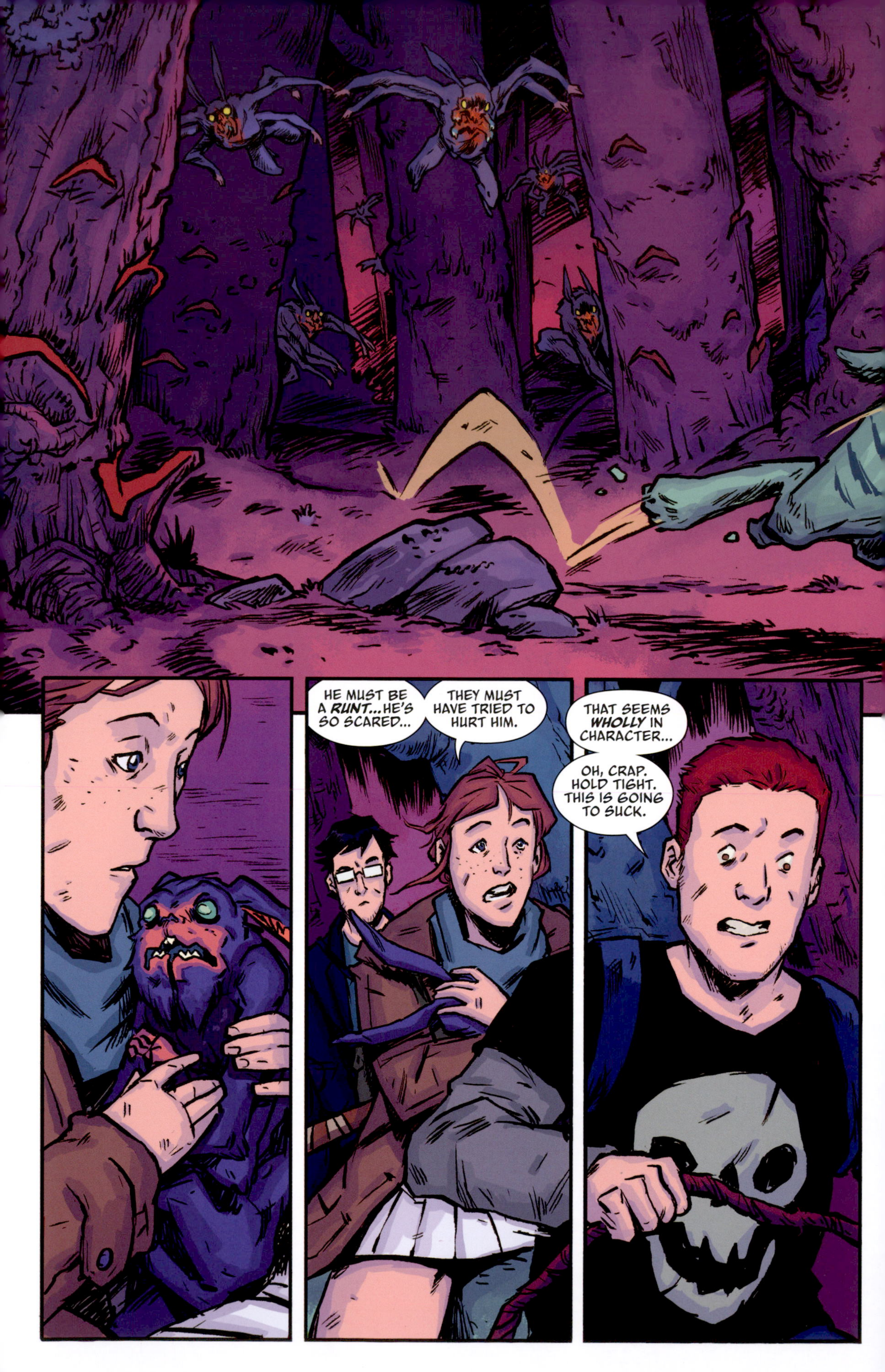
HE MUST BE A *RUNT*...HE'S SO SCARED...
THEY MUST HAVE TRIED TO HURT HIM.
THAT SEEMS *WHOLLY* IN CHARACTER...
OH, CRAP. HOLD TIGHT. THIS IS GOING TO SUCK.

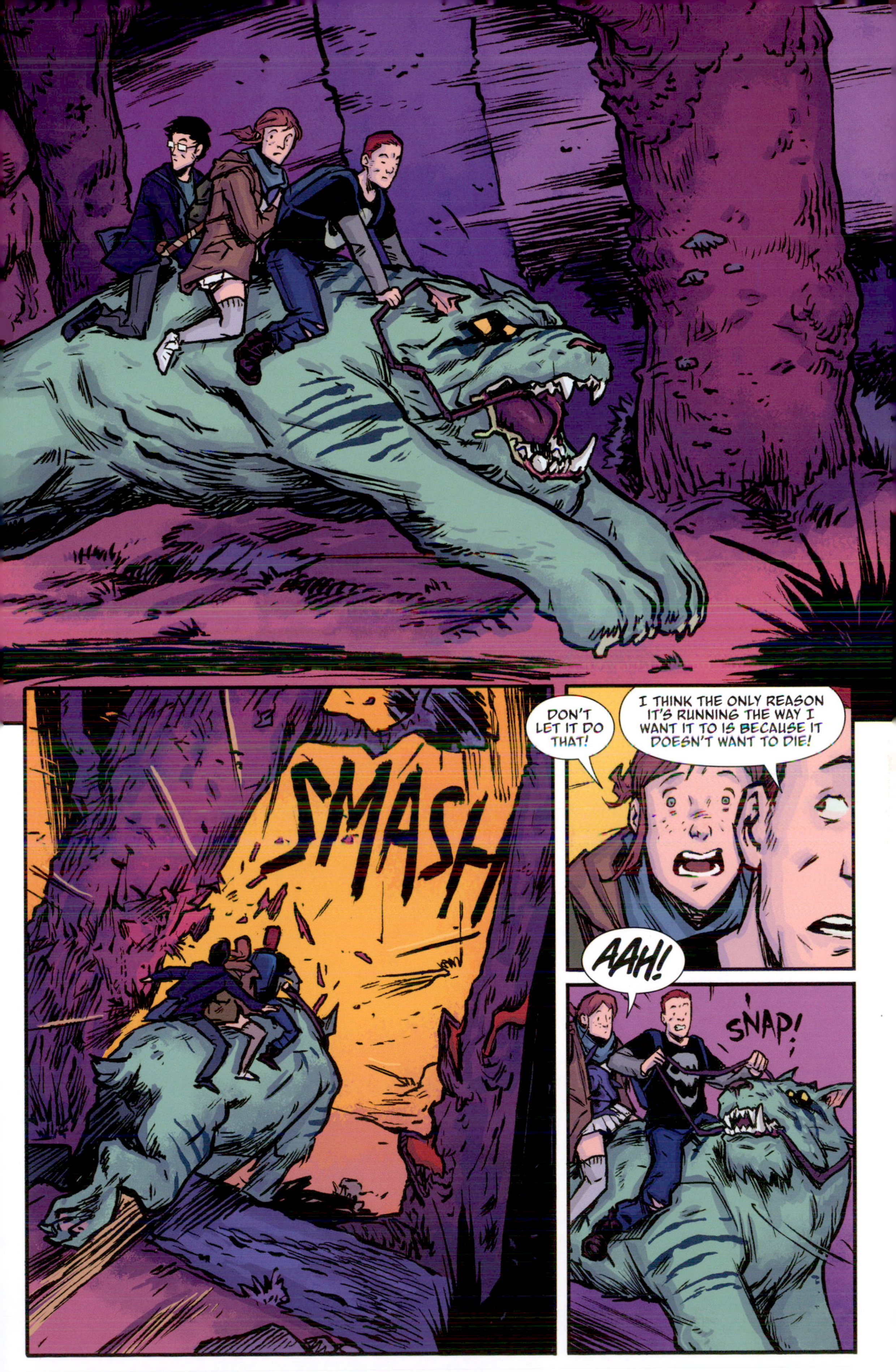
SMASH
DON'T LET IT DO THAT!
I THINK THE ONLY REASON IT'S RUNNING THE WAY I WANT IT TO IS BECAUSE IT DOESN'T WANT TO DIE!
AAH!
SNAP!

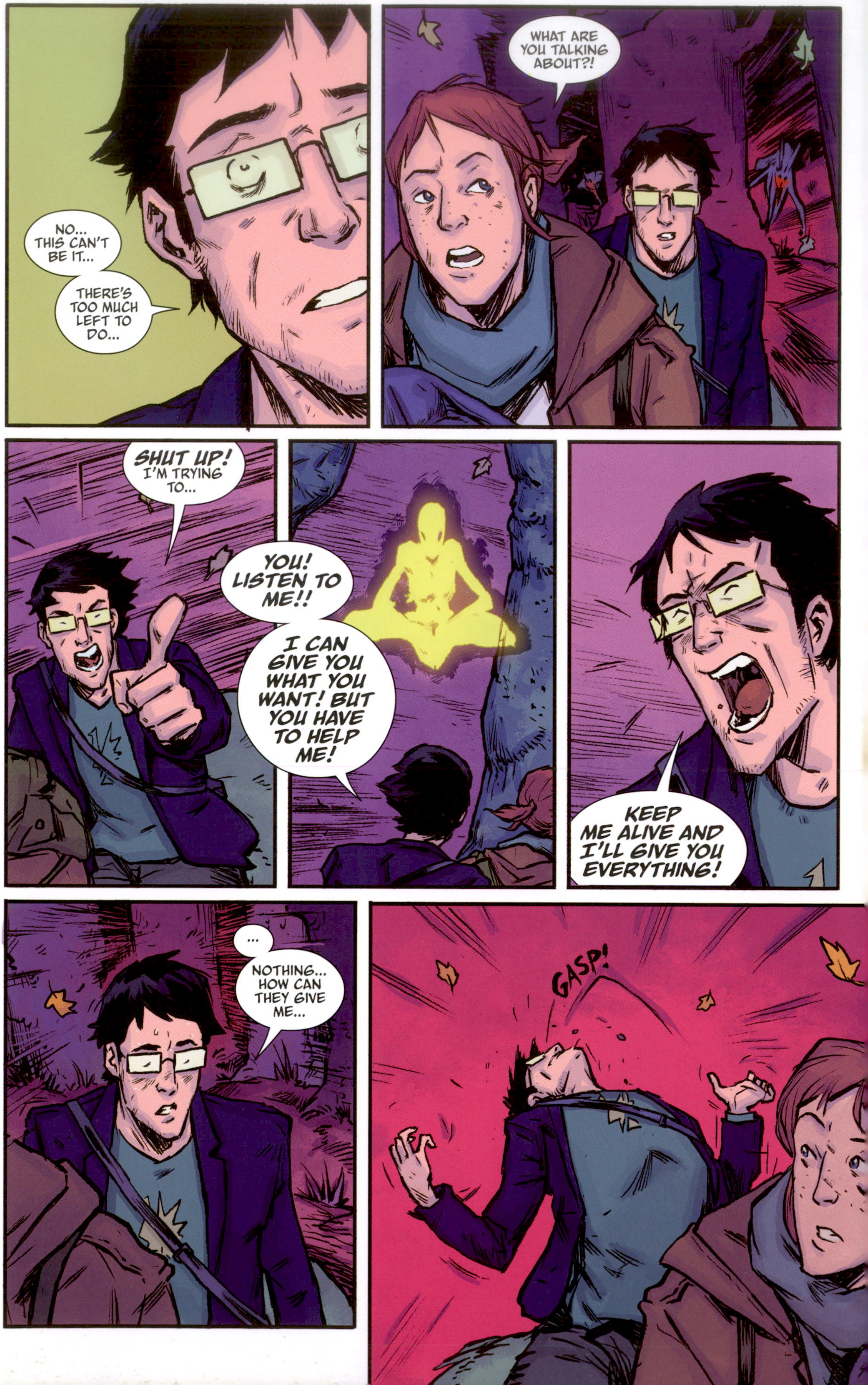
NO... THIS CAN'T BE IT...
THERE'S TOO MUCH LEFT TO DO...
WHAT ARE YOU TALKING ABOUT?!
SHUT UP! I'M TRYING TO...
YOU! LISTEN TO ME!!
I CAN GIVE YOU WHAT YOU WANT! BUT YOU HAVE TO HELP ME!
KEEP ME ALIVE AND I'LL GIVE YOU EVERYTHING!
...
NOTHING... HOW CAN THEY GIVE ME...
GASP!

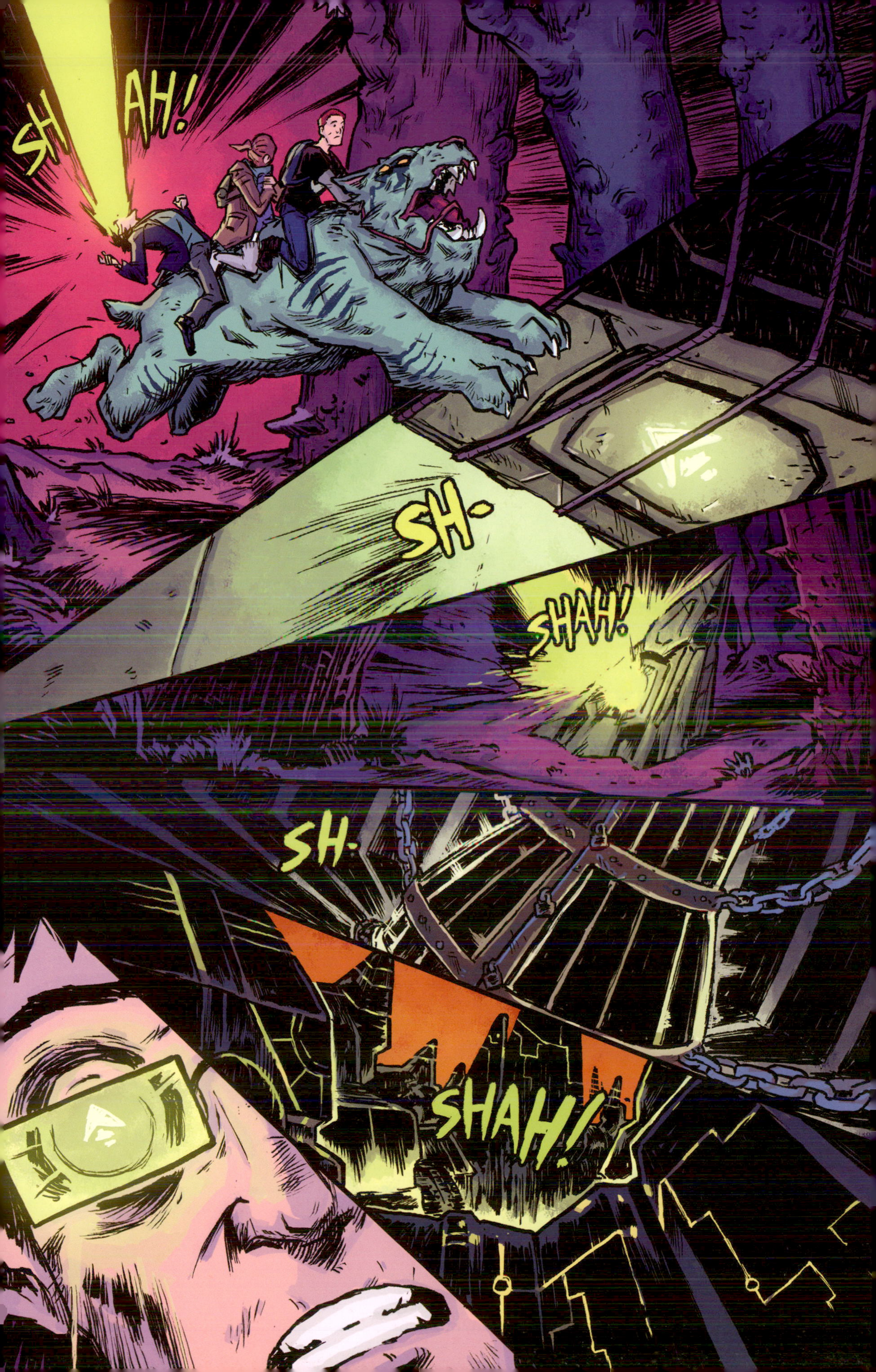
SH
AH!
SH-
SHAH!
SH-
SHAH!

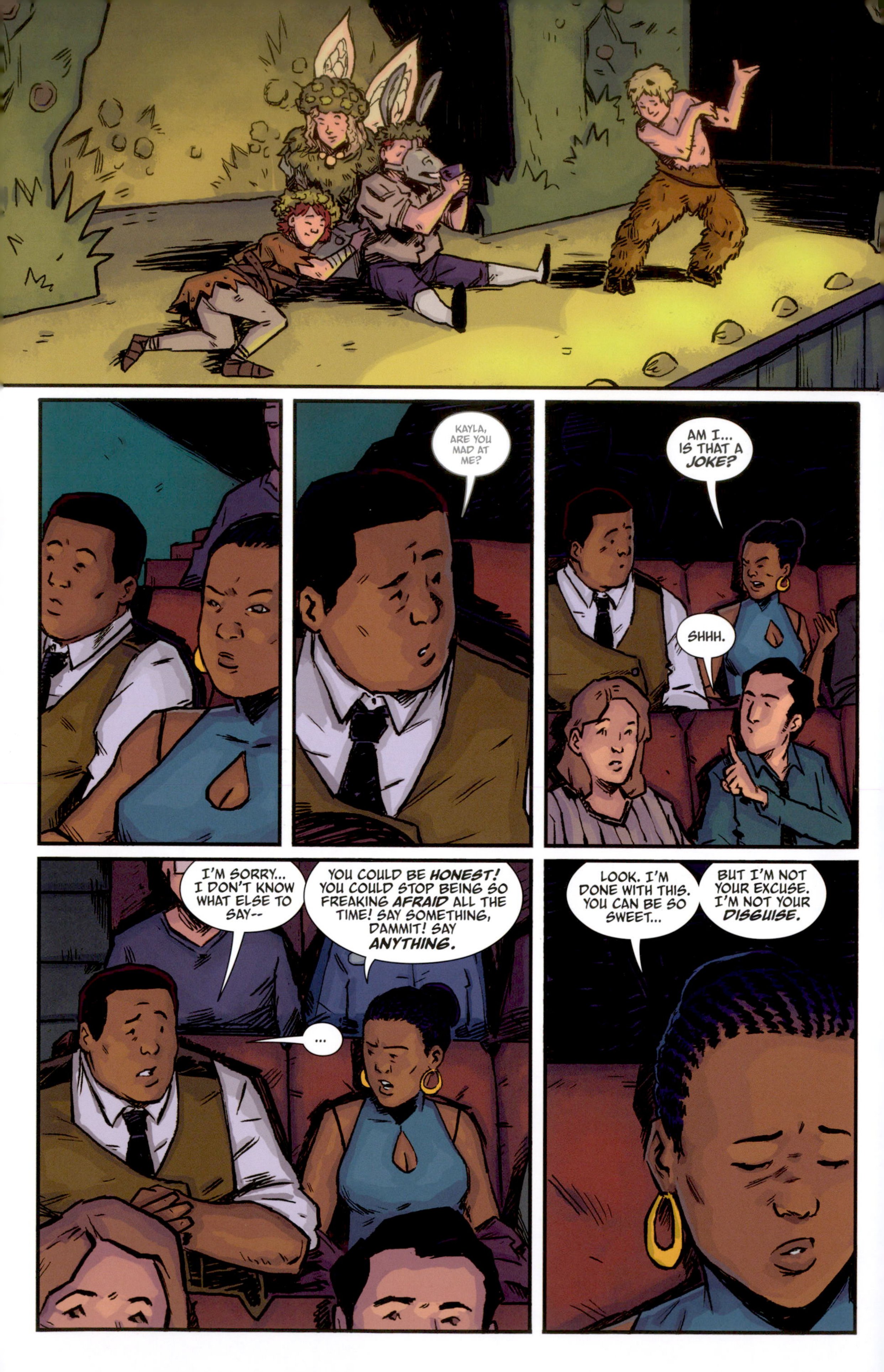
KAYLA, ARE YOU MAD AT ME?
AM I... IS THAT A JOKE?
SHHH.
I'M SORRY... I DON'T KNOW WHAT ELSE TO SAY--
YOU COULD BE HONEST! YOU COULD STOP BEING SO FREAKING AFRAID ALL THE TIME! SAY SOMETHING, DAMMIT! SAY ANYTHING.
...
LOOK. I'M DONE WITH THIS. YOU CAN BE SO SWEET...
BUT I'M NOT YOUR EXCUSE. I'M NOT YOUR DISGUISE.

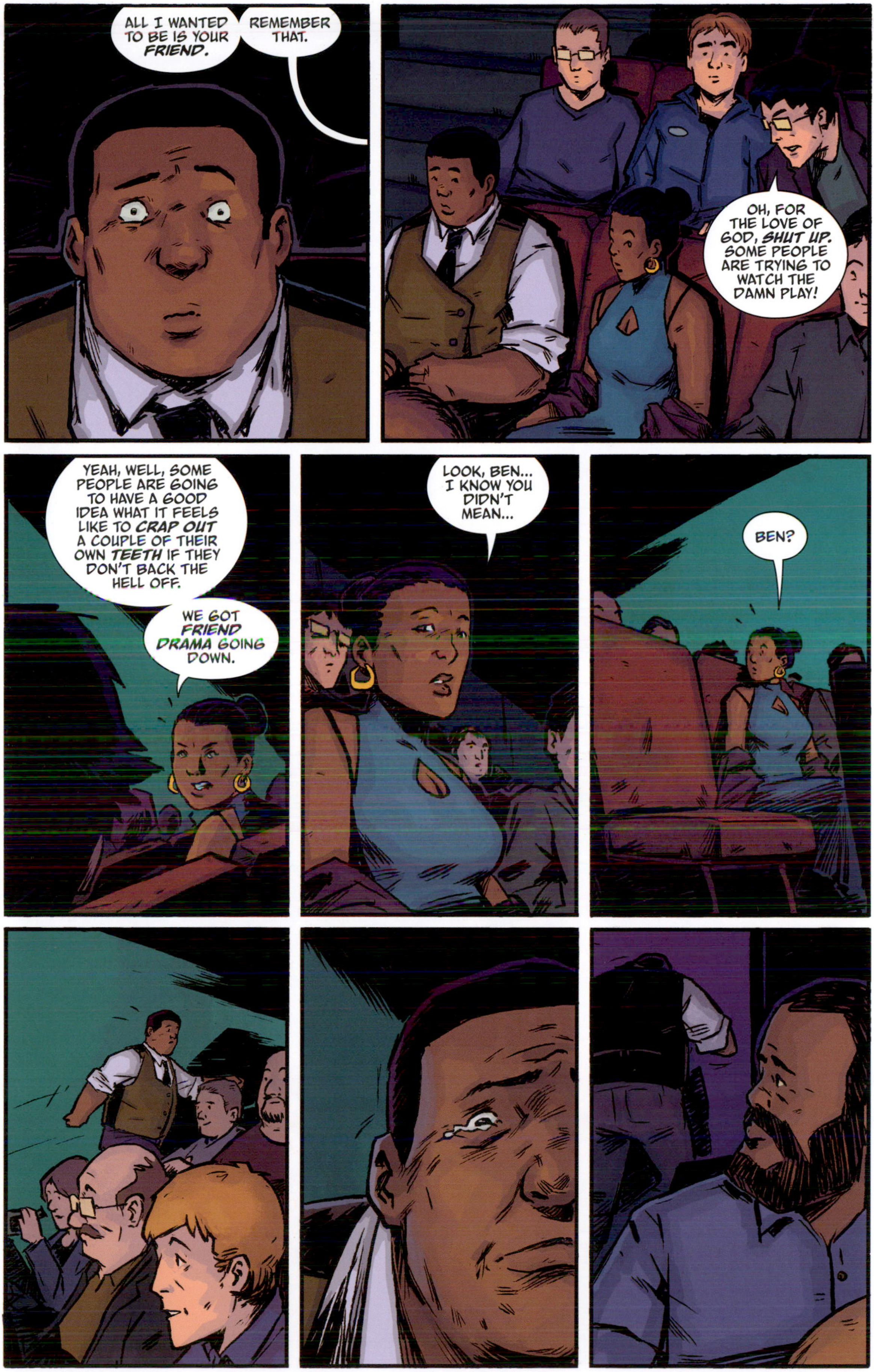
ALL I WANTED TO BE IS YOUR FRIEND.
REMEMBER THAT.
OH, FOR THE LOVE OF GOD, SHUT UP. SOME PEOPLE ARE TRYING TO WATCH THE DAMN PLAY!
YEAH, WELL, SOME PEOPLE ARE GOING TO HAVE A GOOD IDEA WHAT IT FEELS LIKE TO CRAP OUT A COUPLE OF THEIR OWN TEETH IF THEY DON'T BACK THE HELL OFF.
WE GOT FRIEND DRAMA GOING DOWN.
LOOK, BEN... I KNOW YOU DIDN'T MEAN...
BEN?

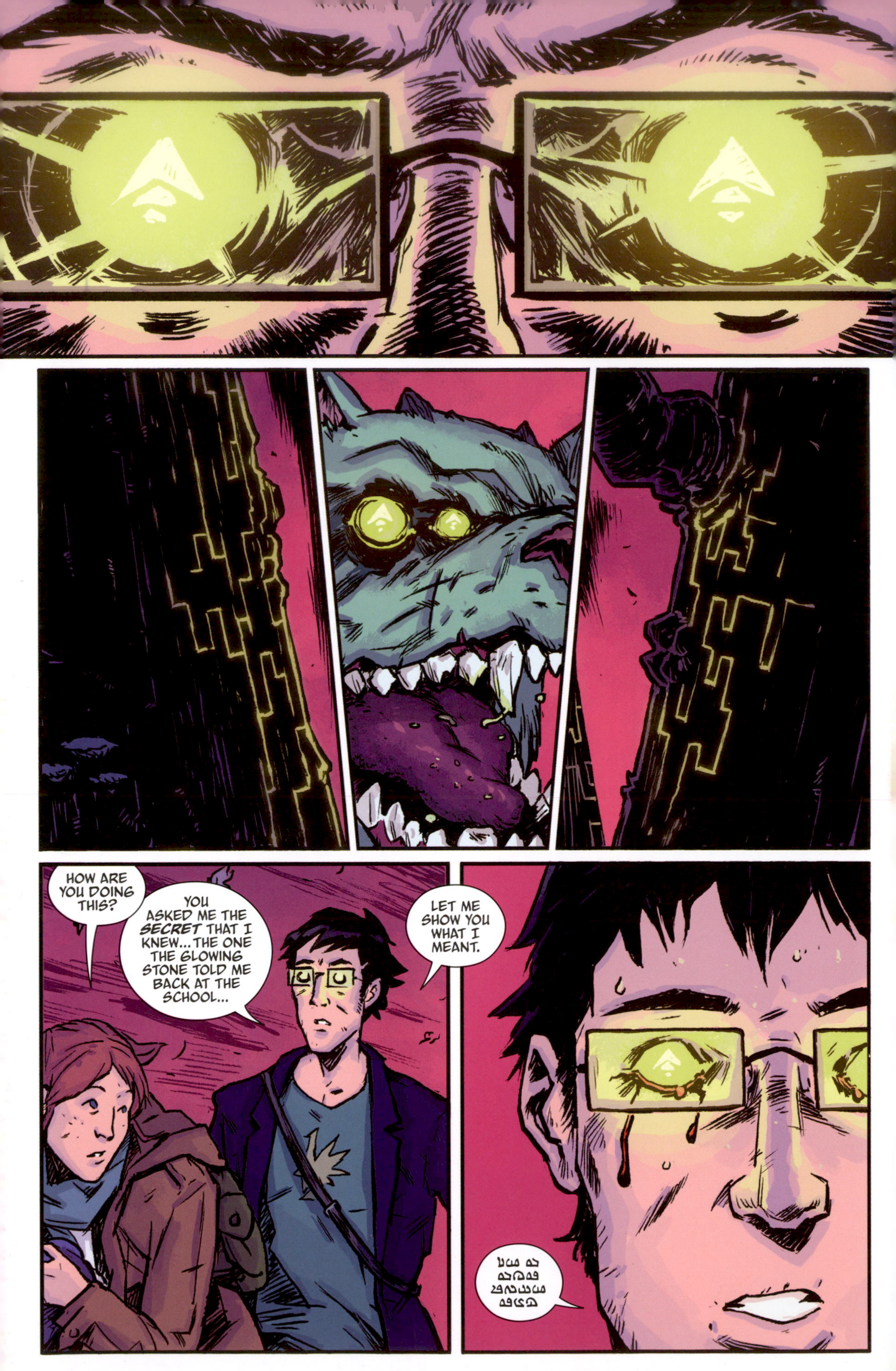
HOW ARE YOU DOING THIS?
YOU ASKED ME THE *SECRET* THAT I KNEW... THE ONE THE GLOWING STONE TOLD ME BACK AT THE SCHOOL...
LET ME SHOW YOU WHAT I MEANT.

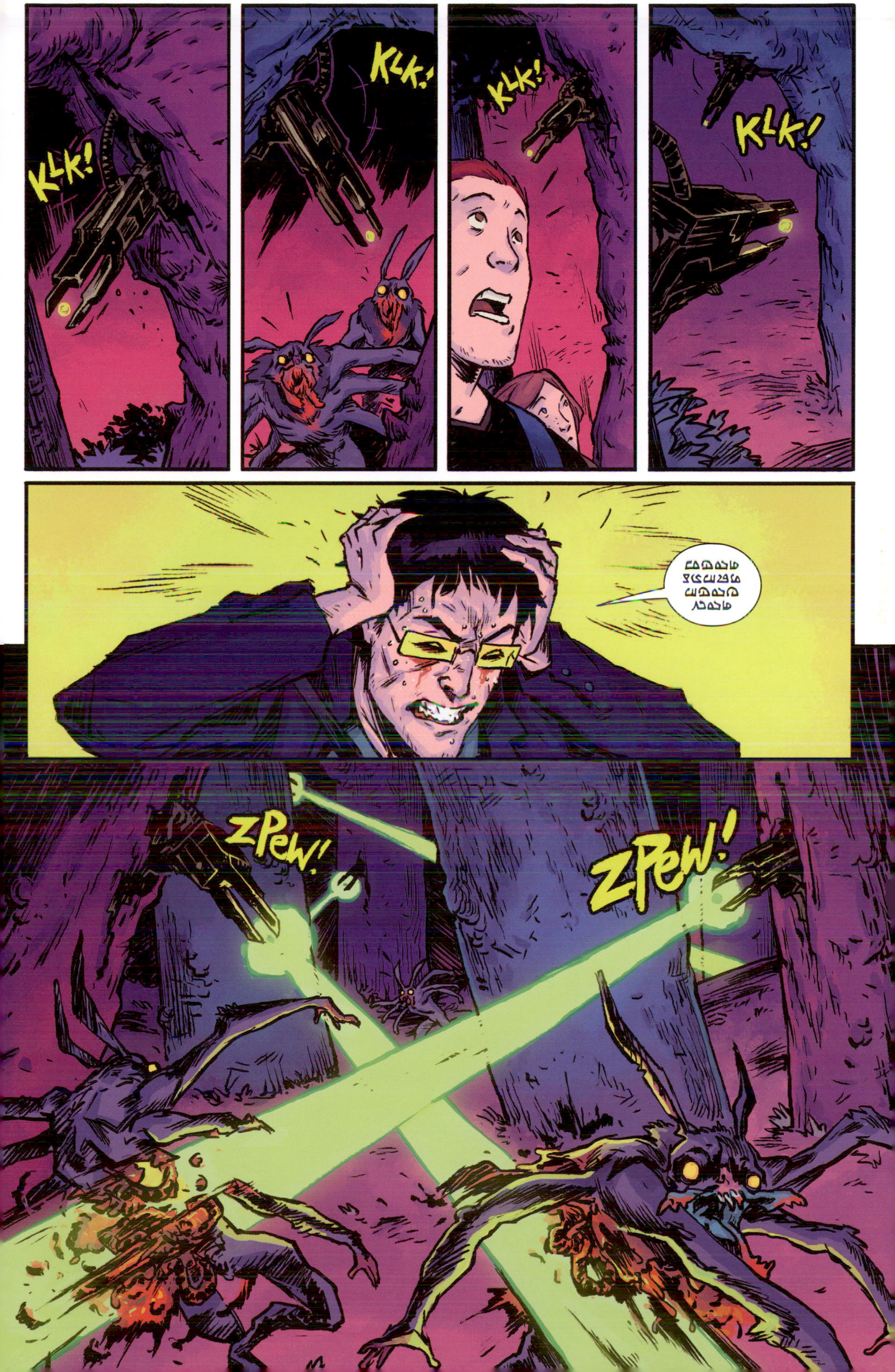
KLK!
KLK!
KLK!
KLK!
ZPEW!
ZPEW!

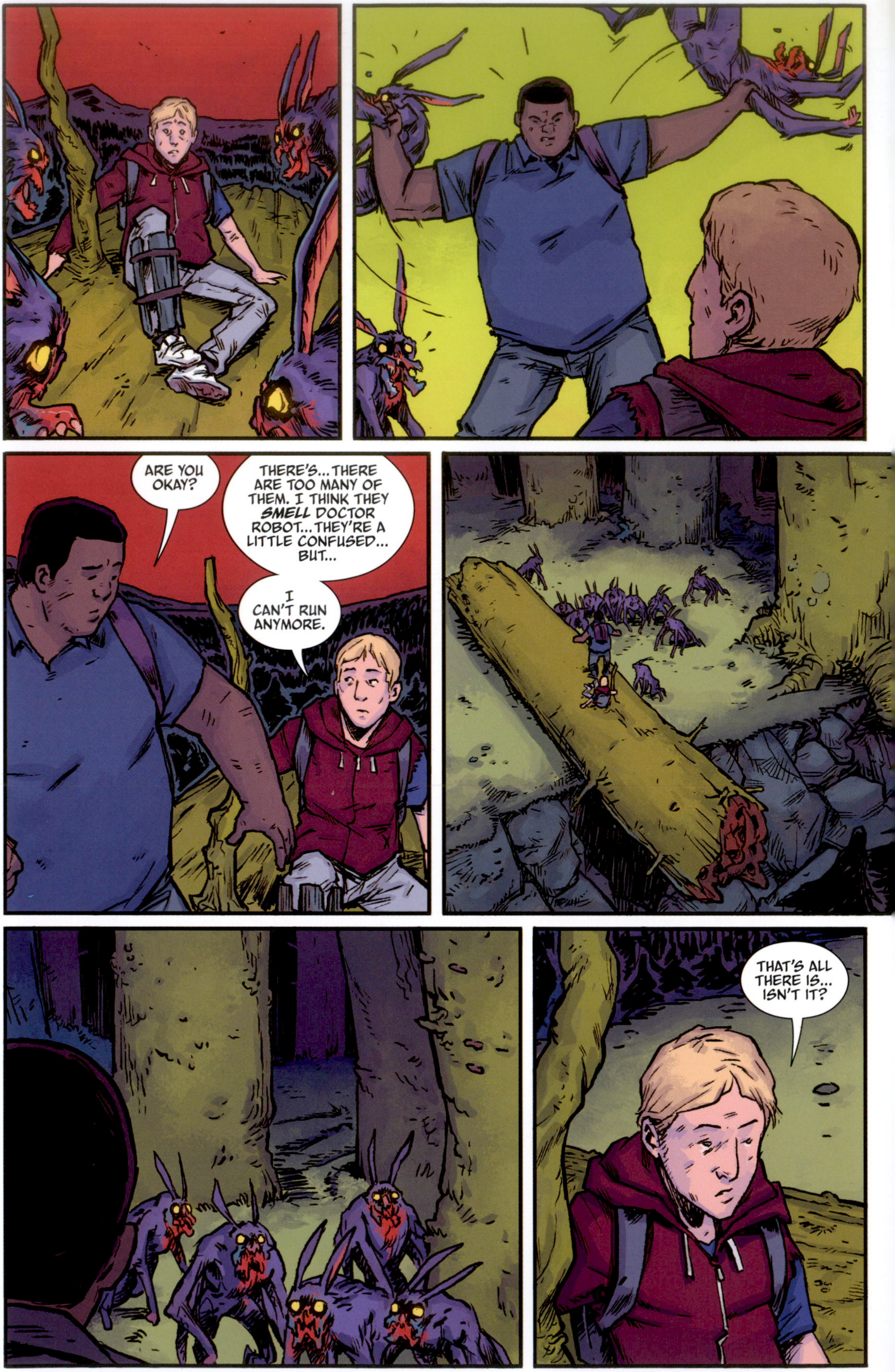
ARE YOU OKAY?
THERE'S... THERE ARE TOO MANY OF THEM. I THINK THEY SMELL DOCTOR ROBOT... THEY'RE A LITTLE CONFUSED... BUT...
I CAN'T RUN ANYMORE.
THAT'S ALL THERE IS... ISN'T IT?

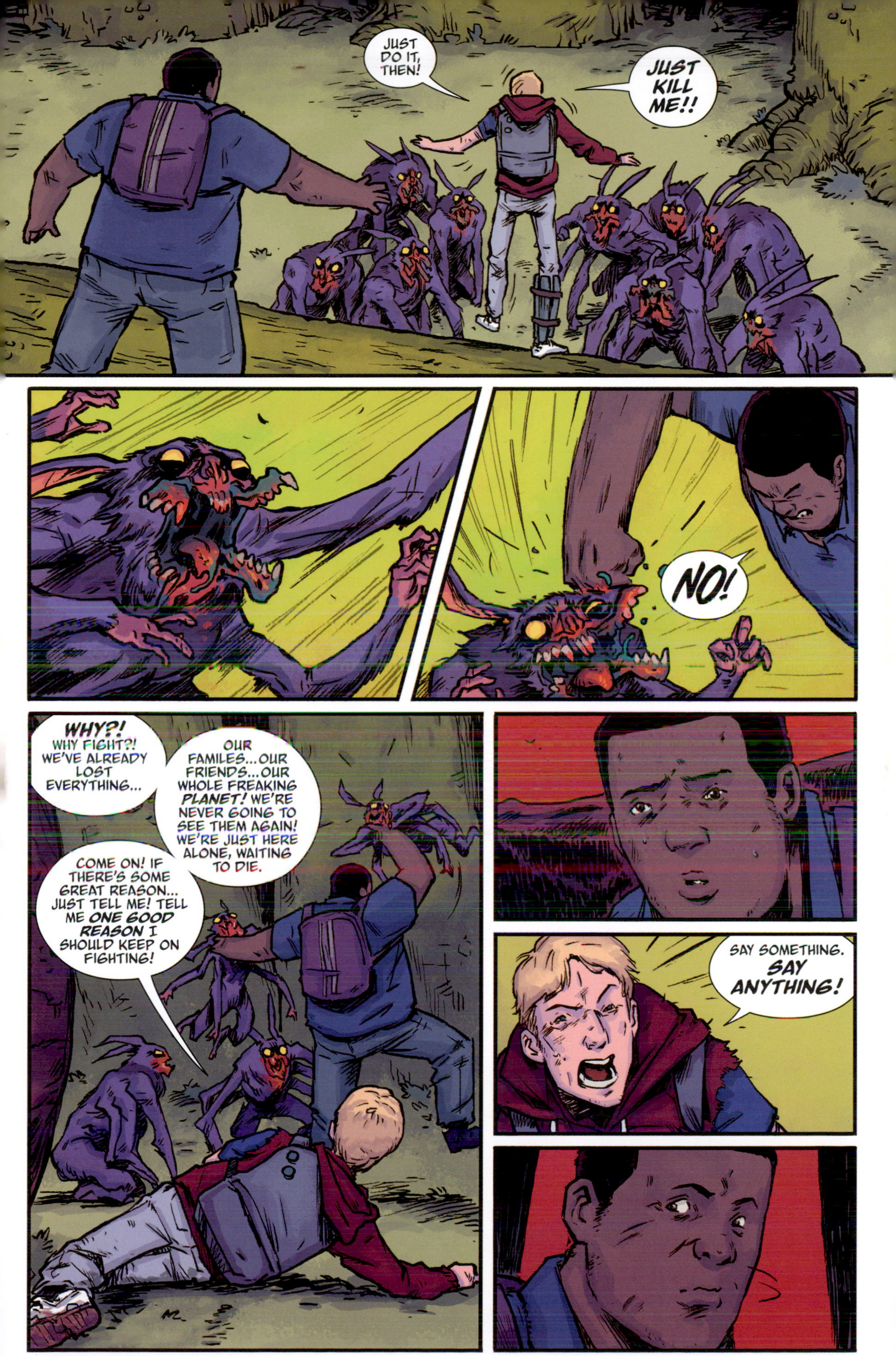
JUST DO IT, THEN!
JUST KILL ME!!
NO!
WHY?! WHY FIGHT?! WE'VE ALREADY LOST EVERYTHING...
OUR FAMILES...OUR FRIENDS...OUR WHOLE FREAKING PLANET! WE'RE NEVER GOING TO SEE THEM AGAIN! WE'RE JUST HERE ALONE, WAITING TO DIE.
COME ON! IF THERE'S SOME GREAT REASON... JUST TELL ME! TELL ME ONE GOOD REASON I SHOULD KEEP ON FIGHTING!
SAY SOMETHING. SAY ANYTHING!

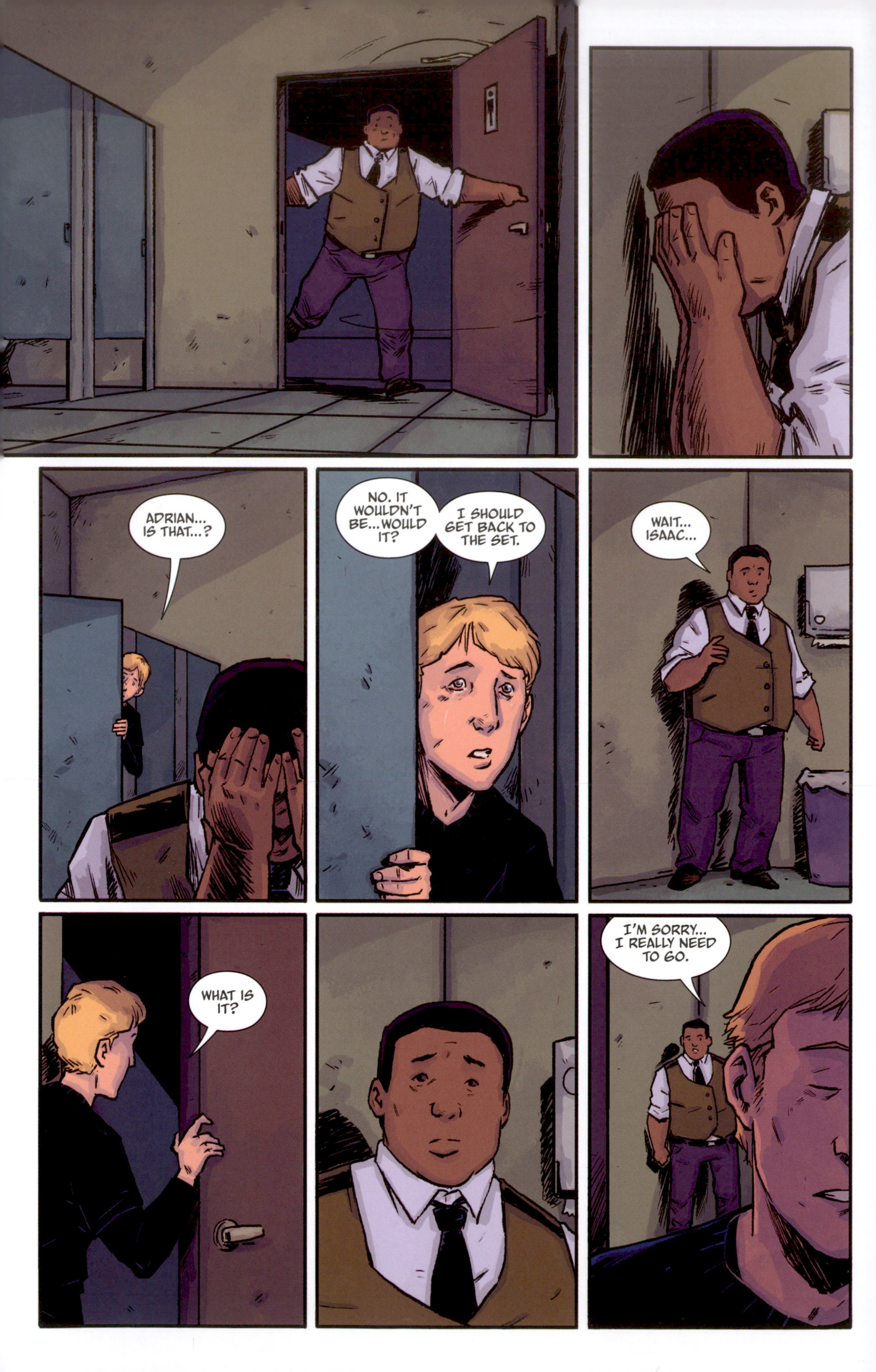
ADRIAN... IS THAT...?
NO. IT WOULDN'T BE...WOULD IT?
I SHOULD GET BACK TO THE SET.
WAIT... ISAAC...
WHAT IS IT?
I'M SORRY... I REALLY NEED TO GO.

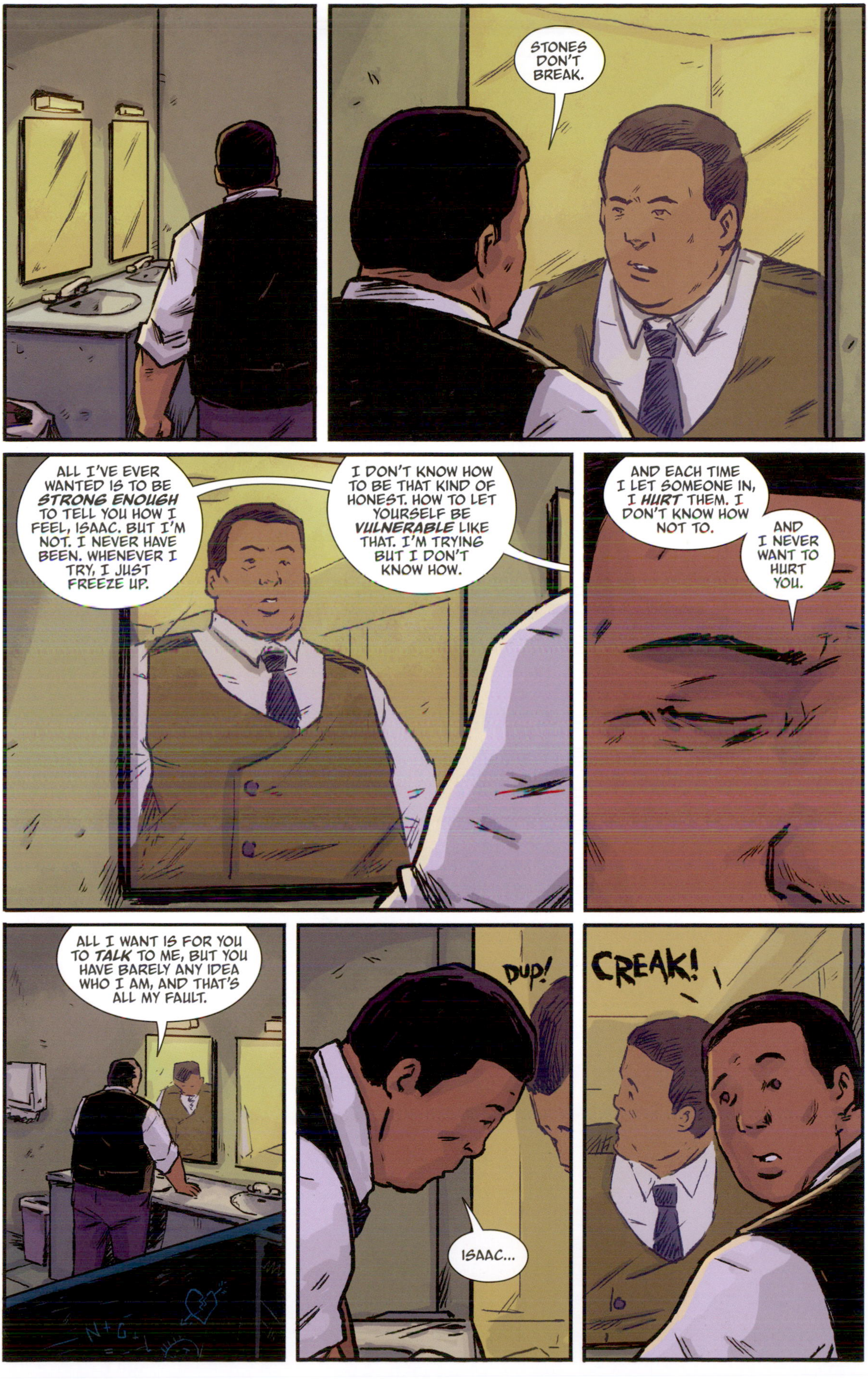
STONES DON'T BREAK.
ALL I'VE EVER WANTED IS TO BE STRONG ENOUGH TO TELL YOU HOW I FEEL, ISAAC. BUT I'M NOT. I NEVER HAVE BEEN. WHENEVER I TRY, I JUST FREEZE UP.
I DON'T KNOW HOW TO BE THAT KIND OF HONEST. HOW TO LET YOURSELF BE VULNERABLE LIKE THAT. I'M TRYING BUT I DON'T KNOW HOW.
AND EACH TIME I LET SOMEONE IN, I HURT THEM. I DON'T KNOW HOW NOT TO.
AND I NEVER WANT TO HURT YOU.
ALL I WANT IS FOR YOU TO TALK TO ME, BUT YOU HAVE BARELY ANY IDEA WHO I AM, AND THAT'S ALL MY FAULT.
DUP!
ISAAC...
CREAK!

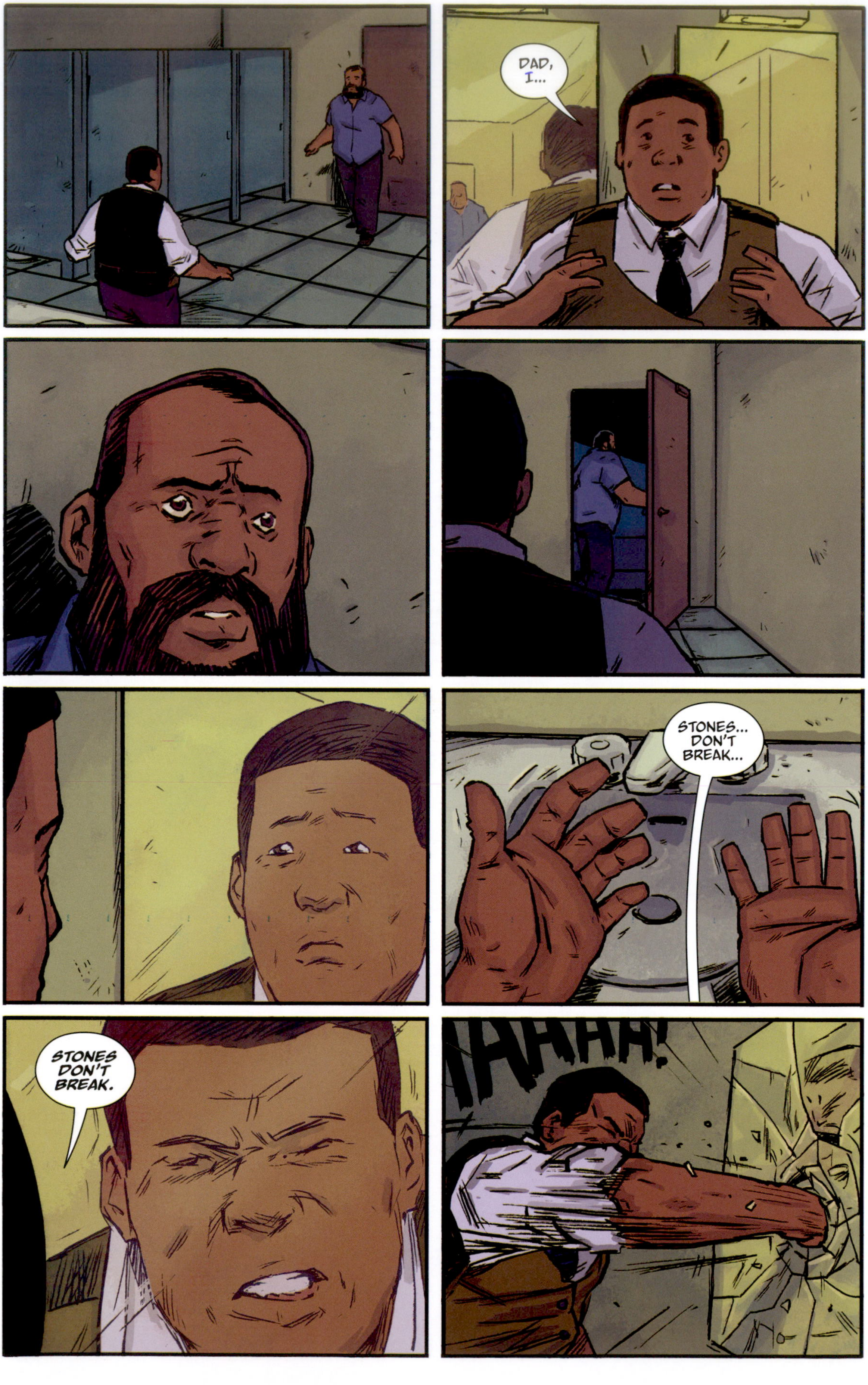
DAD, I...
STONES... DON'T BREAK...
STONES DON'T BREAK.
AAAAH!

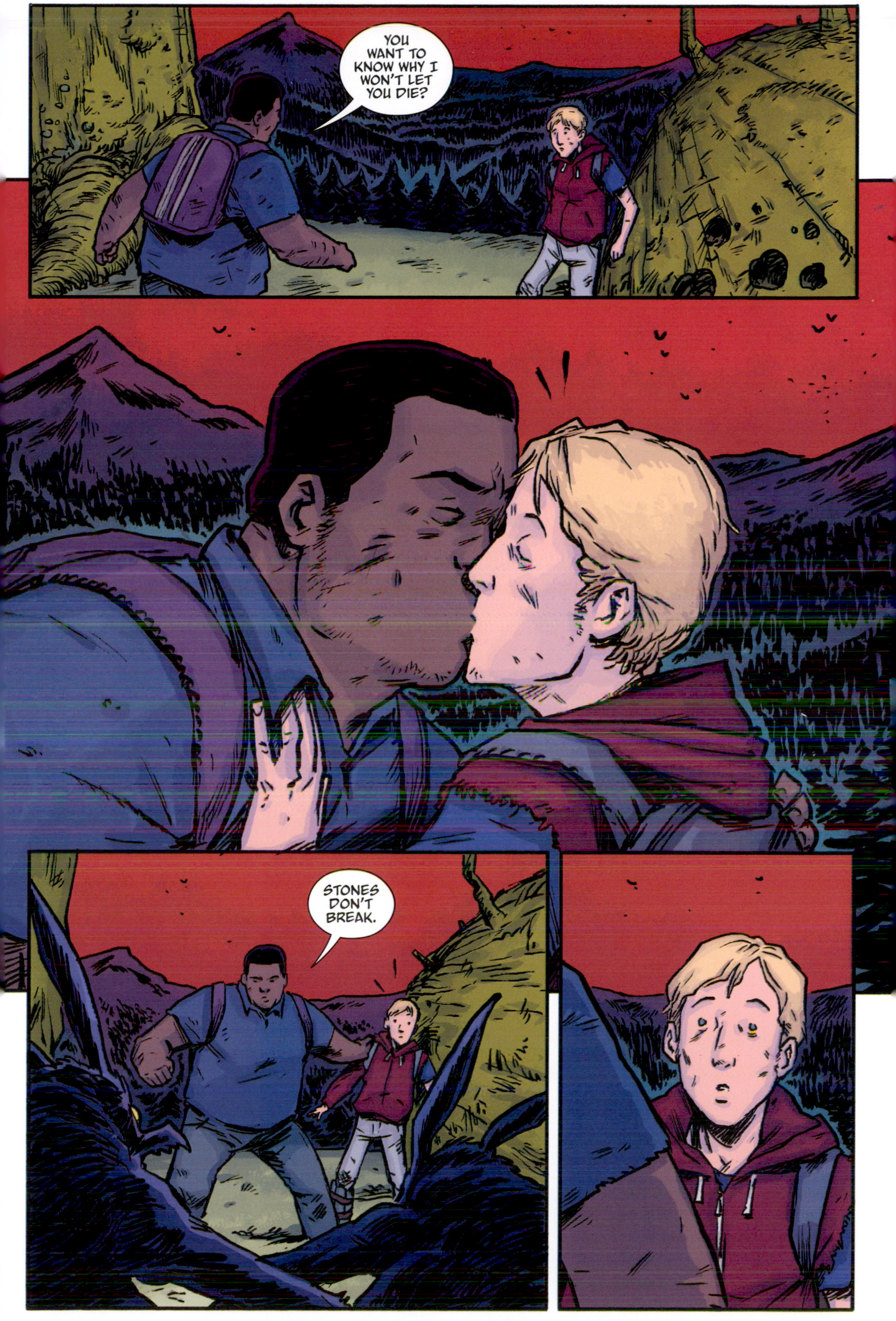
YOU WANT TO KNOW WHY I WON'T LET YOU DIE?
STONES DON'T BREAK.

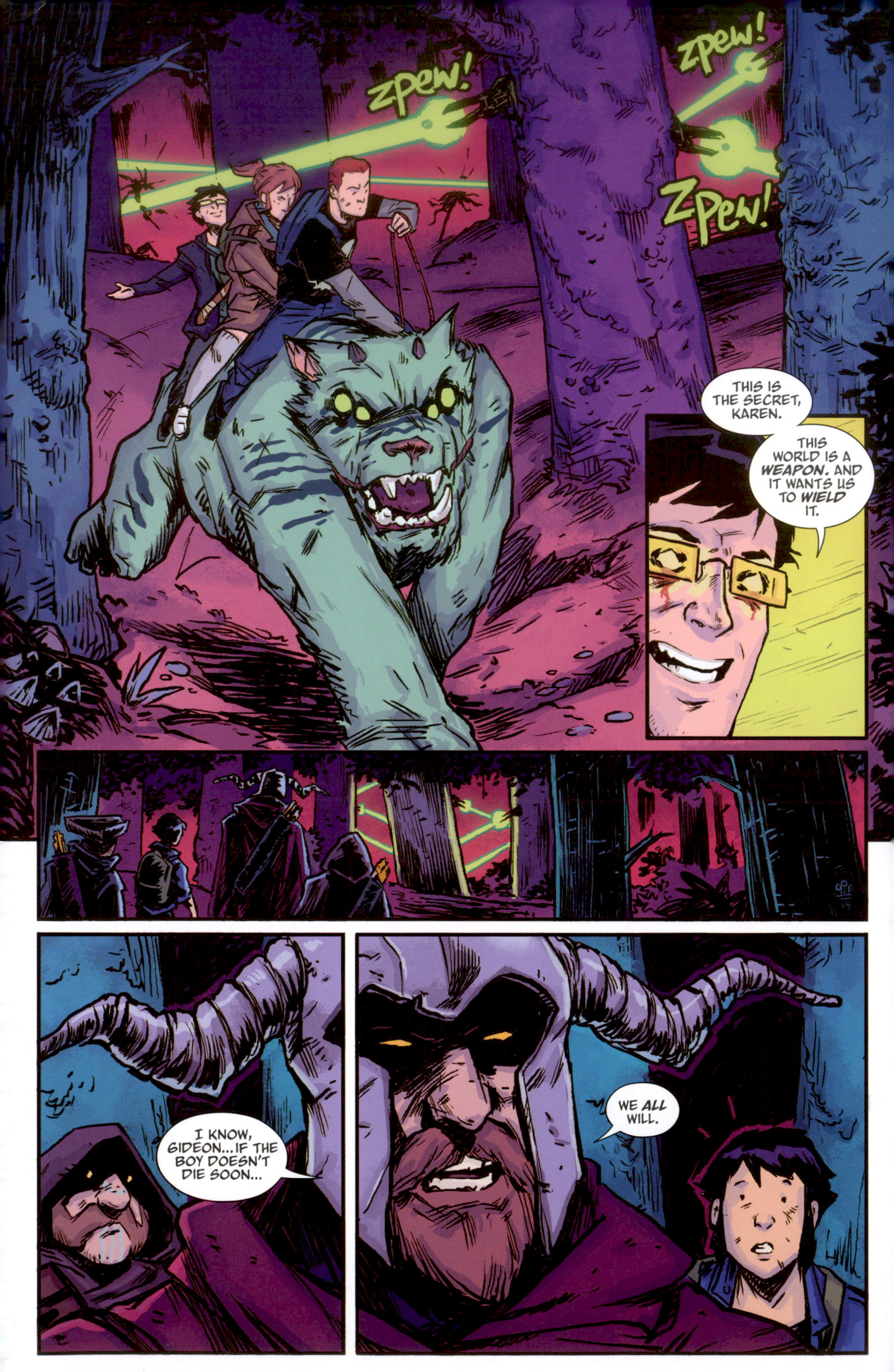
ZPEW!
ZPEW!
ZPEW!
THIS IS THE SECRET, KAREN.
THIS WORLD IS A WEAPON. AND IT WANTS US TO WIELD IT.
I KNOW, GIDEON...IF THE BOY DOESN'T DIE SOON...
WE ALL WILL.

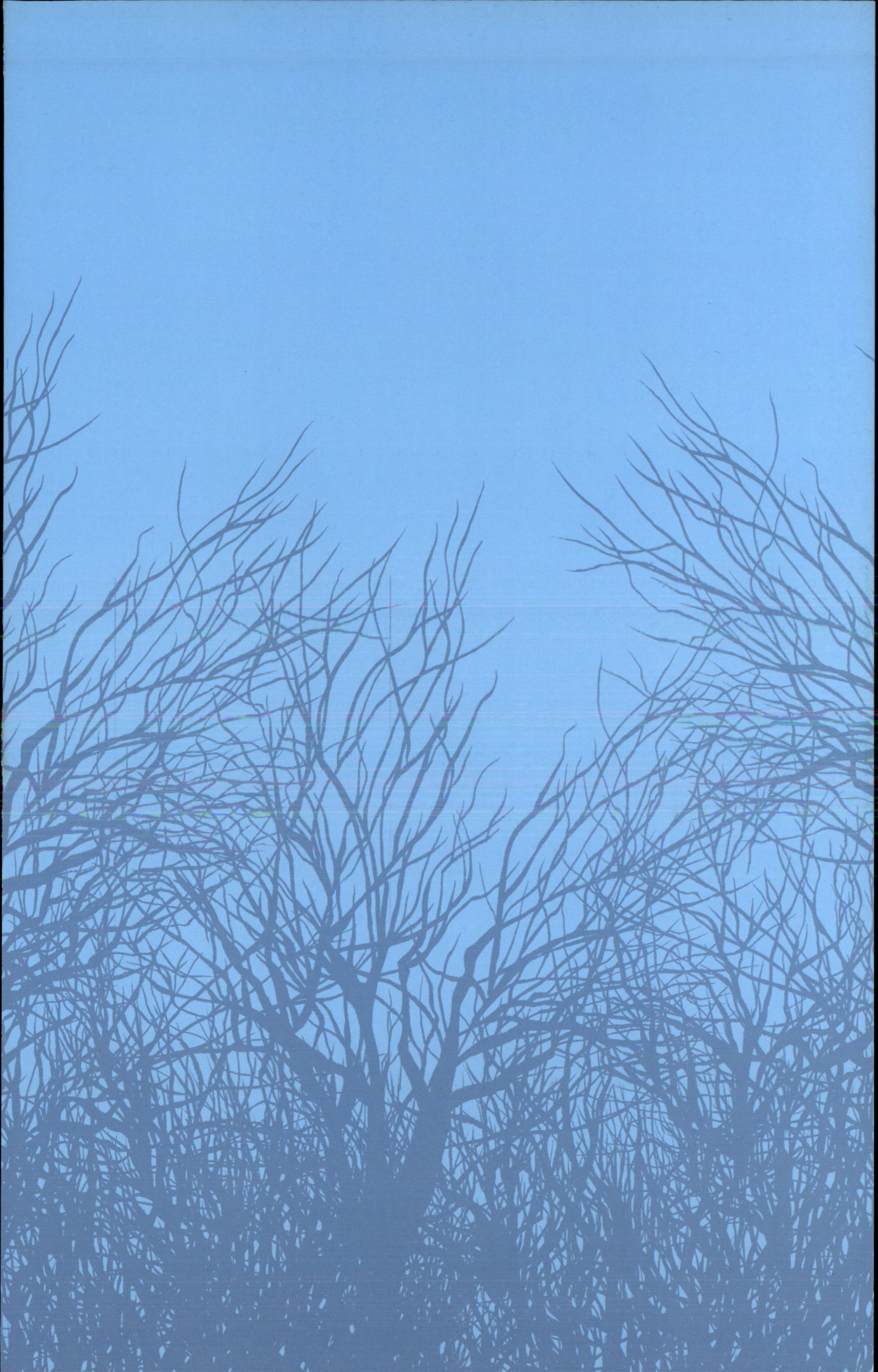

CHAPTER
EIGHT

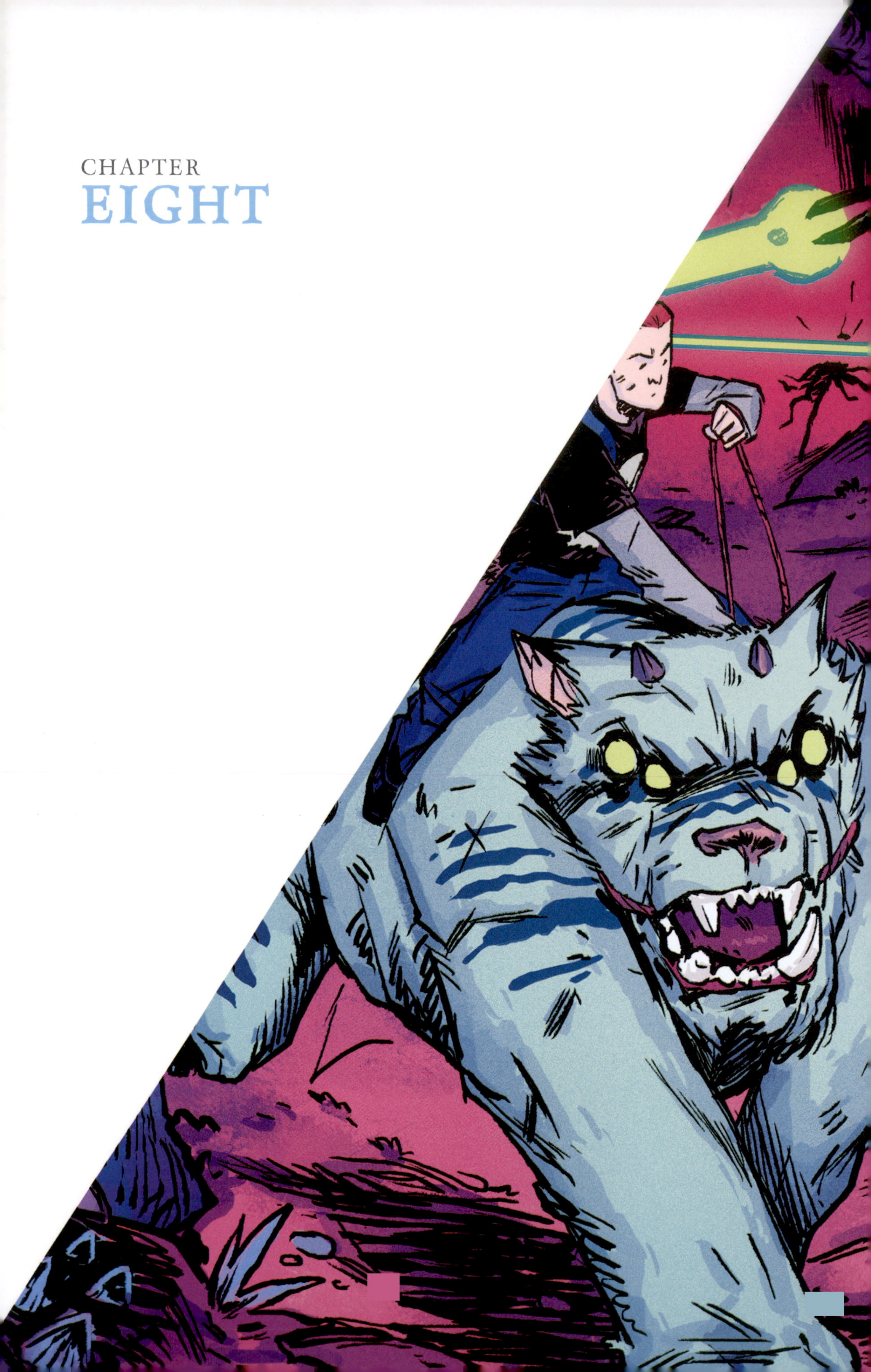

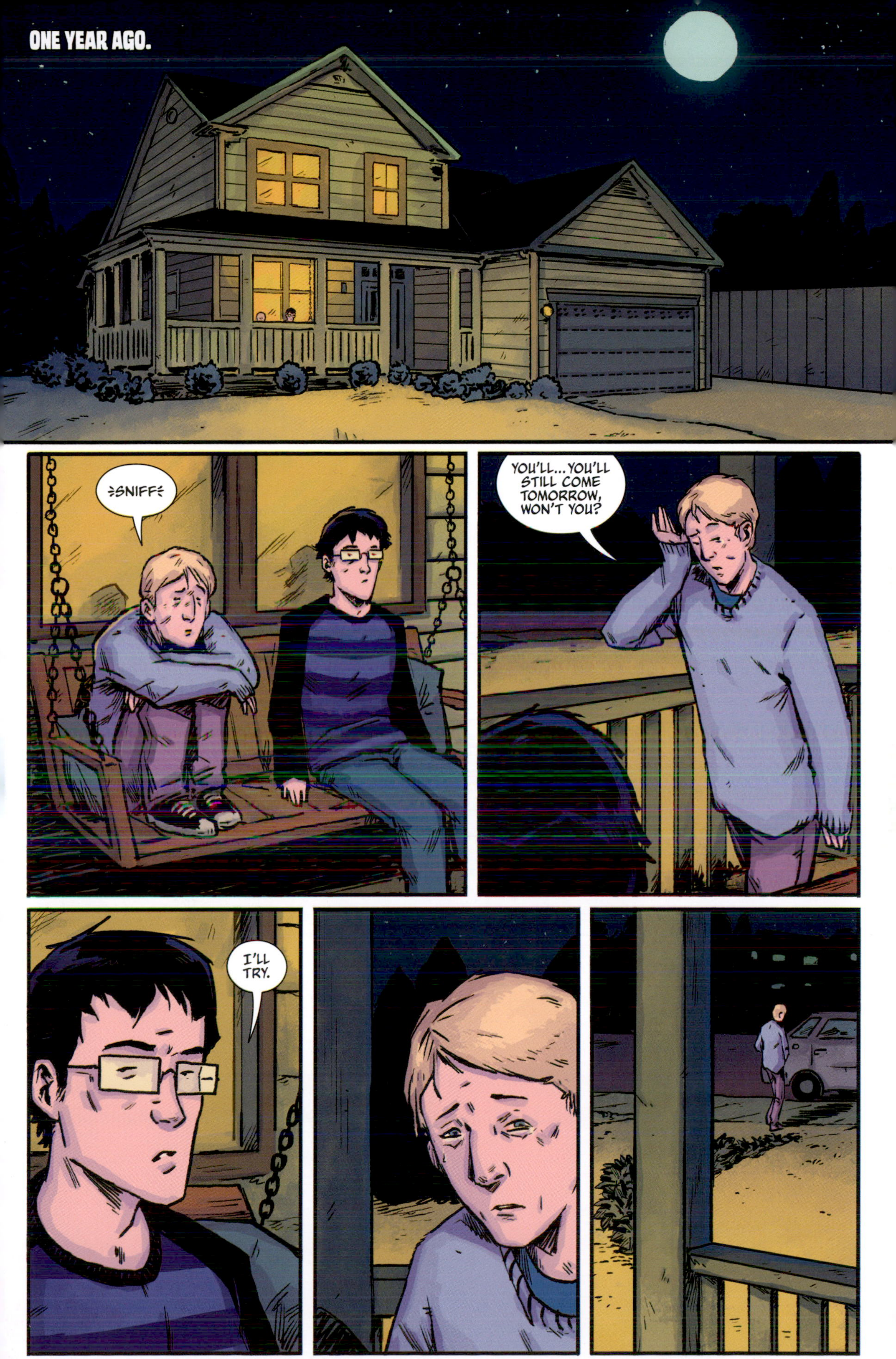
ONE YEAR AGO.
SNIFF
YOU'LL... YOU'LL STILL COME TOMORROW, WON'T YOU?
I'LL TRY.

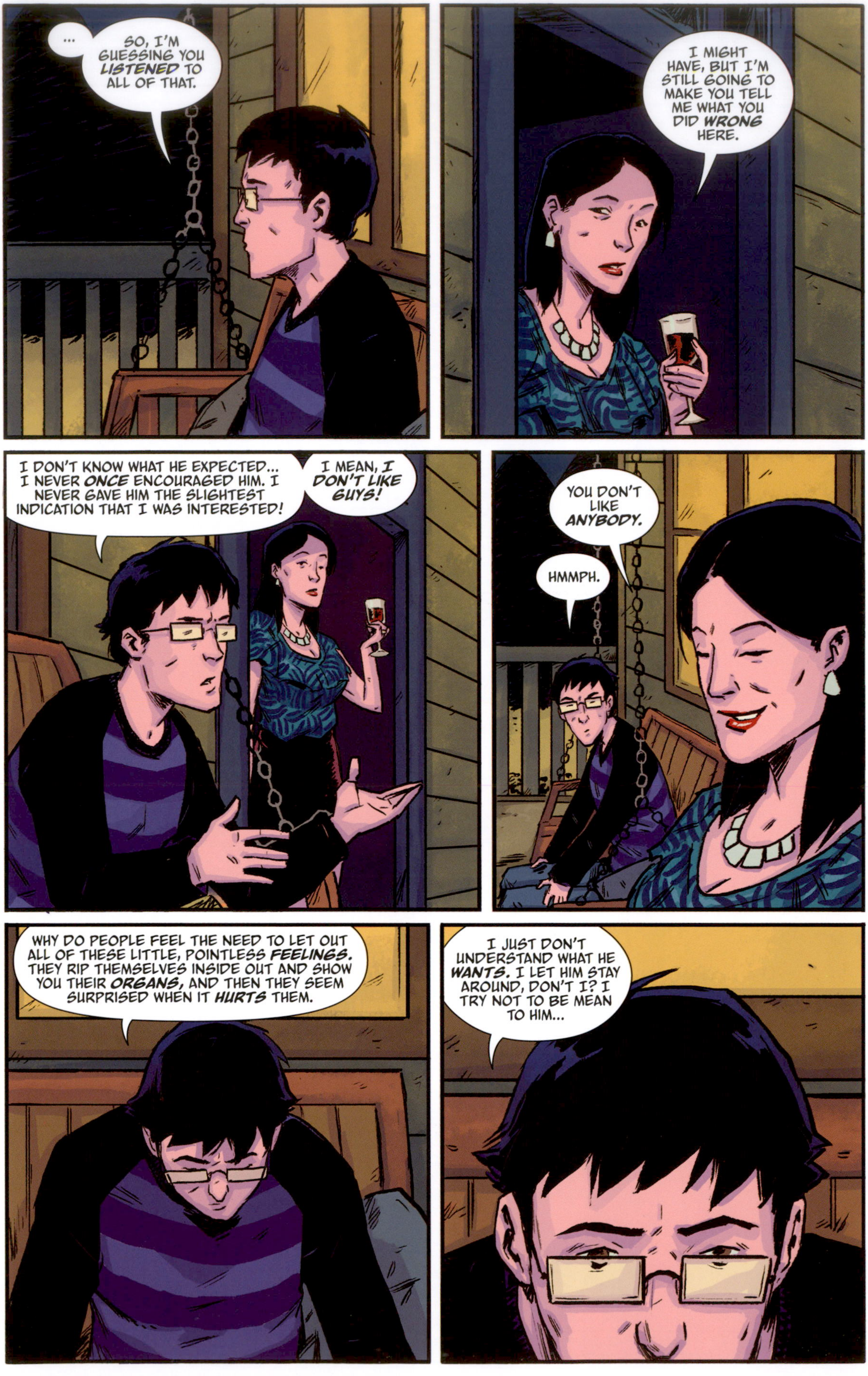
...
SO, I'M GUESSING YOU LISTENED TO ALL OF THAT.
I MIGHT HAVE, BUT I'M STILL GOING TO MAKE YOU TELL ME WHAT YOU DID WRONG HERE.
I DON'T KNOW WHAT HE EXPECTED... I NEVER ONCE ENCOURAGED HIM. I NEVER GAVE HIM THE SLIGHTEST INDICATION THAT I WAS INTERESTED!
I MEAN, I DON'T LIKE GUYS!
YOU DON'T LIKE ANYBODY.
HMMPH.
WHY DO PEOPLE FEEL THE NEED TO LET OUT ALL OF THESE LITTLE, POINTLESS FEELINGS. THEY RIP THEMSELVES INSIDE OUT AND SHOW YOU THEIR ORGANS, AND THEN THEY SEEM SURPRISED WHEN IT HURTS THEM.
I JUST DON'T UNDERSTAND WHAT HE WANTS. I LET HIM STAY AROUND, DON'T I? I TRY NOT TO BE MEAN TO HIM...

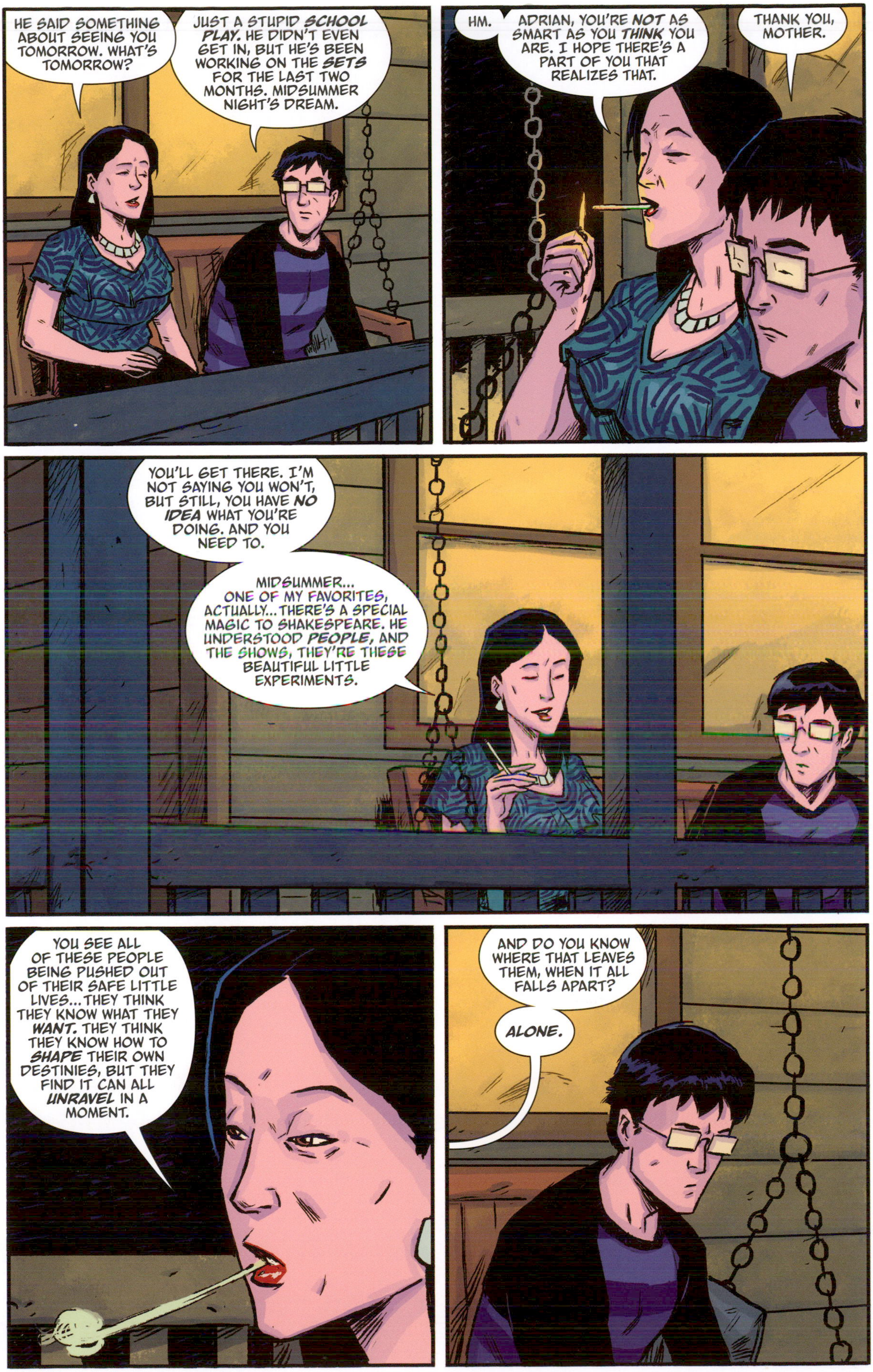
HE SAID SOMETHING ABOUT SEEING YOU TOMORROW. WHAT'S TOMORROW?
JUST A STUPID SCHOOL PLAY. HE DIDN'T EVEN GET IN, BUT HE'S BEEN WORKING ON THE SETS FOR THE LAST TWO MONTHS. MIDSUMMER NIGHT'S DREAM.
HM.
ADRIAN, YOU'RE NOT AS SMART AS YOU THINK YOU ARE. I HOPE THERE'S A PART OF YOU THAT REALIZES THAT.
THANK YOU, MOTHER.
YOU'LL GET THERE. I'M NOT SAYING YOU WON'T, BUT STILL, YOU HAVE NO IDEA WHAT YOU'RE DOING. AND YOU NEED TO.
MIDSUMMER... ONE OF MY FAVORITES, ACTUALLY... THERE'S A SPECIAL MAGIC TO SHAKESPEARE. HE UNDERSTOOD PEOPLE, AND THE SHOWS, THEY'RE THESE BEAUTIFUL LITTLE EXPERIMENTS.
YOU SEE ALL OF THESE PEOPLE BEING PUSHED OUT OF THEIR SAFE LITTLE LIVES... THEY THINK THEY KNOW WHAT THEY WANT. THEY THINK THEY KNOW HOW TO SHAPE THEIR OWN DESTINIES, BUT THEY FIND IT CAN ALL UNRAVEL IN A MOMENT.
AND DO YOU KNOW WHERE THAT LEAVES THEM, WHEN IT ALL FALLS APART?
ALONE.

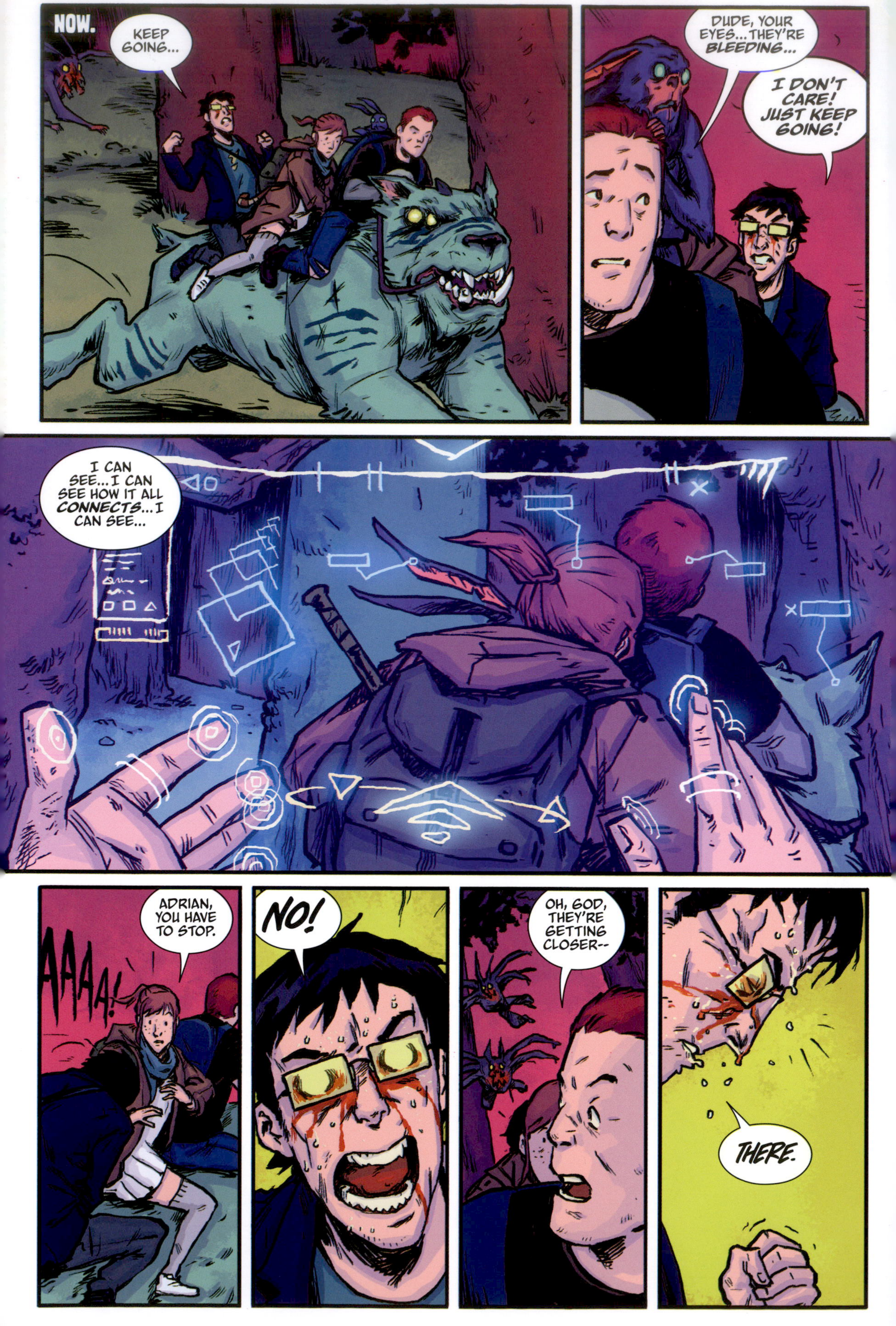
NOW.
KEEP GOING...
DUDE, YOUR EYES... THEY'RE BLEEDING...
I DON'T CARE! JUST KEEP GOING!
I CAN SEE... I CAN SEE HOW IT ALL CONNECTS... I CAN SEE...
AAAA!
ADRIAN, YOU HAVE TO STOP.
NO!
OH, GOD, THEY'RE GETTING CLOSER--
THERE.

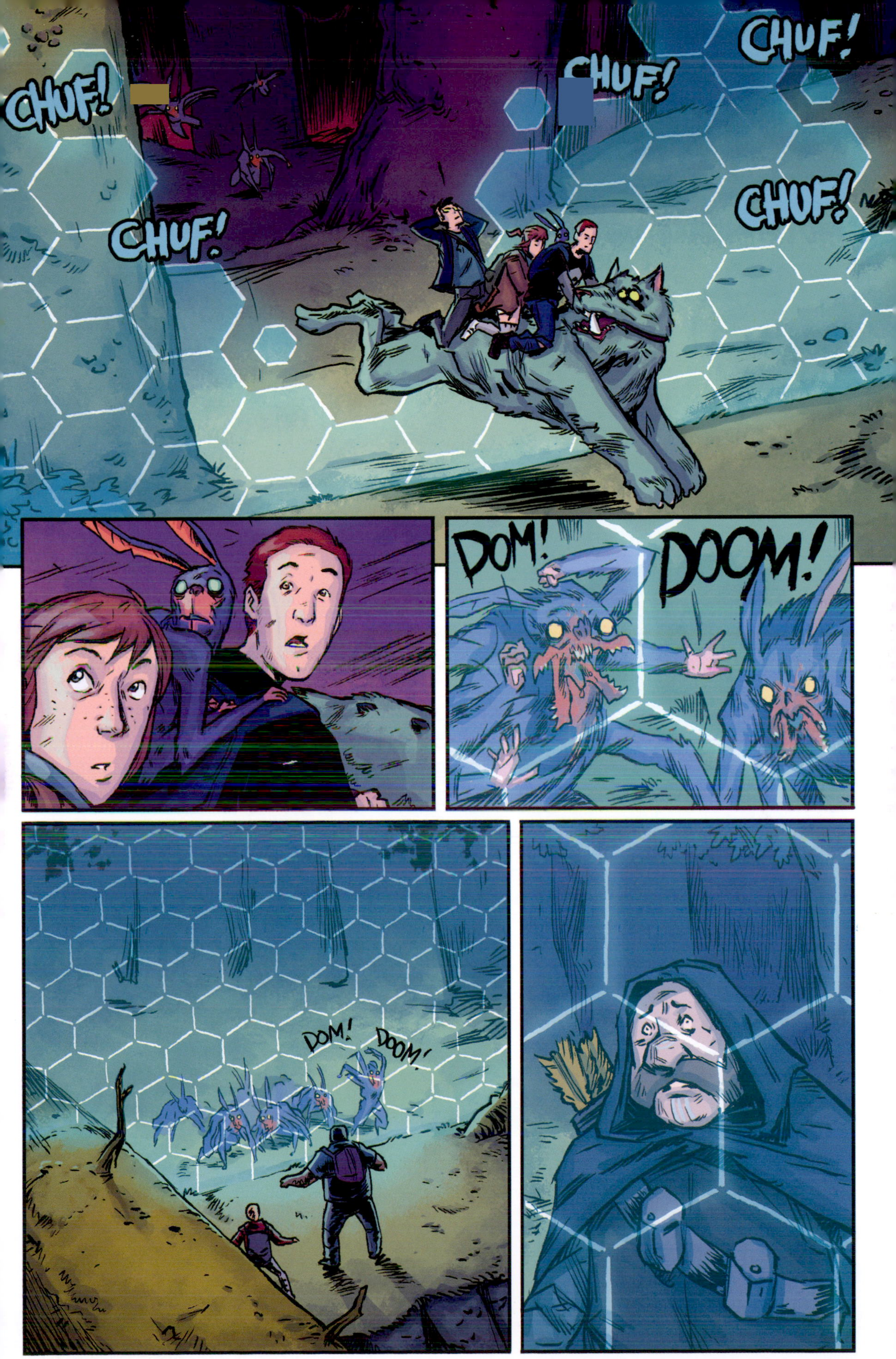
CHUF!
CHUF!
CHUF!
CHUF!
CHUF!
DOM!
DOOM!
DOM!
DOOM!

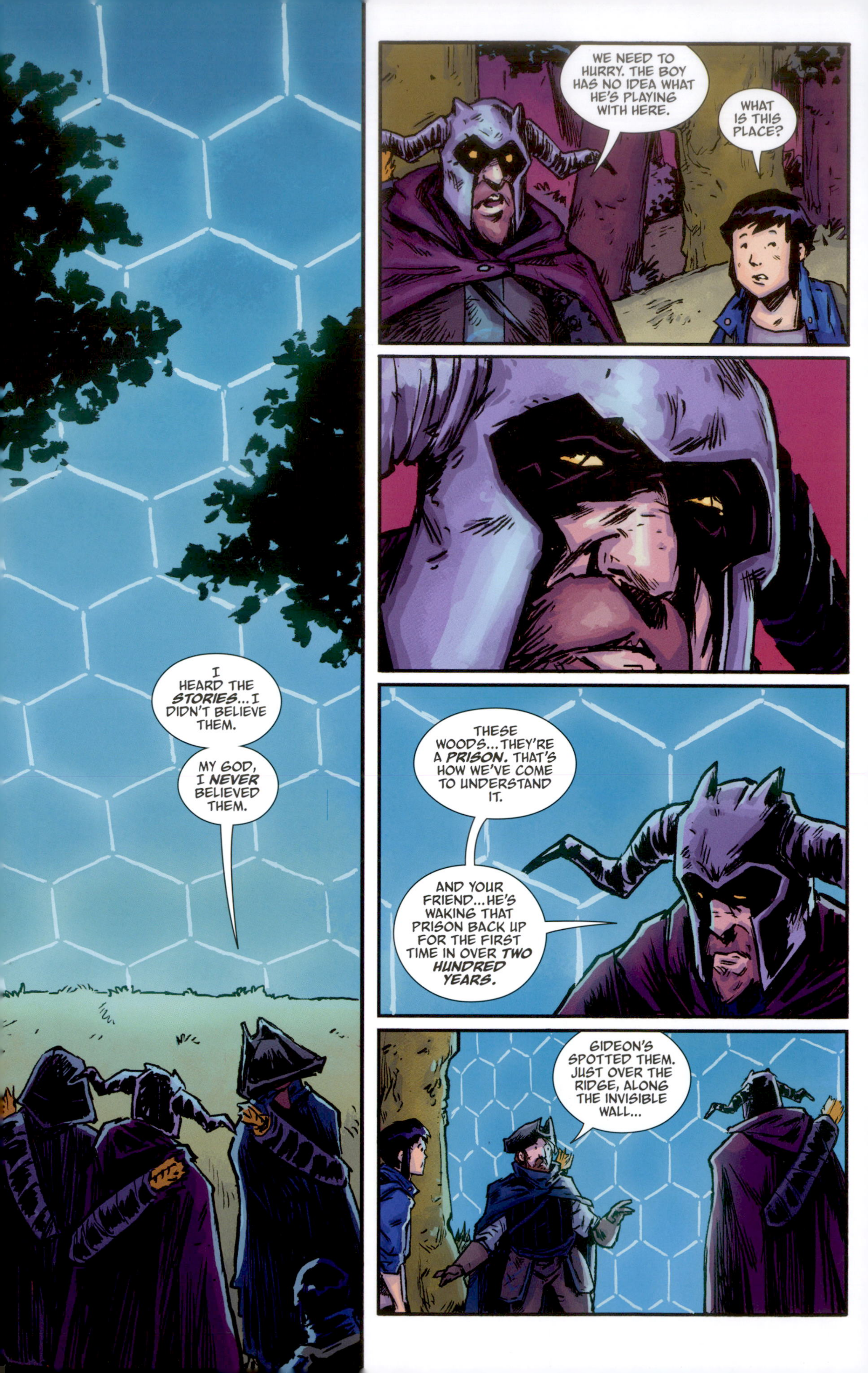
I HEARD THE STORIES... I DIDN'T BELIEVE THEM.
MY GOD, I NEVER BELIEVED THEM.
WE NEED TO HURRY. THE BOY HAS NO IDEA WHAT HE'S PLAYING WITH HERE.
WHAT IS THIS PLACE?
THESE WOODS... THEY'RE A PRISON. THAT'S HOW WE'VE COME TO UNDERSTAND IT.
AND YOUR FRIEND... HE'S WAKING THAT PRISON BACK UP FOR THE FIRST TIME IN OVER TWO HUNDRED YEARS.
GIDEON'S SPOTTED THEM. JUST OVER THE RIDGE, ALONG THE INVISIBLE WALL...

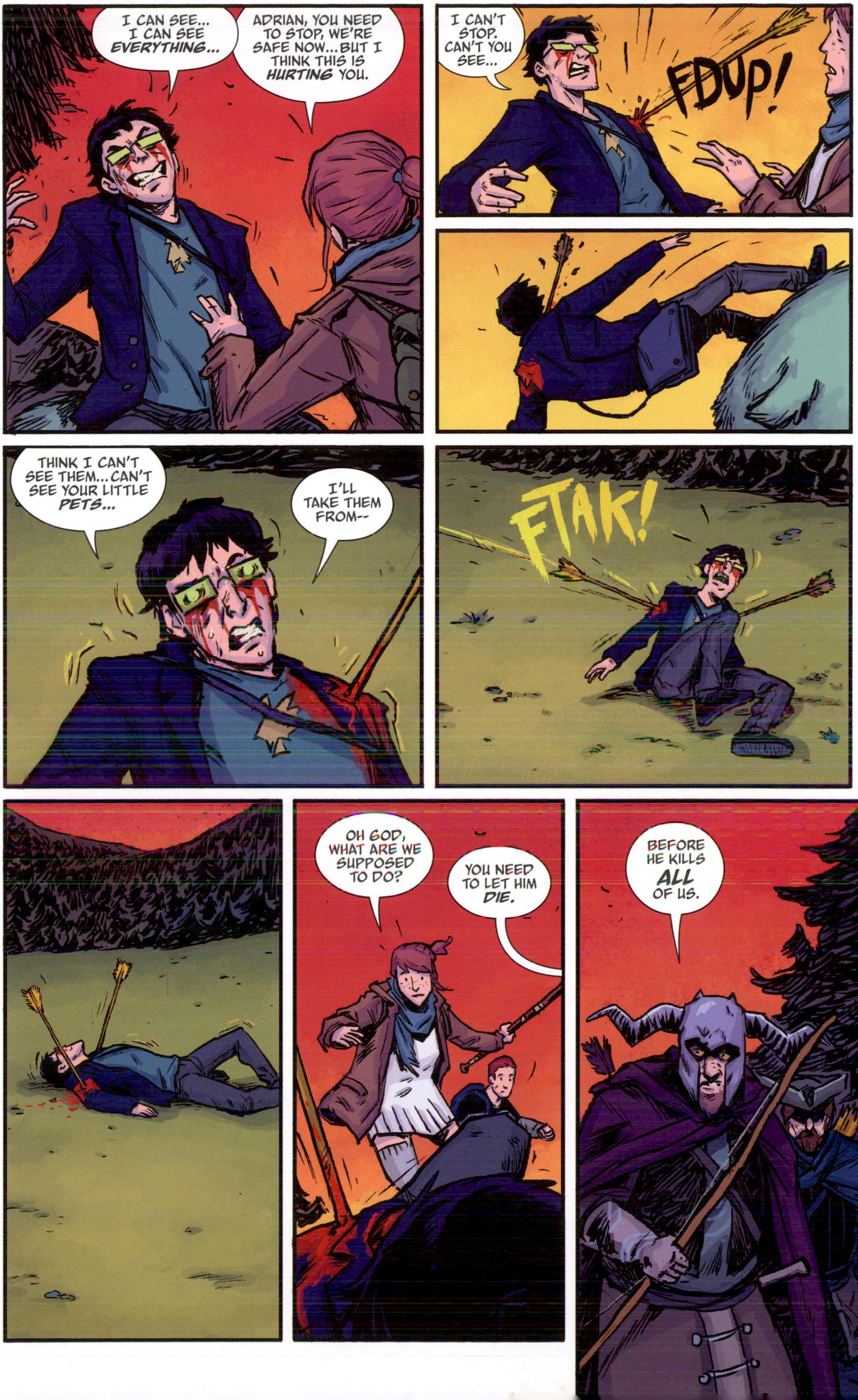

I CAN SEE... I CAN SEE EVERYTHING...
ADRIAN, YOU NEED TO STOP, WE'RE SAFE NOW...BUT I THINK THIS IS HURTING YOU.
I CAN'T STOP. CAN'T YOU SEE...
FDUP!
THINK I CAN'T SEE THEM...CAN'T SEE YOUR LITTLE PETS...
I'LL TAKE THEM FROM--
FTAK!
OH GOD, WHAT ARE WE SUPPOSED TO DO?
YOU NEED TO LET HIM DIE.
BEFORE HE KILLS ALL OF US.

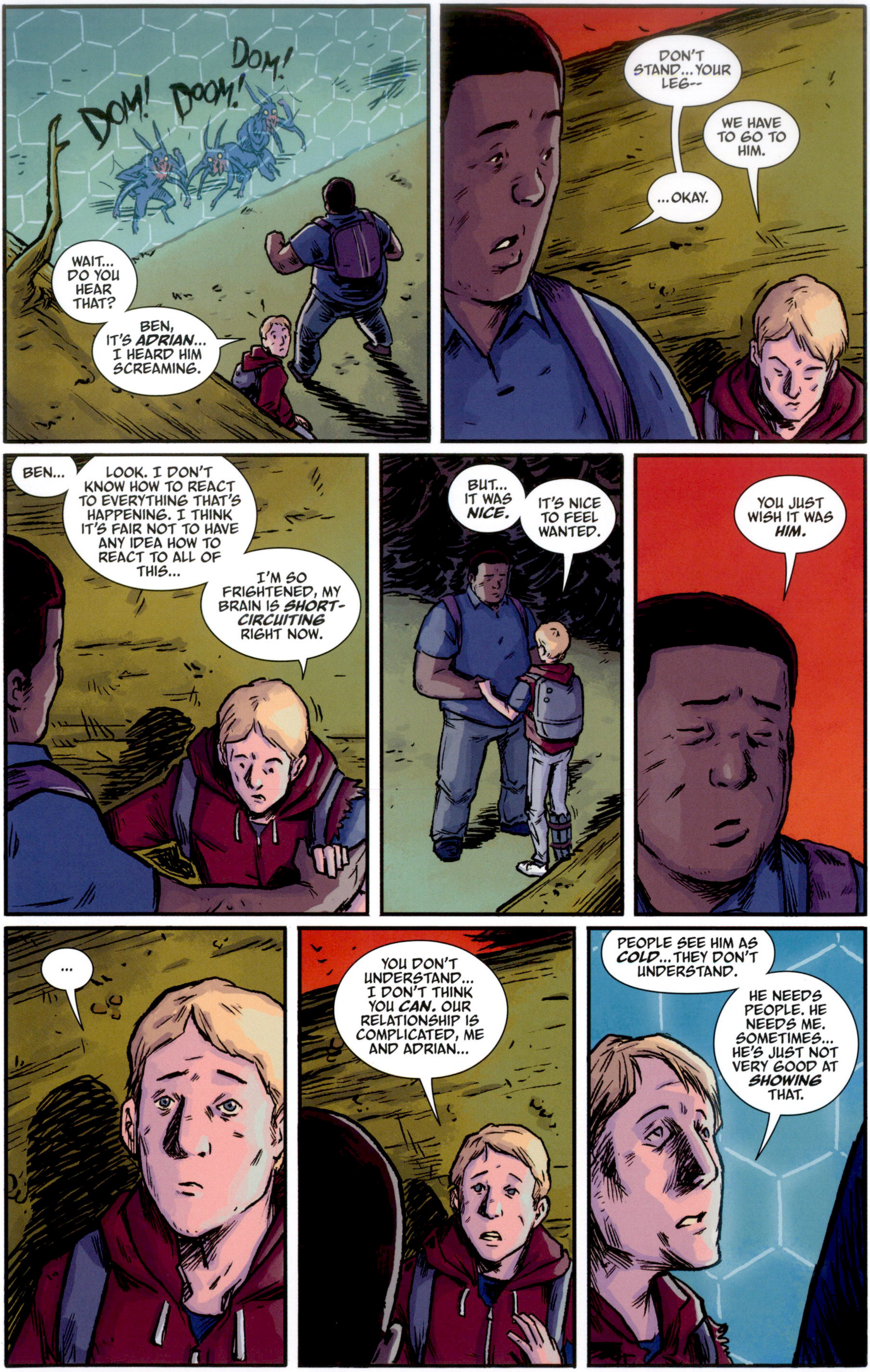
DOM! DOOM! DOM!
WAIT... DO YOU HEAR THAT?
BEN, IT'S ADRIAN... I HEARD HIM SCREAMING.
DON'T STAND... YOUR LEG--
...OKAY.
WE HAVE TO GO TO HIM.
BEN...
LOOK. I DON'T KNOW HOW TO REACT TO EVERYTHING THAT'S HAPPENING. I THINK IT'S FAIR NOT TO HAVE ANY IDEA HOW TO REACT TO ALL OF THIS...
I'M SO FRIGHTENED, MY BRAIN IS SHORT-CIRCUITING RIGHT NOW.
BUT... IT WAS NICE.
IT'S NICE TO FEEL WANTED.
YOU JUST WISH IT WAS HIM.
...
YOU DON'T UNDERSTAND... I DON'T THINK YOU CAN. OUR RELATIONSHIP IS COMPLICATED, ME AND ADRIAN...
PEOPLE SEE HIM AS COLD... THEY DON'T UNDERSTAND.
HE NEEDS PEOPLE. HE NEEDS ME. SOMETIMES... HE'S JUST NOT VERY GOOD AT SHOWING THAT.

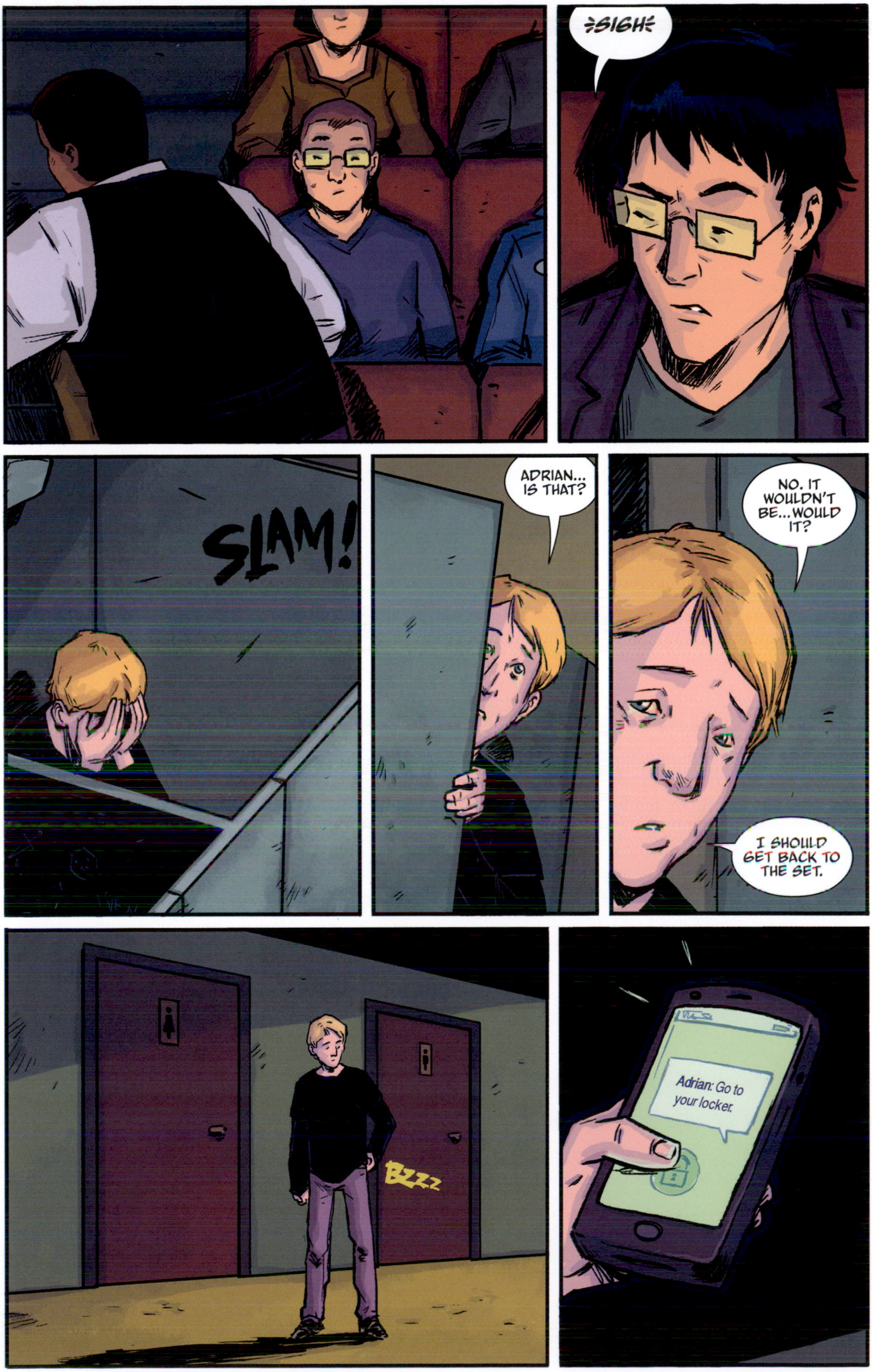
SIGH
SLAM!
ADRIAN... IS THAT?
NO. IT WOULDN'T BE...WOULD IT?
I SHOULD GET BACK TO THE SET.
BZZZ
Adrian: Go to your locker.

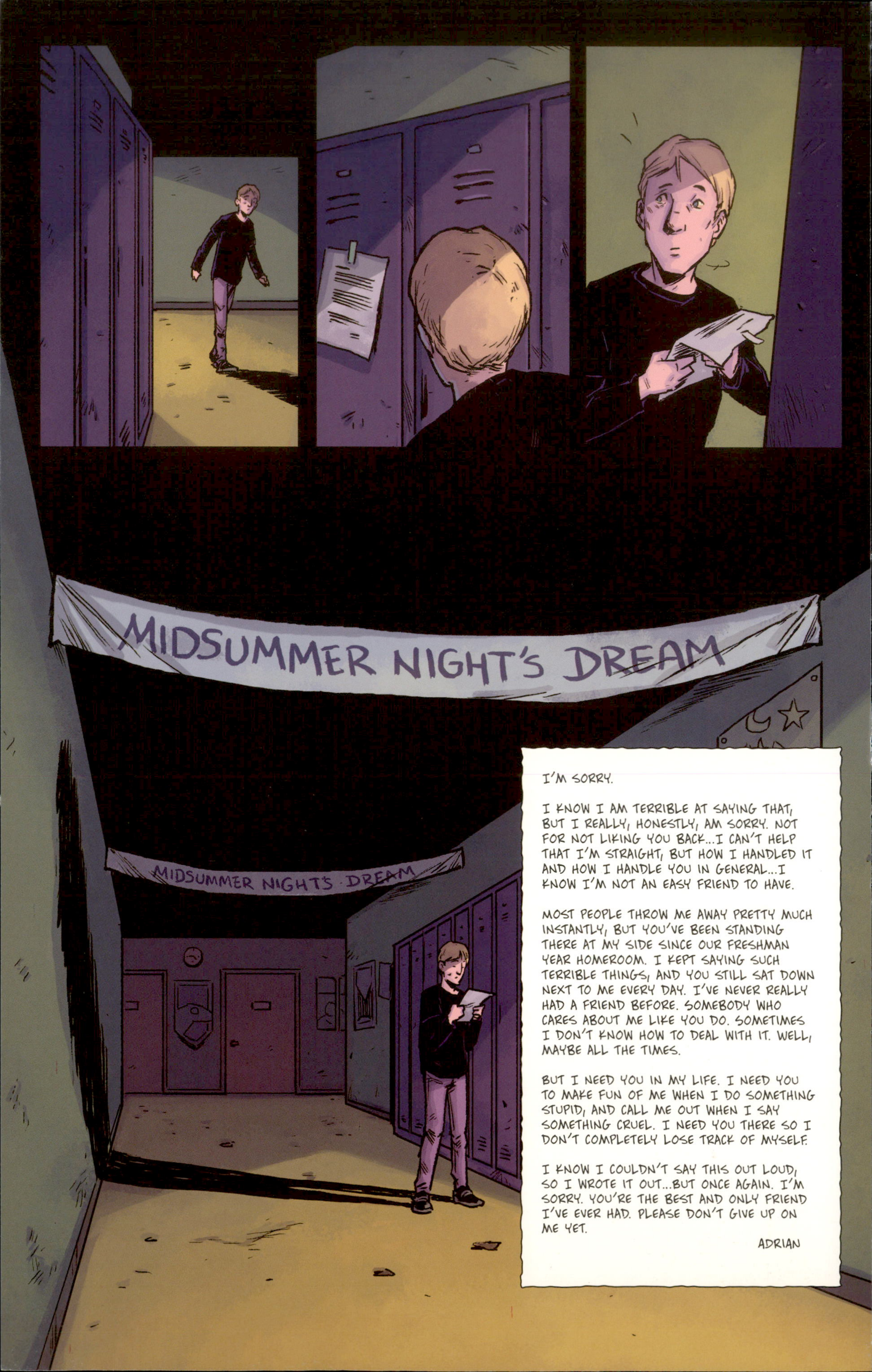
MIDSUMMER NIGHT'S DREAM
MIDSUMMER NIGHT'S DREAM
I'M SORRY.
I KNOW I AM TERRIBLE AT SAYING THAT, BUT I REALLY, HONESTLY, AM SORRY. NOT FOR NOT LIKING YOU BACK...I CAN'T HELP THAT I'M STRAIGHT, BUT HOW I HANDLED IT AND HOW I HANDLE YOU IN GENERAL...I KNOW I'M NOT AN EASY FRIEND TO HAVE.
MOST PEOPLE THROW ME AWAY PRETTY MUCH INSTANTLY, BUT YOU'VE BEEN STANDING THERE AT MY SIDE SINCE OUR FRESHMAN YEAR HOMEROOM. I KEPT SAYING SUCH TERRIBLE THINGS, AND YOU STILL SAT DOWN NEXT TO ME EVERY DAY. I'VE NEVER REALLY HAD A FRIEND BEFORE. SOMEBODY WHO CARES ABOUT ME LIKE YOU DO. SOMETIMES I DON'T KNOW HOW TO DEAL WITH IT. WELL, MAYBE ALL THE TIMES.
BUT I NEED YOU IN MY LIFE. I NEED YOU TO MAKE FUN OF ME WHEN I DO SOMETHING STUPID, AND CALL ME OUT WHEN I SAY SOMETHING CRUEL. I NEED YOU THERE SO I DON'T COMPLETELY LOSE TRACK OF MYSELF.
I KNOW I COULDN'T SAY THIS OUT LOUD, SO I WROTE IT OUT...BUT ONCE AGAIN. I'M SORRY. YOU'RE THE BEST AND ONLY FRIEND I'VE EVER HAD. PLEASE DON'T GIVE UP ON ME YET.
ADRIAN

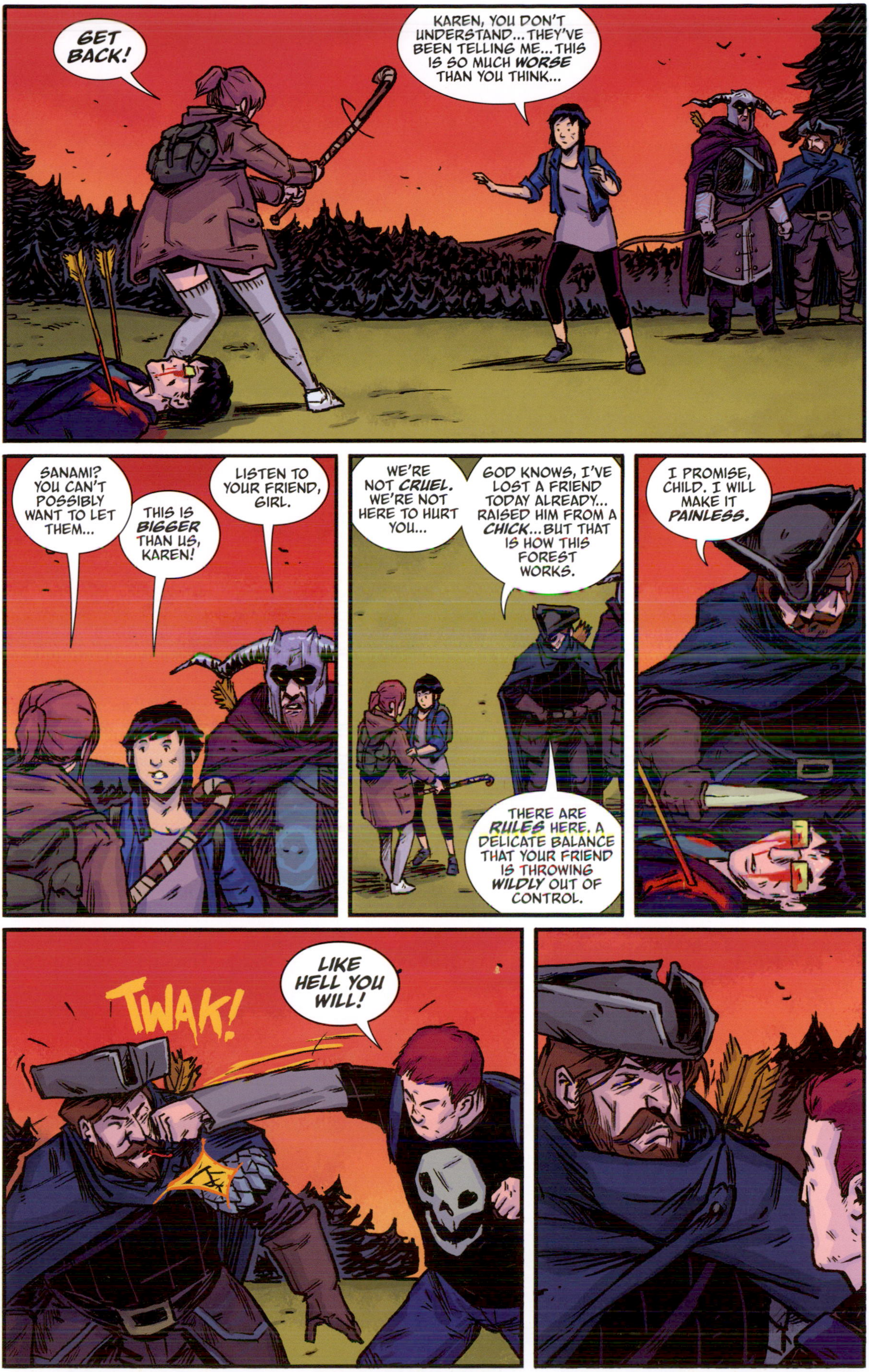
GET BACK!
KAREN, YOU DON'T UNDERSTAND... THEY'VE BEEN TELLING ME... THIS IS SO MUCH WORSE THAN YOU THINK...
SANAMI? YOU CAN'T POSSIBLY WANT TO LET THEM...
THIS IS BIGGER THAN US, KAREN!
LISTEN TO YOUR FRIEND, GIRL.
WE'RE NOT CRUEL. WE'RE NOT HERE TO HURT YOU...
GOD KNOWS, I'VE LOST A FRIEND TODAY ALREADY... RAISED HIM FROM A CHICK... BUT THAT IS HOW THIS FOREST WORKS.
THERE ARE RULES HERE. A DELICATE BALANCE THAT YOUR FRIEND IS THROWING WILDLY OUT OF CONTROL.
I PROMISE, CHILD. I WILL MAKE IT PAINLESS.
TWAK!
LIKE HELL YOU WILL!

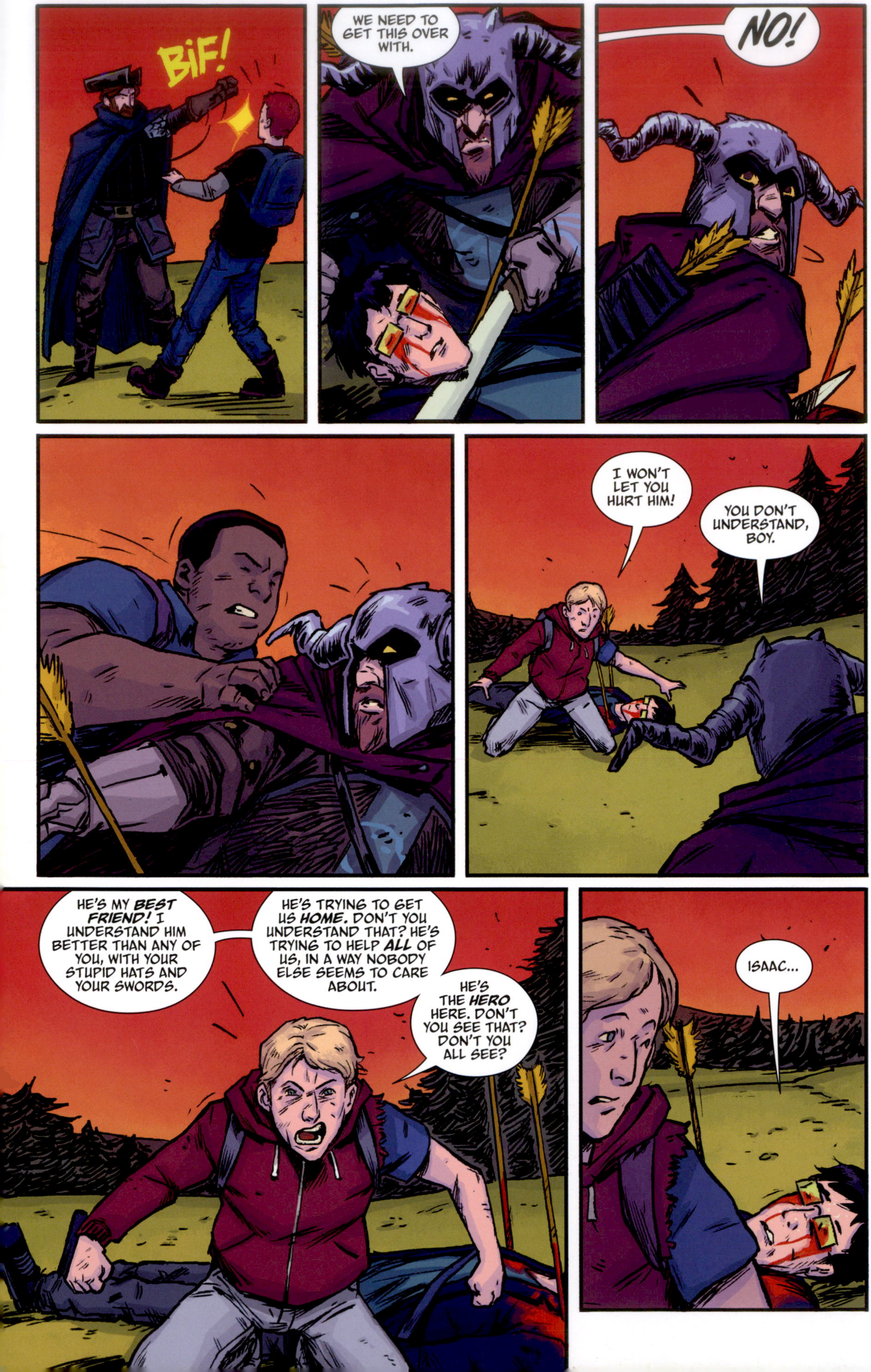
BIF!
WE NEED TO GET THIS OVER WITH.
NO!
I WON'T LET YOU HURT HIM!
YOU DON'T UNDERSTAND, BOY.
HE'S MY *BEST FRIEND!* I UNDERSTAND HIM BETTER THAN ANY OF YOU, WITH YOUR STUPID HATS AND YOUR SWORDS.
HE'S TRYING TO GET US *HOME.* DON'T YOU UNDERSTAND THAT? HE'S TRYING TO HELP *ALL* OF US, IN A WAY NOBODY ELSE SEEMS TO CARE ABOUT.
HE'S THE *HERO* HERE. DON'T YOU SEE THAT? DON'T YOU ALL SEE?
ISAAC...

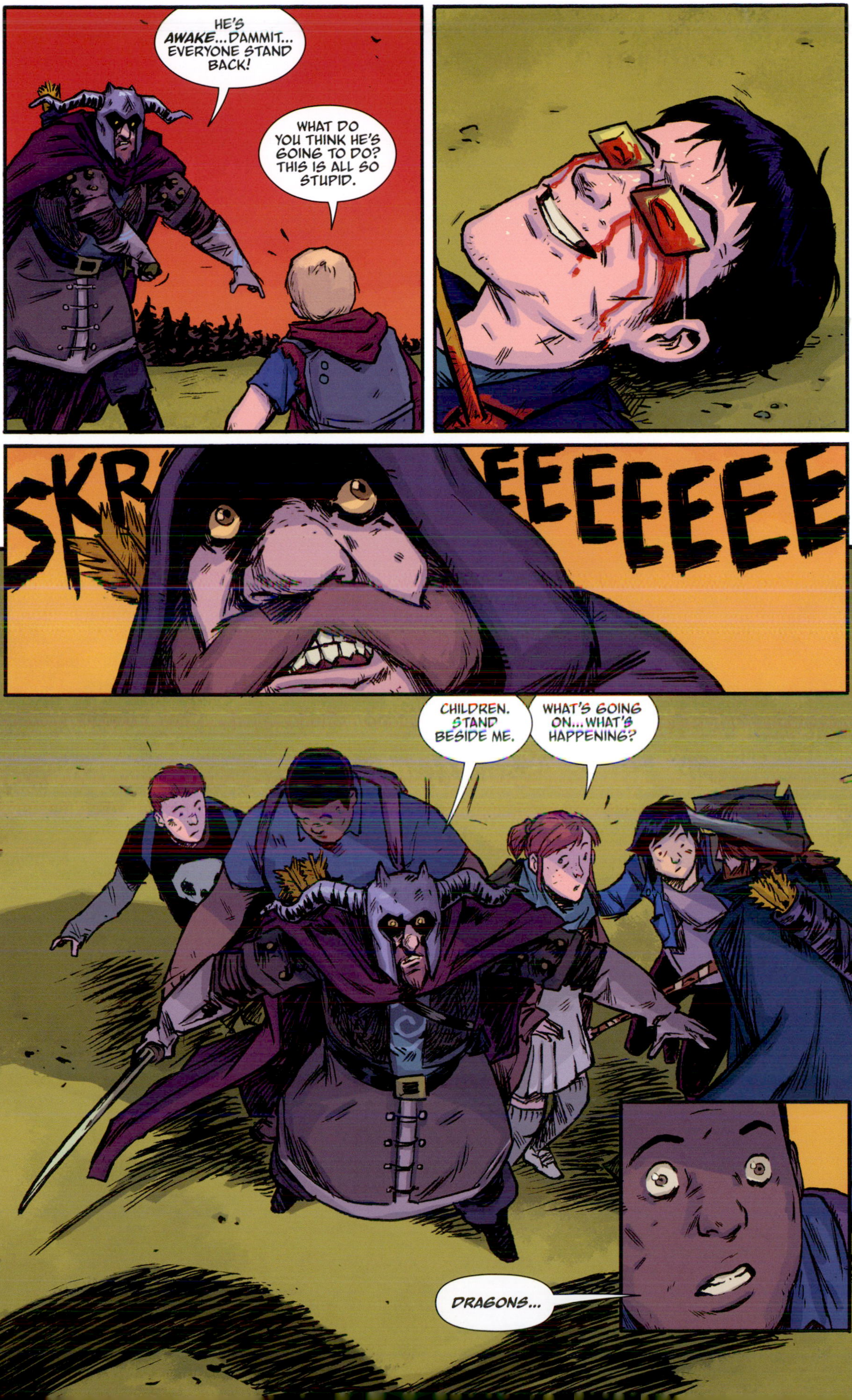
HE'S AWAKE...DAMMIT... EVERYONE STAND BACK!
WHAT DO YOU THINK HE'S GOING TO DO? THIS IS ALL SO STUPID.
SKREEEEEEEEEE
CHILDREN. STAND BESIDE ME.
WHAT'S GOING ON...WHAT'S HAPPENING?
DRAGONS...

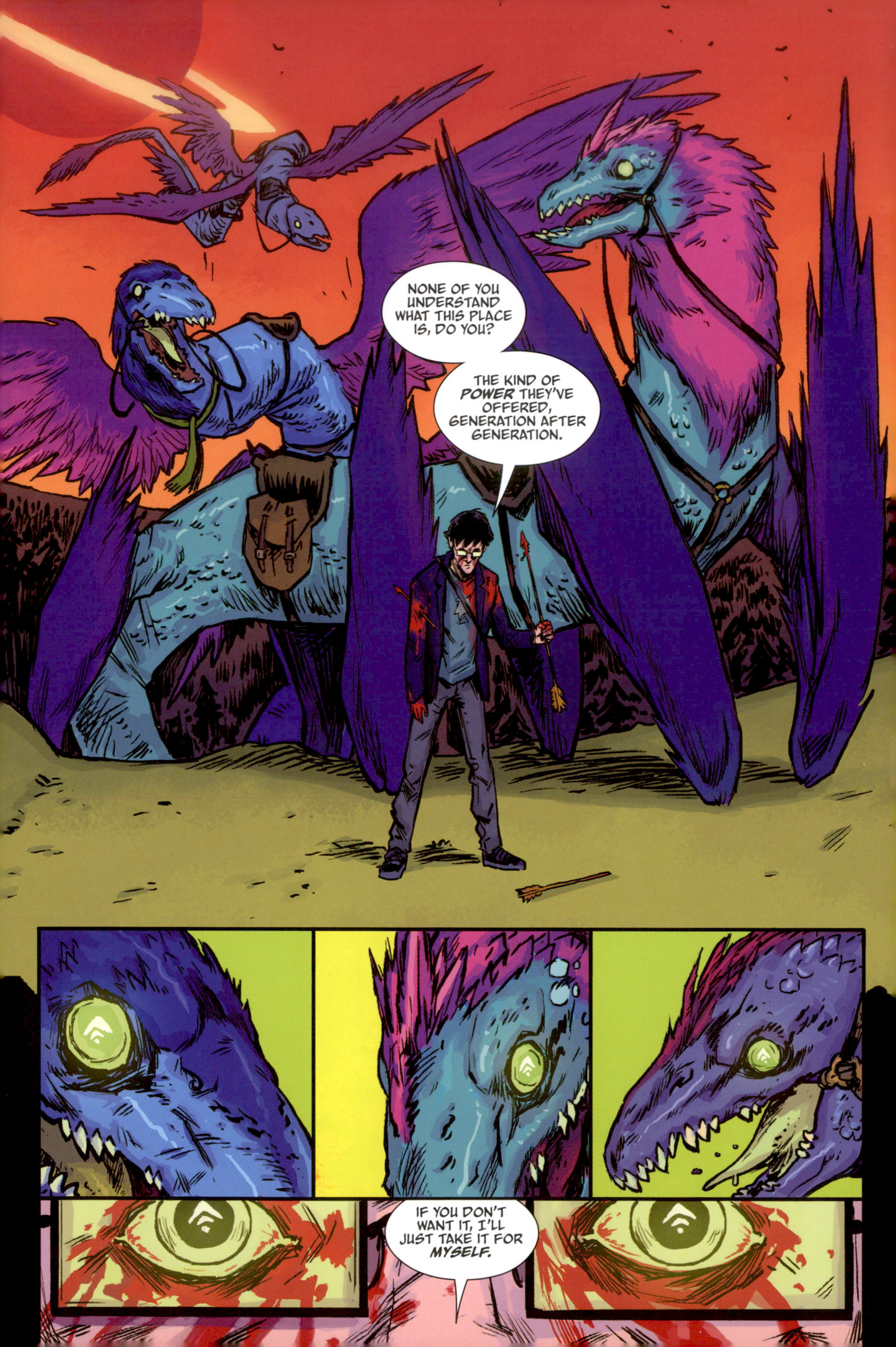
NONE OF YOU UNDERSTAND WHAT THIS PLACE IS, DO YOU?
THE KIND OF *POWER* THEY'VE OFFERED, GENERATION AFTER GENERATION.
IF YOU DON'T WANT IT, I'LL JUST TAKE IT FOR *MYSELF*.

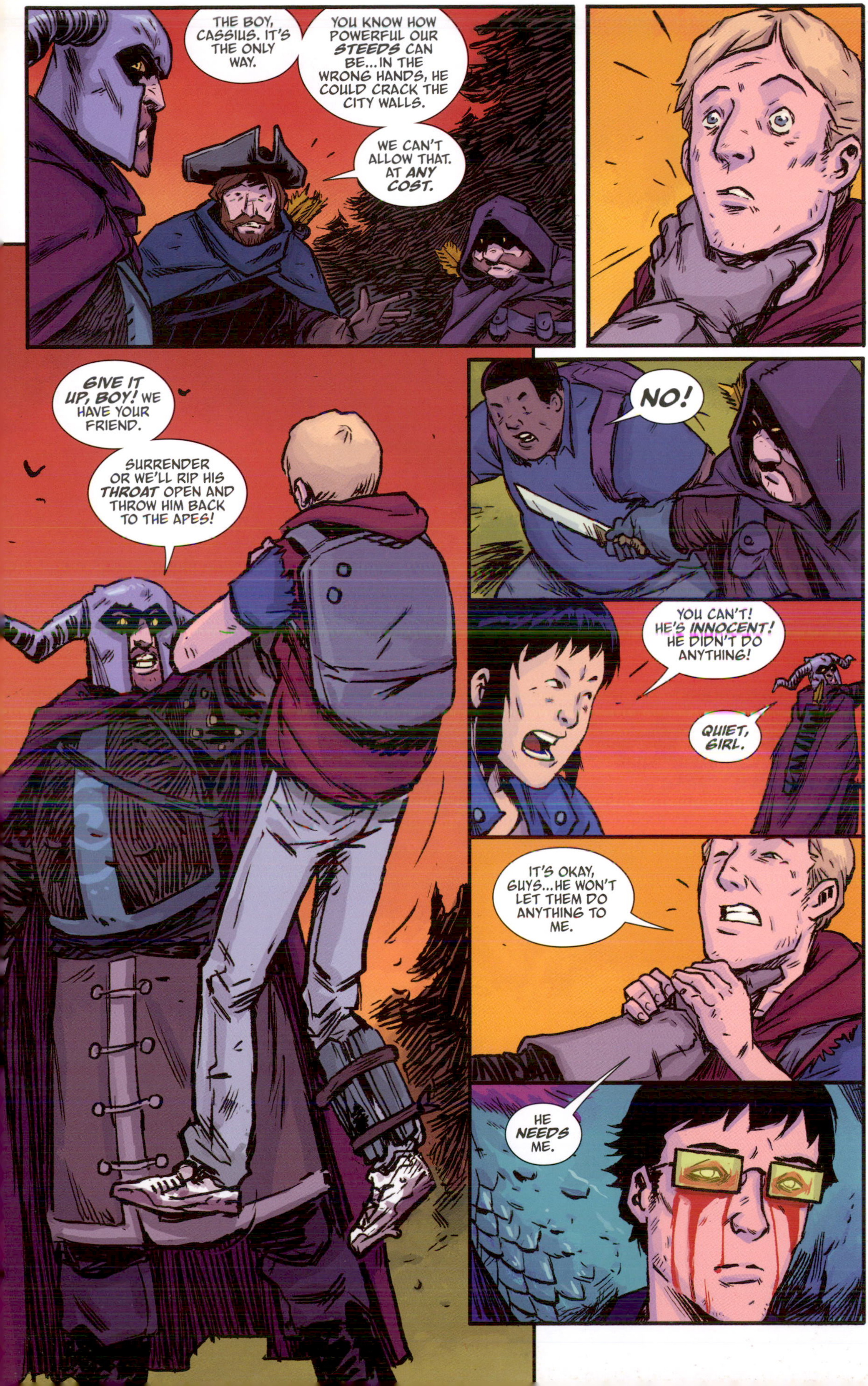
THE BOY, CASSIUS. IT'S THE ONLY WAY.
YOU KNOW HOW POWERFUL OUR STEEDS CAN BE...IN THE WRONG HANDS, HE COULD CRACK THE CITY WALLS.
WE CAN'T ALLOW THAT. AT ANY COST.
GIVE IT UP, BOY! WE HAVE YOUR FRIEND.
SURRENDER OR WE'LL RIP HIS THROAT OPEN AND THROW HIM BACK TO THE APES!
NO!
YOU CAN'T! HE'S INNOCENT! HE DIDN'T DO ANYTHING!
QUIET, GIRL.
IT'S OKAY, GUYS...HE WON'T LET THEM DO ANYTHING TO ME.
HE NEEDS ME.

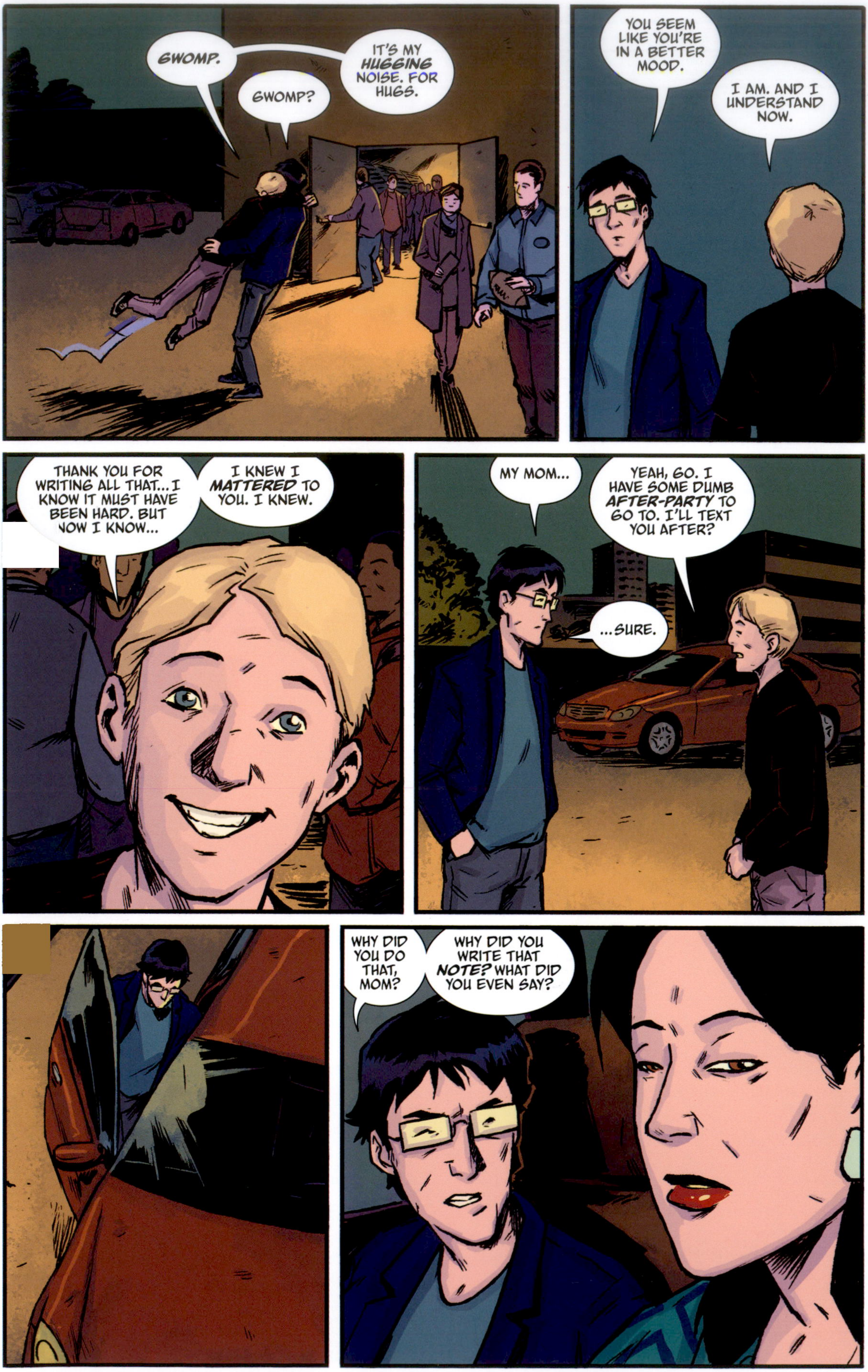
GWOMP.
GWOMP?
IT'S MY HUGGING NOISE. FOR HUGS.
YOU SEEM LIKE YOU'RE IN A BETTER MOOD.
I AM. AND I UNDERSTAND NOW.
THANK YOU FOR WRITING ALL THAT... I KNOW IT MUST HAVE BEEN HARD. BUT NOW I KNOW...
I KNEW I MATTERED TO YOU. I KNEW.
MY MOM...
YEAH, GO. I HAVE SOME DUMB AFTER-PARTY TO GO TO. I'LL TEXT YOU AFTER?
...SURE.
WHY DID YOU DO THAT, MOM?
WHY DID YOU WRITE THAT NOTE? WHAT DID YOU EVEN SAY?

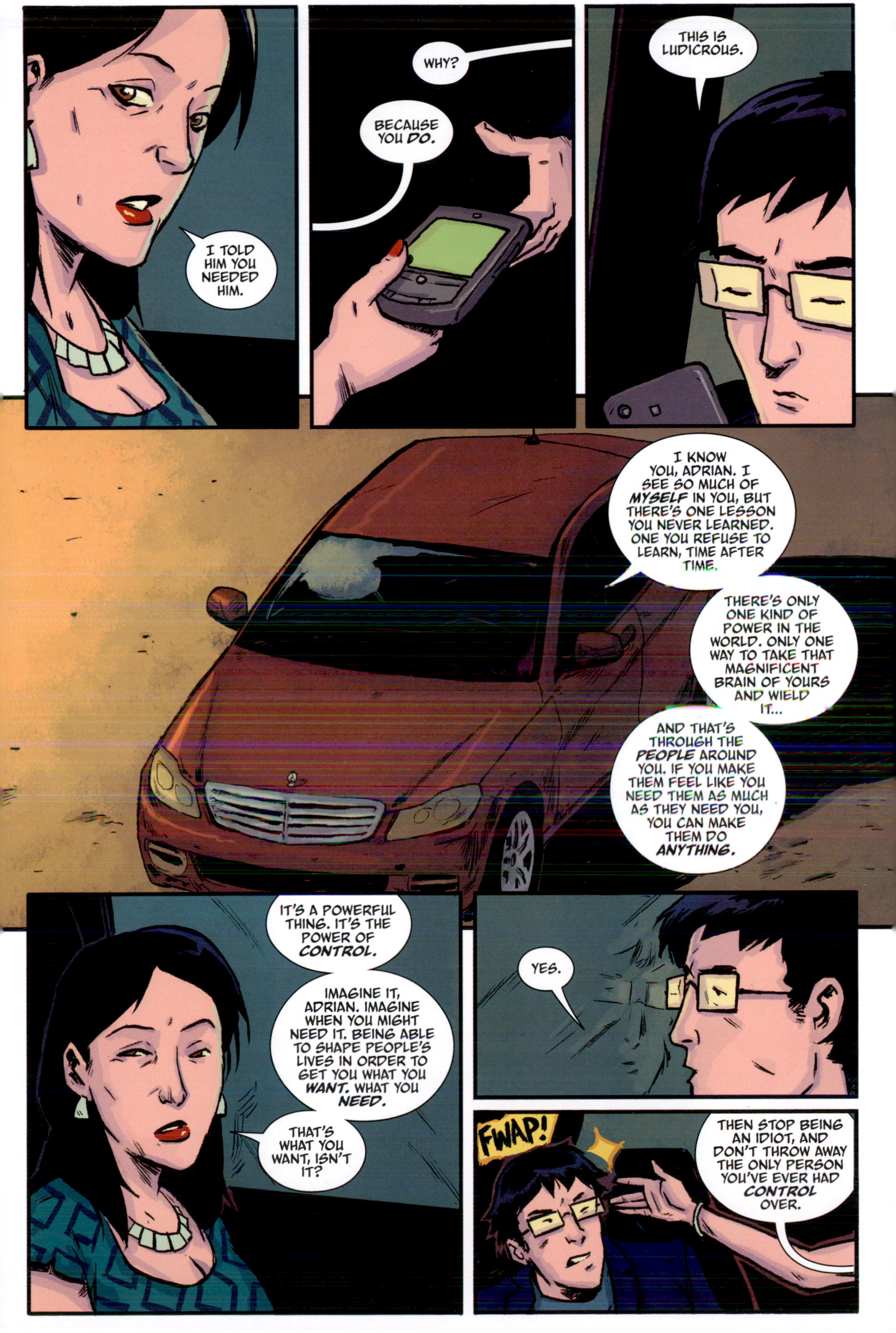
I TOLD HIM YOU NEEDED HIM.
WHY?
BECAUSE YOU *DO.*
THIS IS LUDICROUS.
I KNOW YOU, ADRIAN. I SEE SO MUCH OF *MYSELF* IN YOU, BUT THERE'S ONE LESSON YOU NEVER LEARNED. ONE YOU REFUSE TO LEARN, TIME AFTER TIME.
THERE'S ONLY ONE KIND OF POWER IN THE WORLD. ONLY ONE WAY TO TAKE THAT MAGNIFICENT BRAIN OF YOURS AND WIELD IT...
AND THAT'S THROUGH THE *PEOPLE* AROUND YOU. IF YOU MAKE THEM FEEL LIKE YOU NEED THEM AS MUCH AS THEY NEED YOU, YOU CAN MAKE THEM DO *ANYTHING.*
IT'S A POWERFUL THING. IT'S THE POWER OF *CONTROL.*
IMAGINE IT, ADRIAN. IMAGINE WHEN YOU MIGHT NEED IT. BEING ABLE TO SHAPE PEOPLE'S LIVES IN ORDER TO GET YOU WHAT YOU *WANT.* WHAT YOU *NEED.*
THAT'S WHAT YOU WANT, ISN'T IT?
YES.
FWAP!
THEN STOP BEING AN IDIOT, AND DON'T THROW AWAY THE ONLY PERSON YOU'VE EVER HAD *CONTROL* OVER.

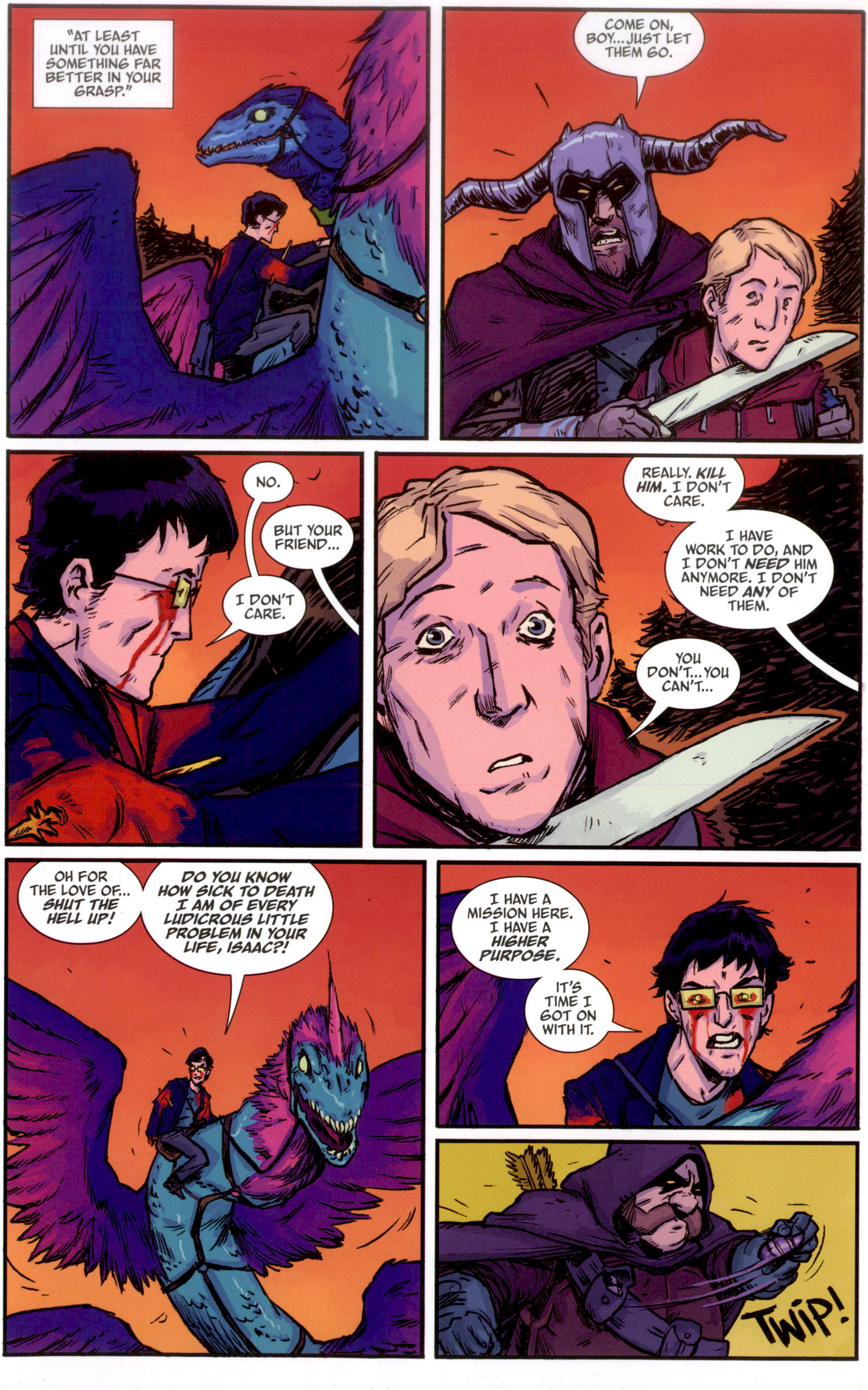
"AT LEAST UNTIL YOU HAVE SOMETHING FAR BETTER IN YOUR GRASP."
COME ON, BOY...JUST LET THEM GO.
NO.
BUT YOUR FRIEND...
I DON'T CARE.
REALLY. KILL HIM. I DON'T CARE.
I HAVE WORK TO DO, AND I DON'T NEED HIM ANYMORE. I DON'T NEED ANY OF THEM.
YOU DON'T...YOU CAN'T...
OH FOR THE LOVE OF... SHUT THE HELL UP!
DO YOU KNOW HOW SICK TO DEATH I AM OF EVERY LUDICROUS LITTLE PROBLEM IN YOUR LIFE, ISAAC?!
I HAVE A MISSION HERE. I HAVE A HIGHER PURPOSE.
IT'S TIME I GOT ON WITH IT.
TWIP!

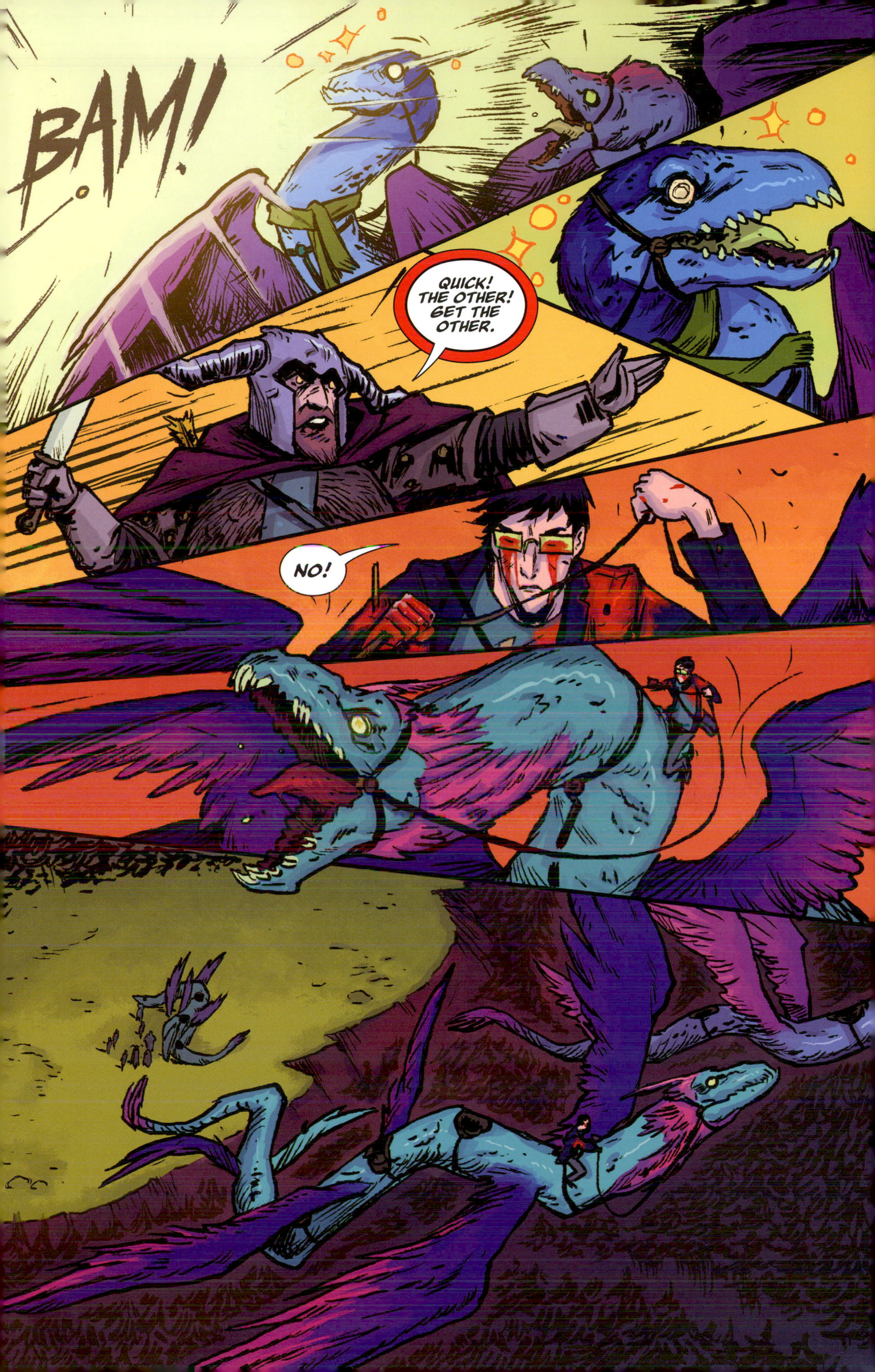
BAM!
QUICK! THE OTHER! GET THE OTHER.
NO!

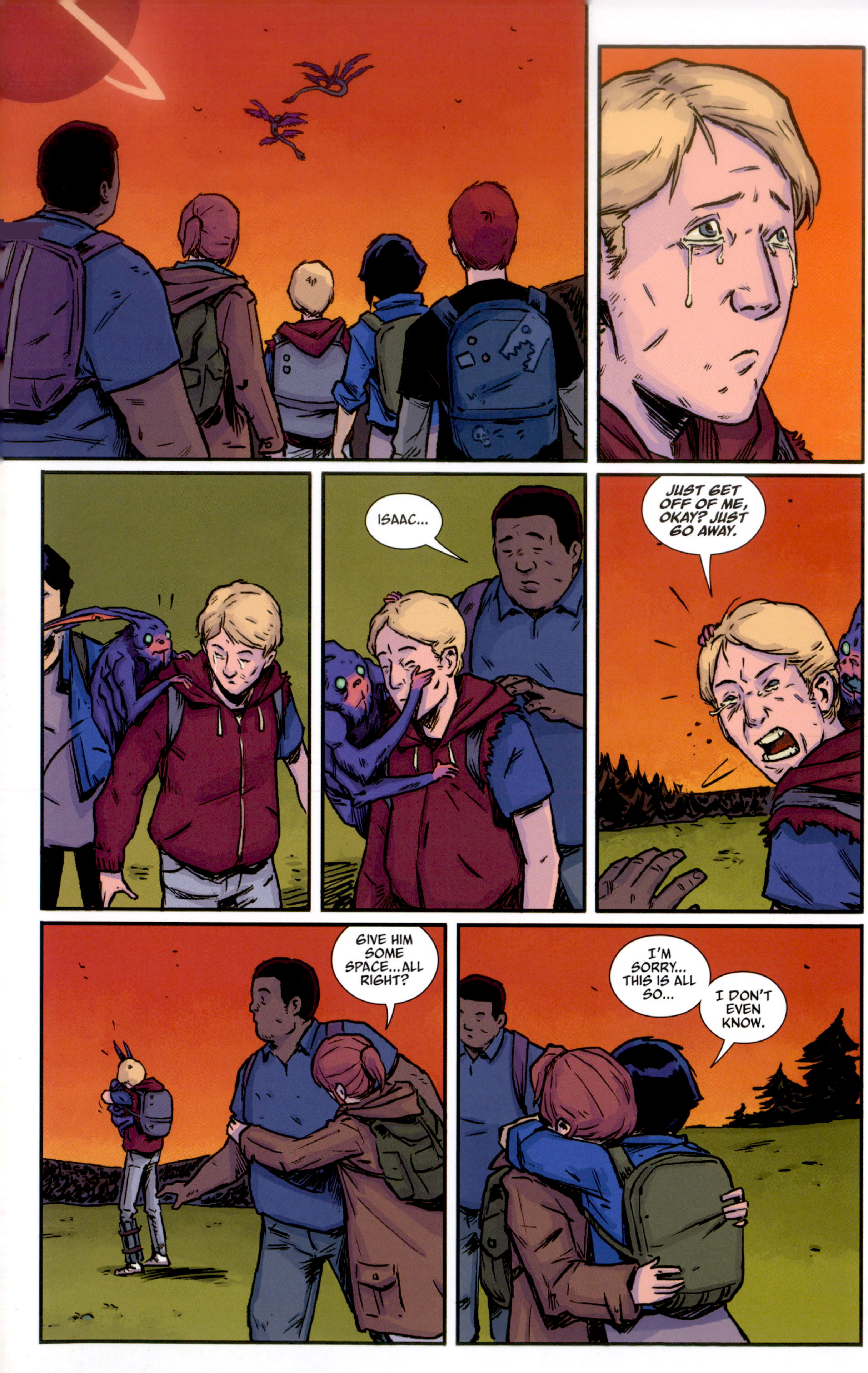
ISAAC...
JUST GET OFF OF ME, OKAY? JUST GO AWAY.
GIVE HIM SOME SPACE...ALL RIGHT?
I'M SORRY... THIS IS ALL SO...
I DON'T EVEN KNOW.

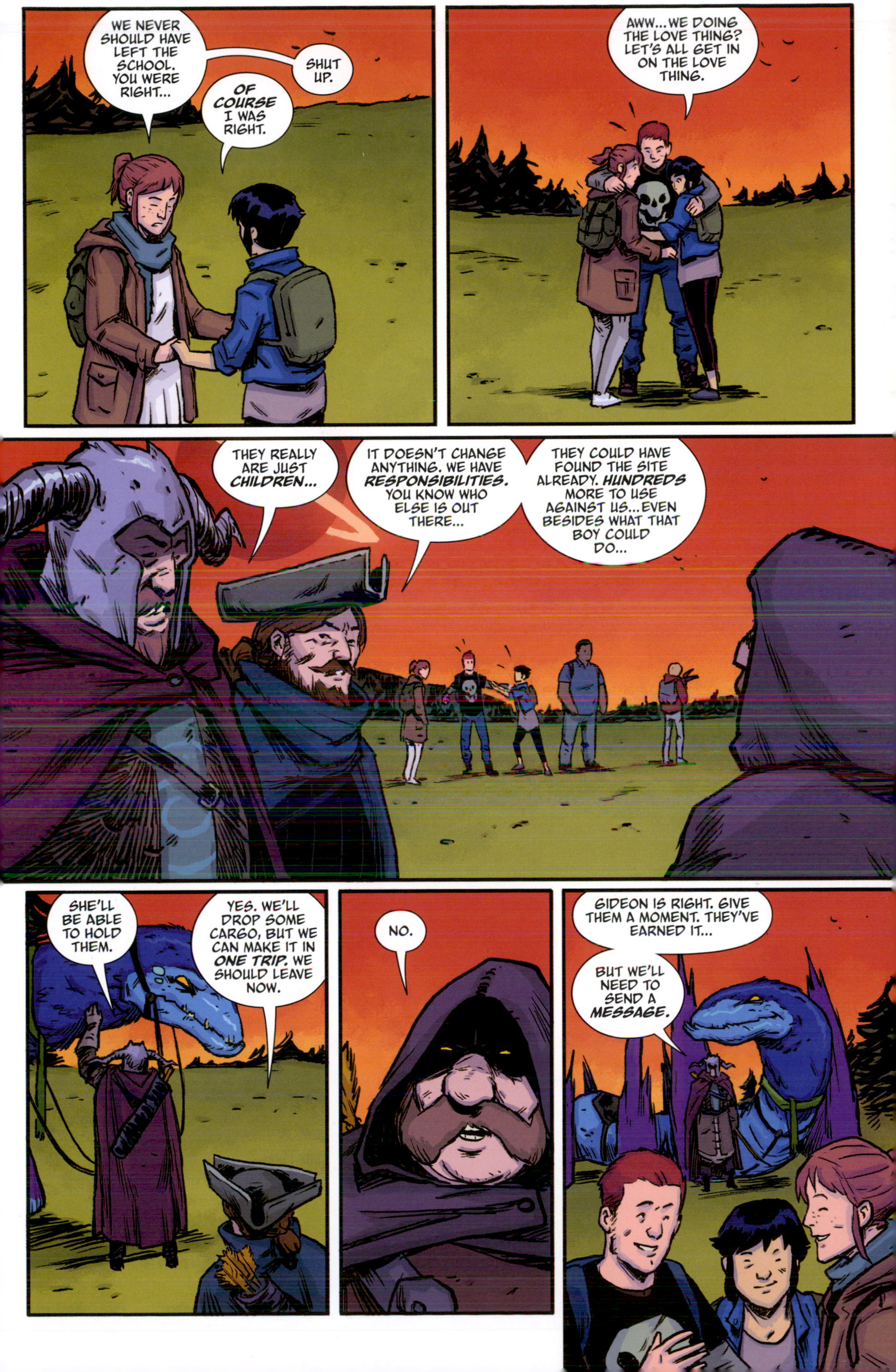
WE NEVER SHOULD HAVE LEFT THE SCHOOL. YOU WERE RIGHT...
SHUT UP.
OF COURSE I WAS RIGHT.
AWW...WE DOING THE LOVE THING? LET'S ALL GET IN ON THE LOVE THING.
THEY REALLY ARE JUST CHILDREN...
IT DOESN'T CHANGE ANYTHING. WE HAVE RESPONSIBILITIES. YOU KNOW WHO ELSE IS OUT THERE...
THEY COULD HAVE FOUND THE SITE ALREADY. HUNDREDS MORE TO USE AGAINST US...EVEN BESIDES WHAT THAT BOY COULD DO...
SHE'LL BE ABLE TO HOLD THEM.
YES. WE'LL DROP SOME CARGO, BUT WE CAN MAKE IT IN ONE TRIP. WE SHOULD LEAVE NOW.
NO.
GIDEON IS RIGHT. GIVE THEM A MOMENT. THEY'VE EARNED IT...
BUT WE'LL NEED TO SEND A MESSAGE.

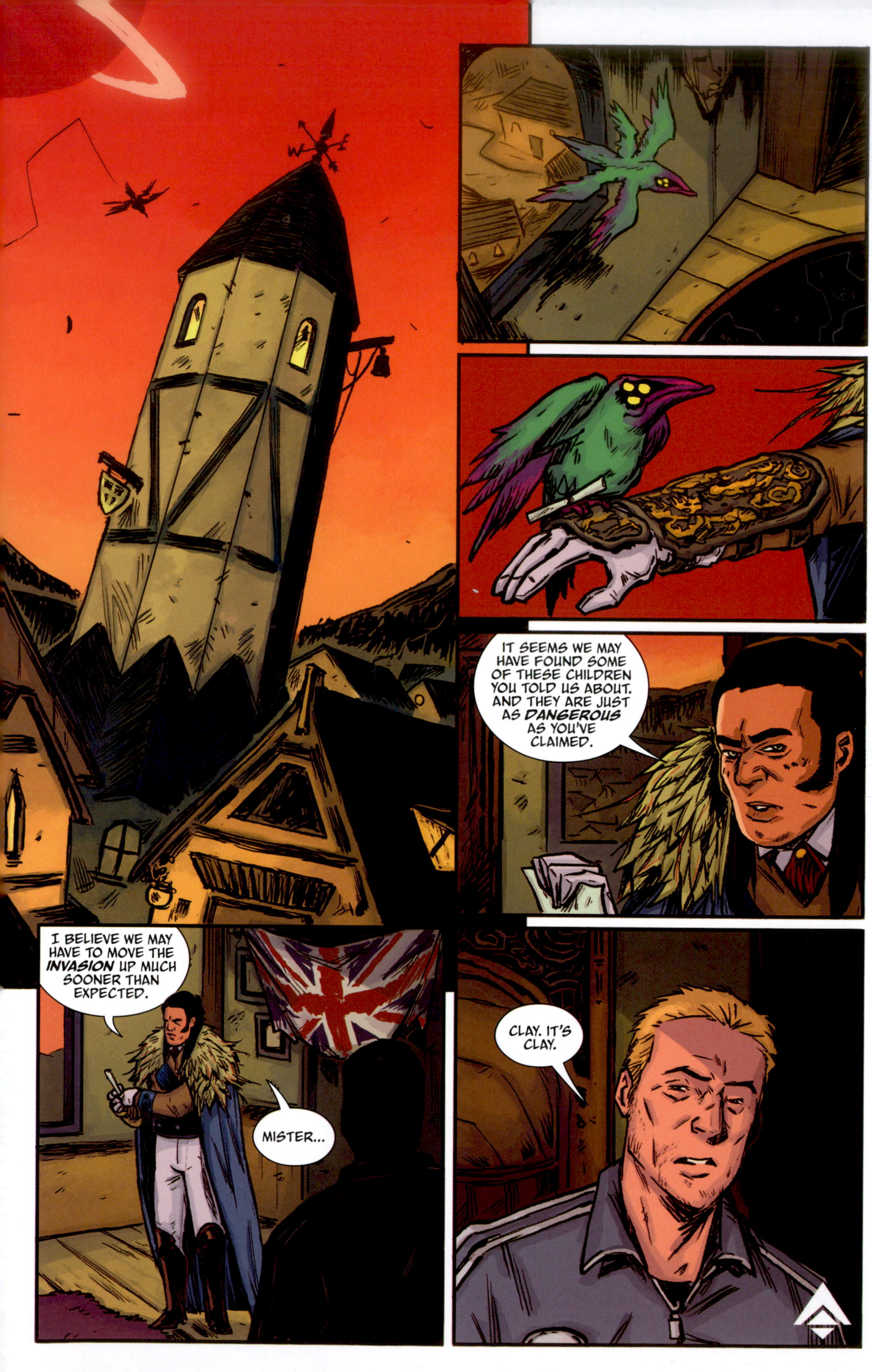
IT SEEMS WE MAY HAVE FOUND SOME OF THESE CHILDREN YOU TOLD US ABOUT. AND THEY ARE JUST AS DANGEROUS AS YOU'VE CLAIMED.
I BELIEVE WE MAY HAVE TO MOVE THE INVASION UP MUCH SOONER THAN EXPECTED.
MISTER...
CLAY. IT'S CLAY.

COVER GALLERY

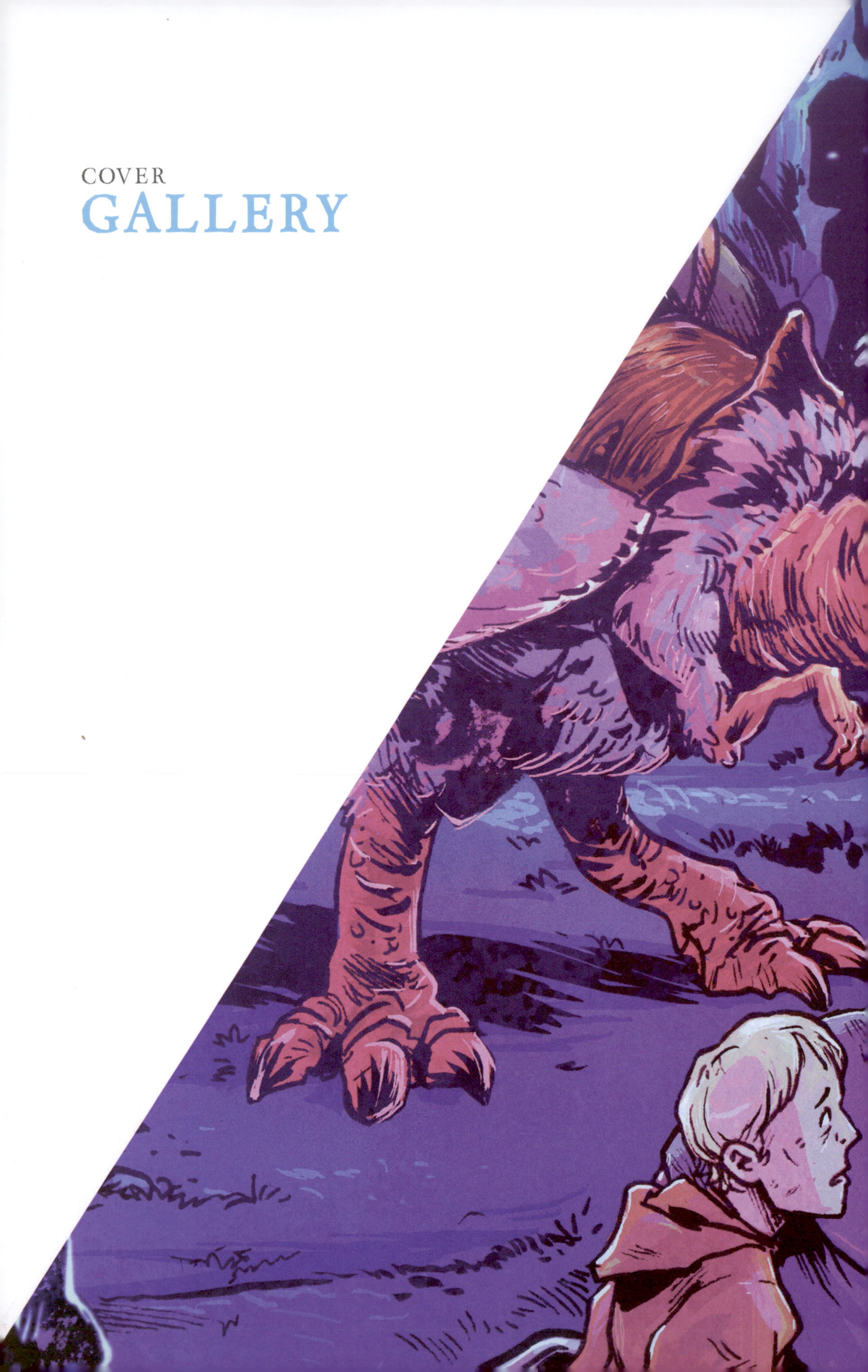

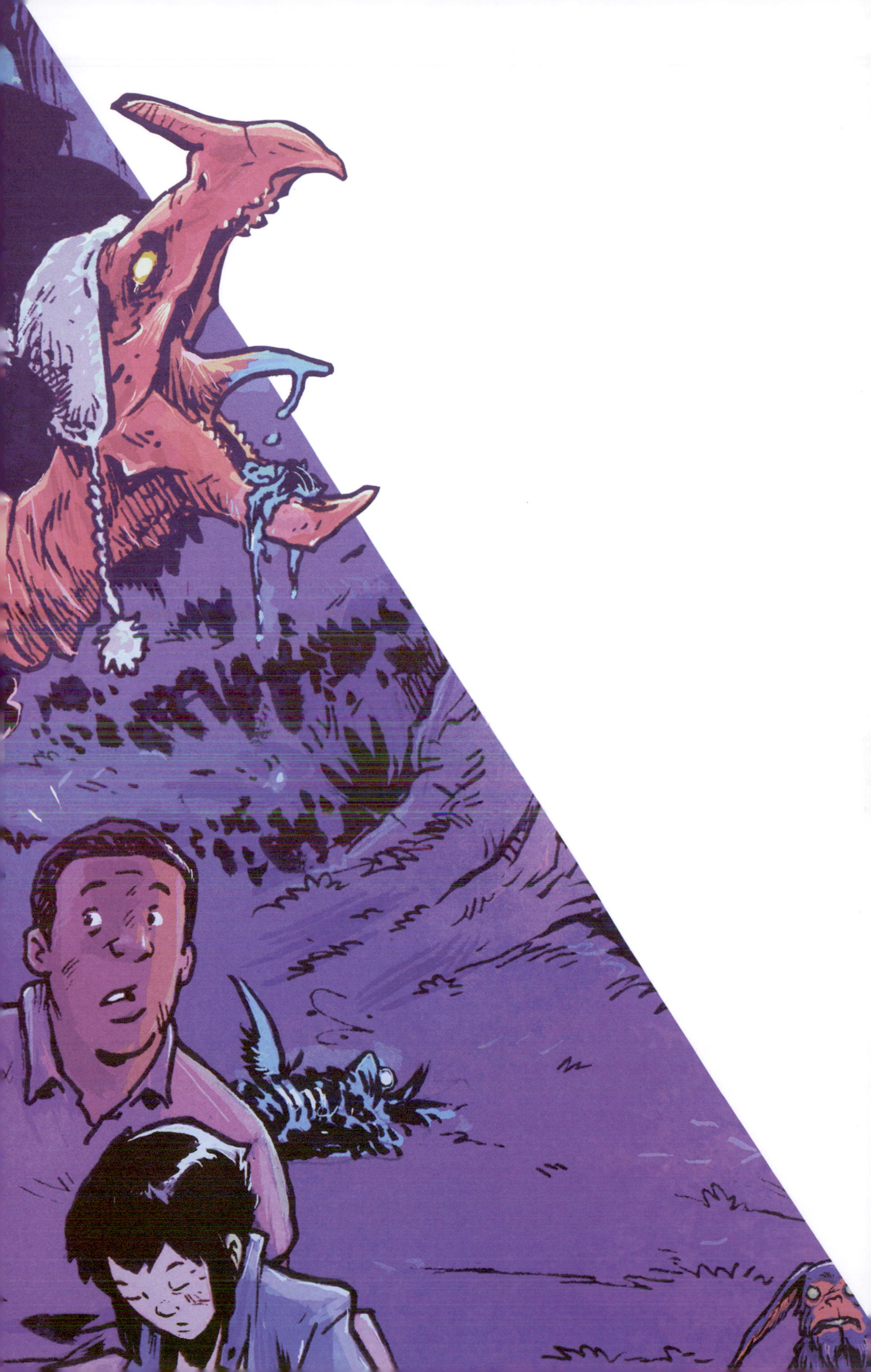

ISSUE FIVE COVER **MICHAEL DIALYNAS**

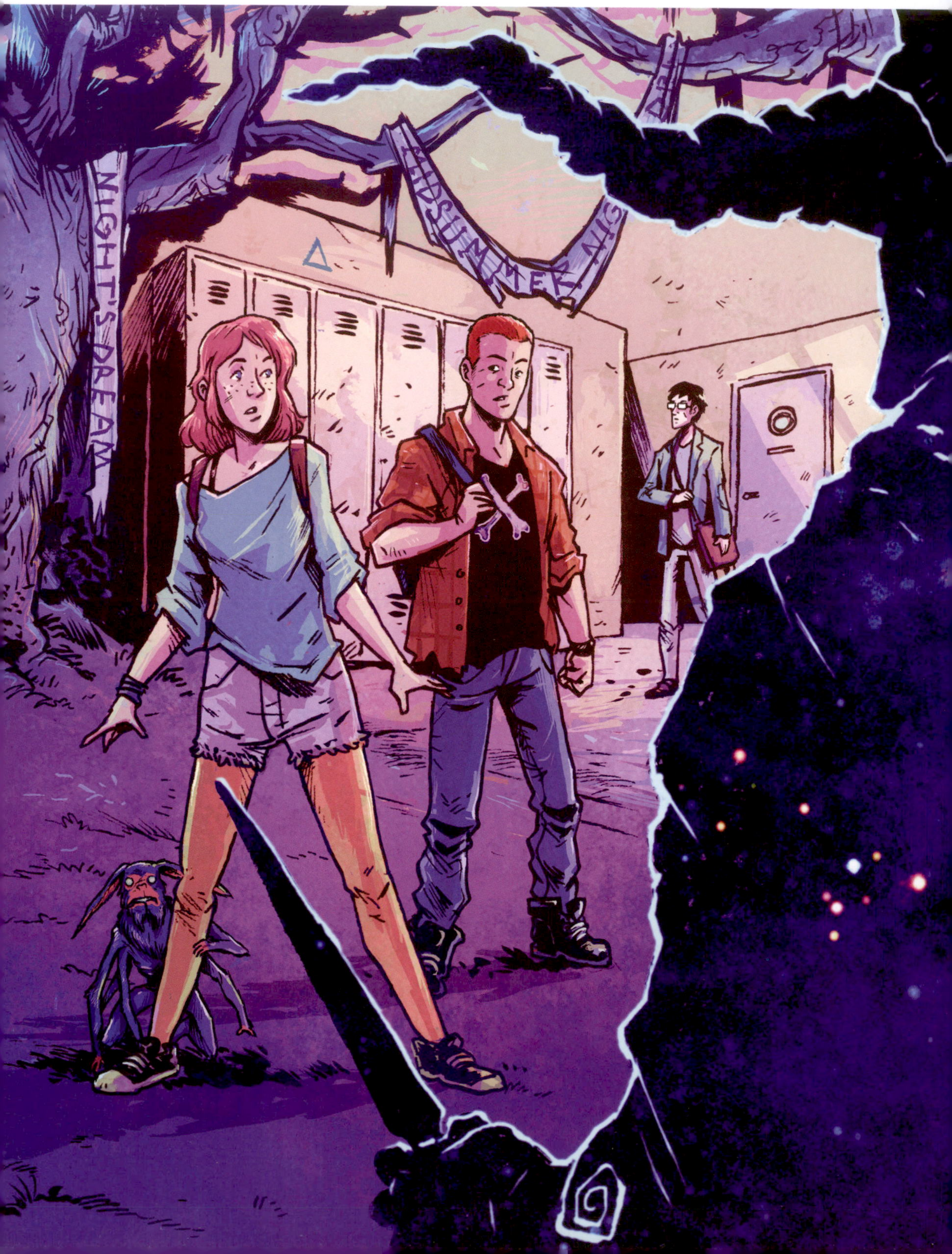
NIGHT'S DREAM

ISSUE SIX COVER **MICHAEL DIALYNAS**

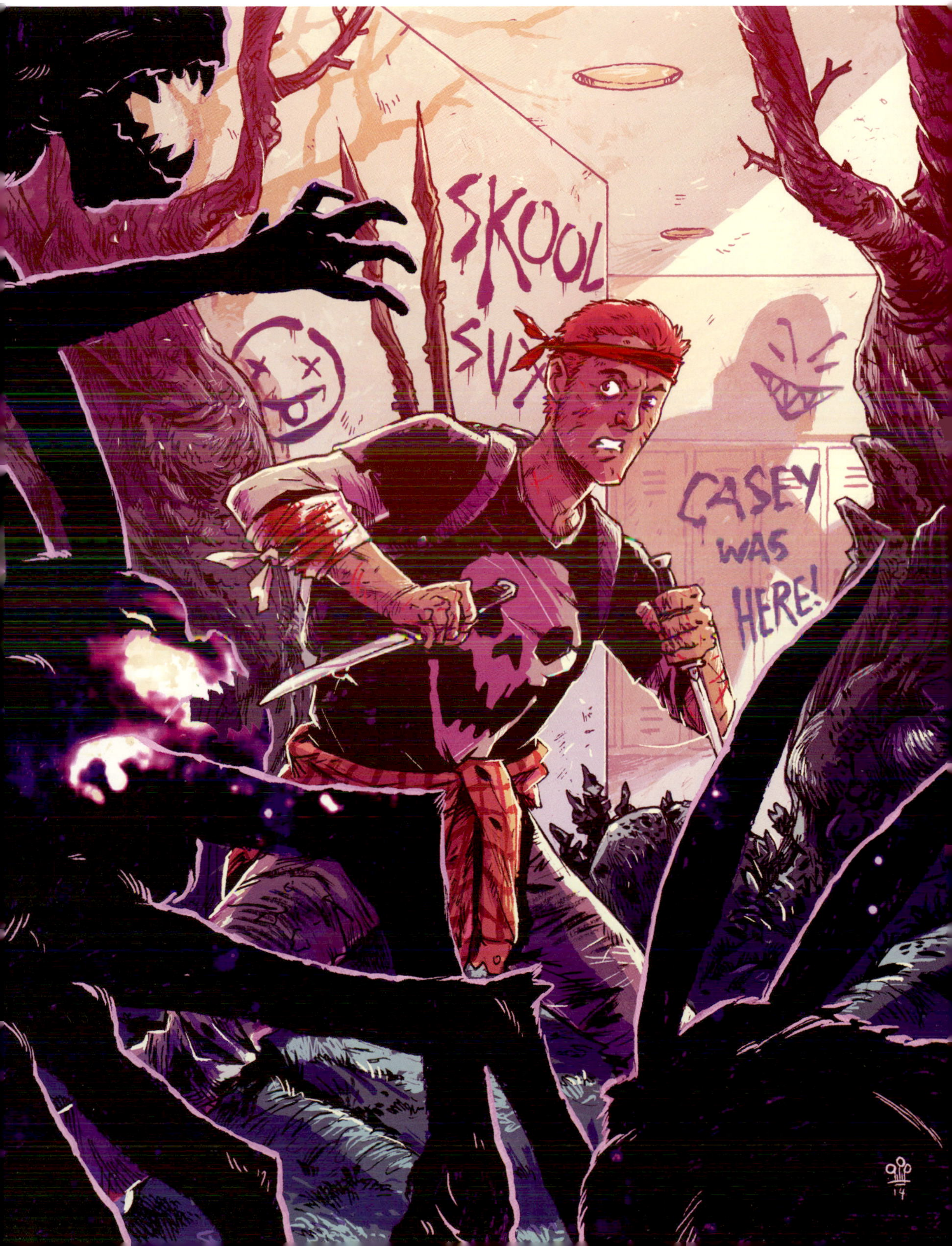
SKOOL
CASEY WAS HERE!

ISSUE SEVEN COVER **MICHAEL DIALYNAS**

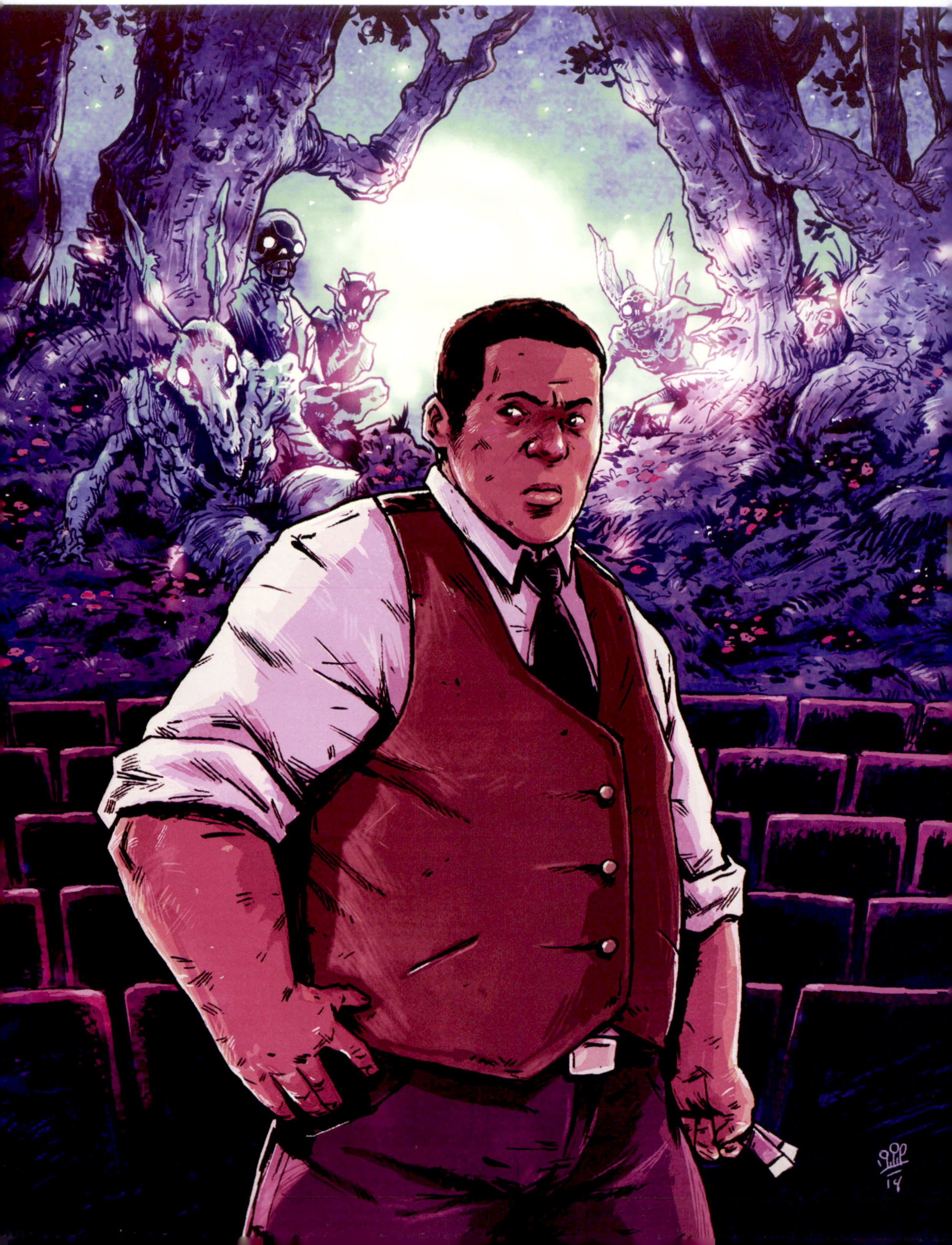

ISSUE EIGHT COVER **MICHAEL DIALYNAS**

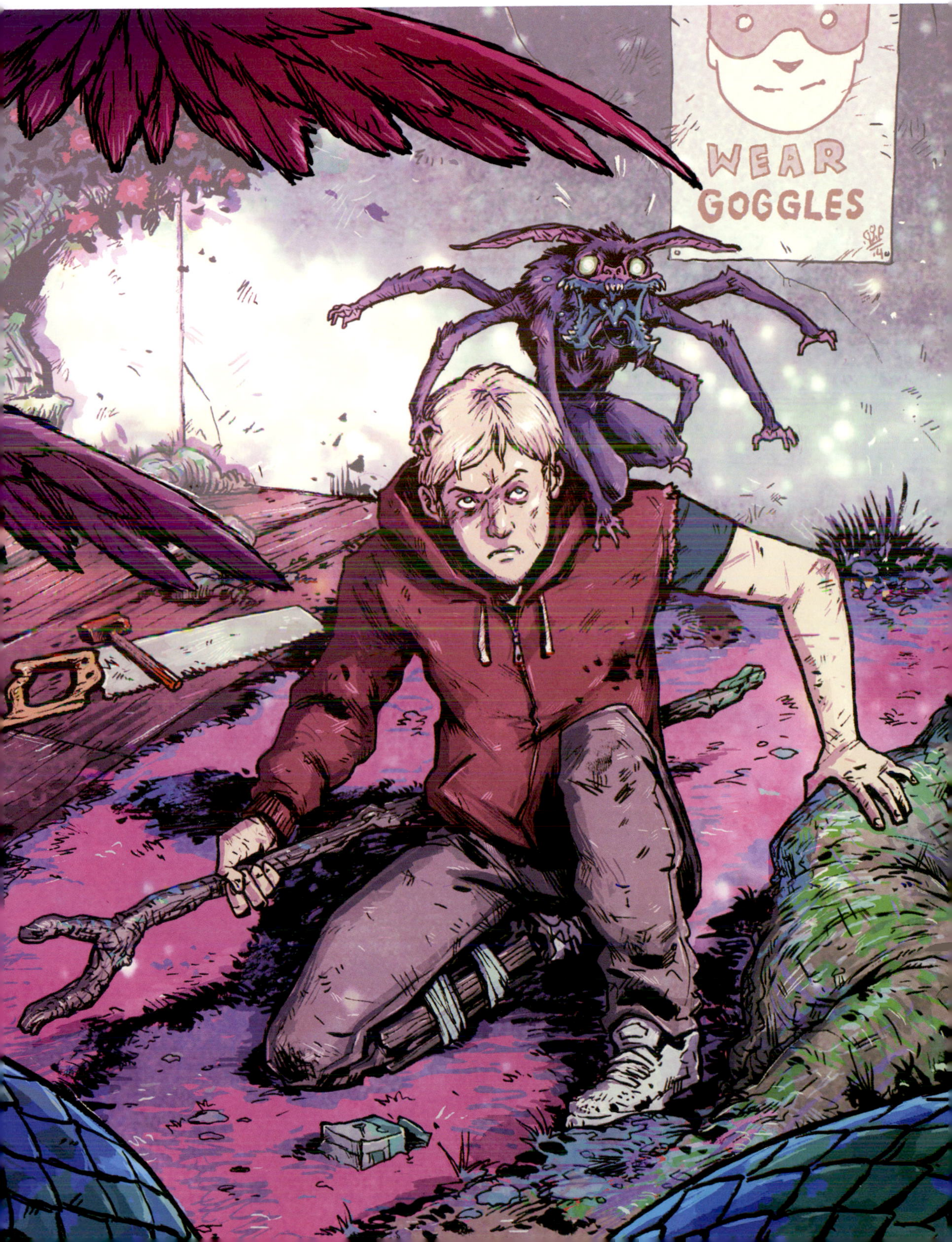
WEAR
GOGGLES

MICHAEL DIALYNAS

SKETCHBOOK

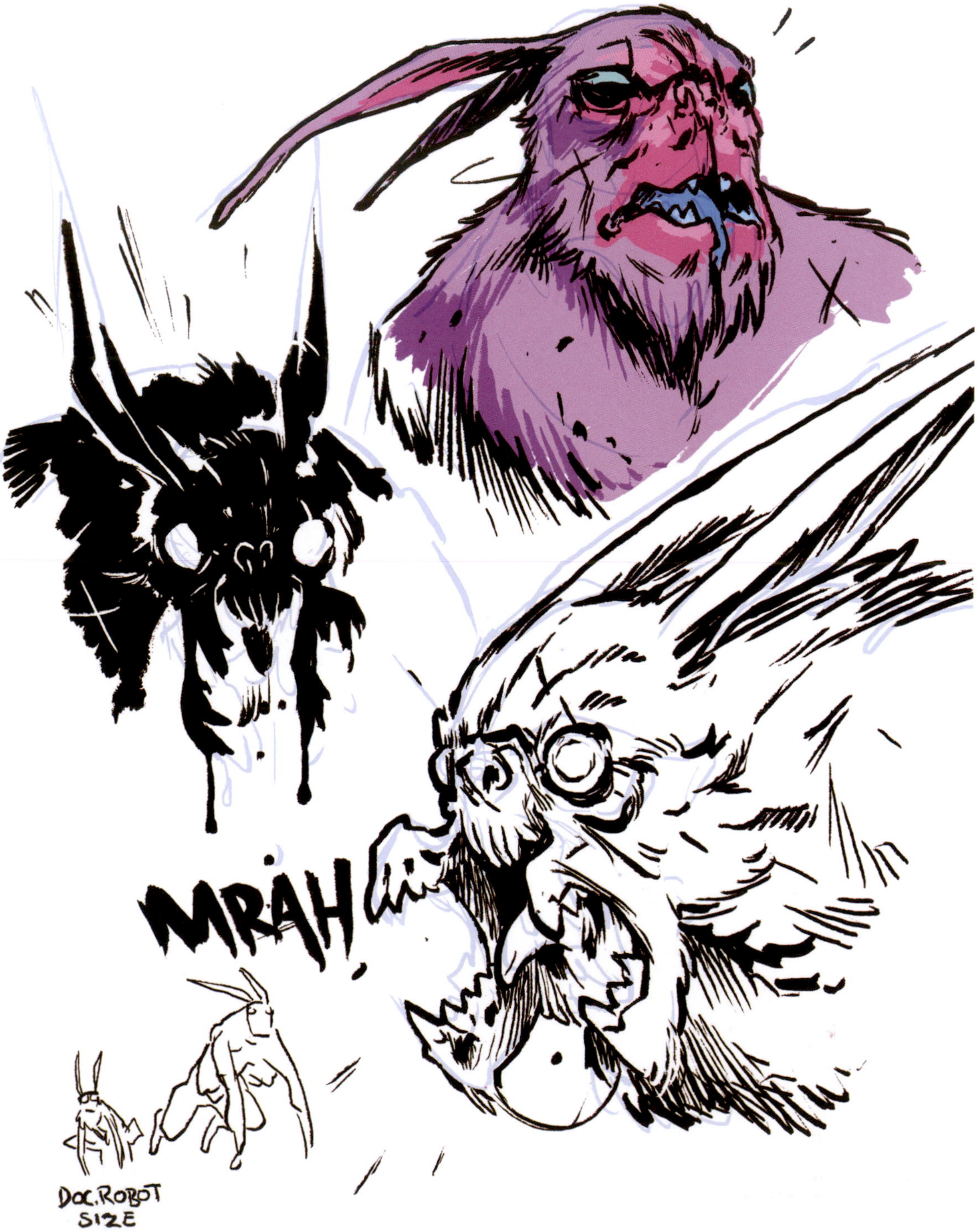
MRAH!
DOC.ROBOT SIZE

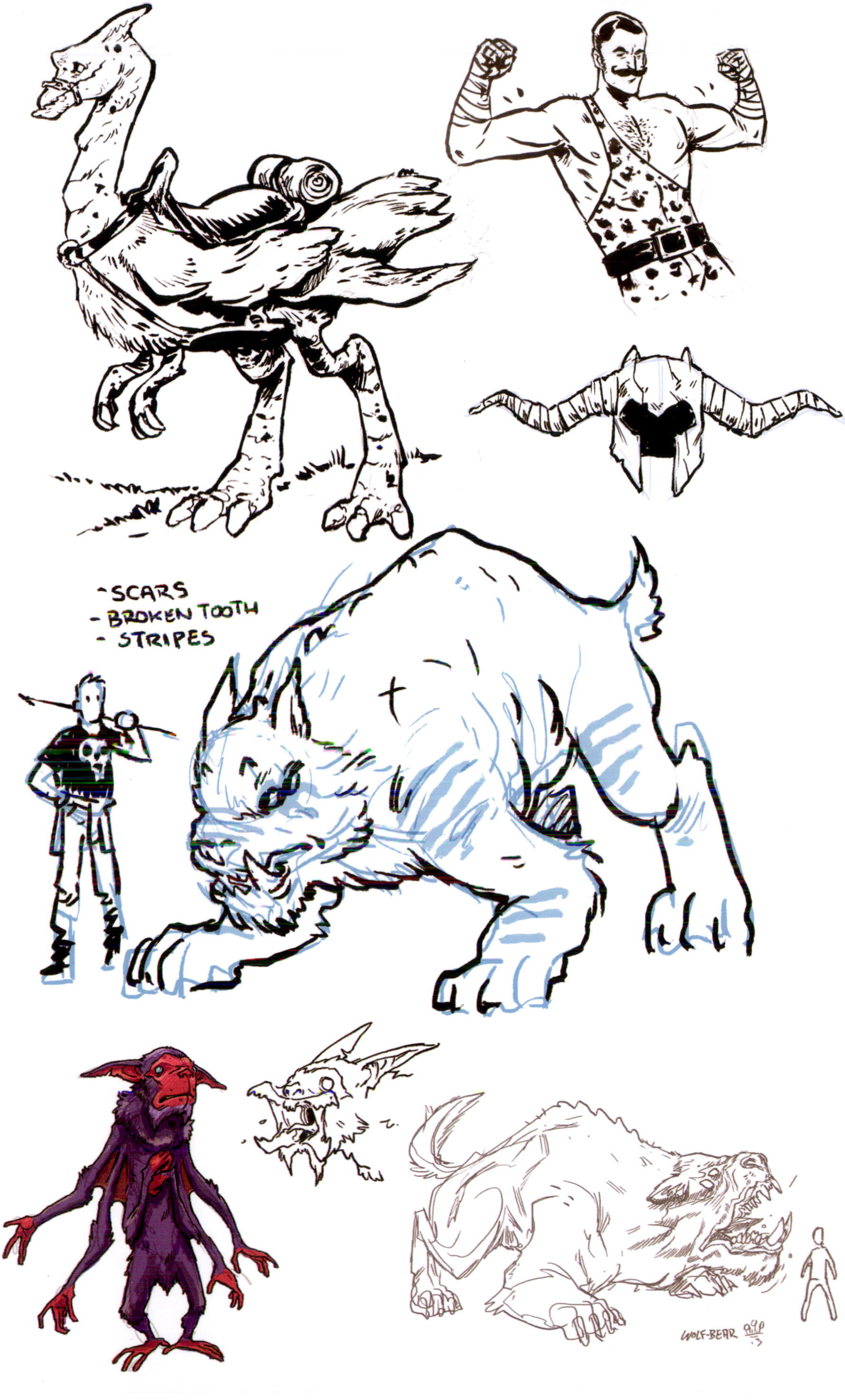

- SCARS
- BROKEN TOOTH
- STRIPES
WOLF-BEAR

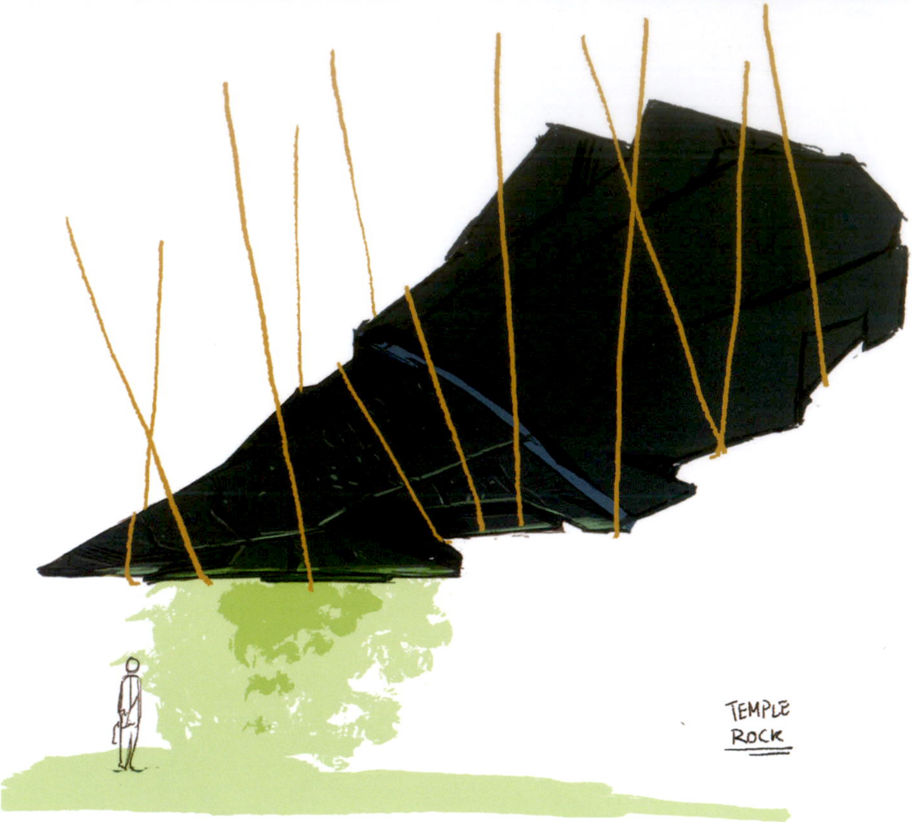
TEMPLE
ROCK

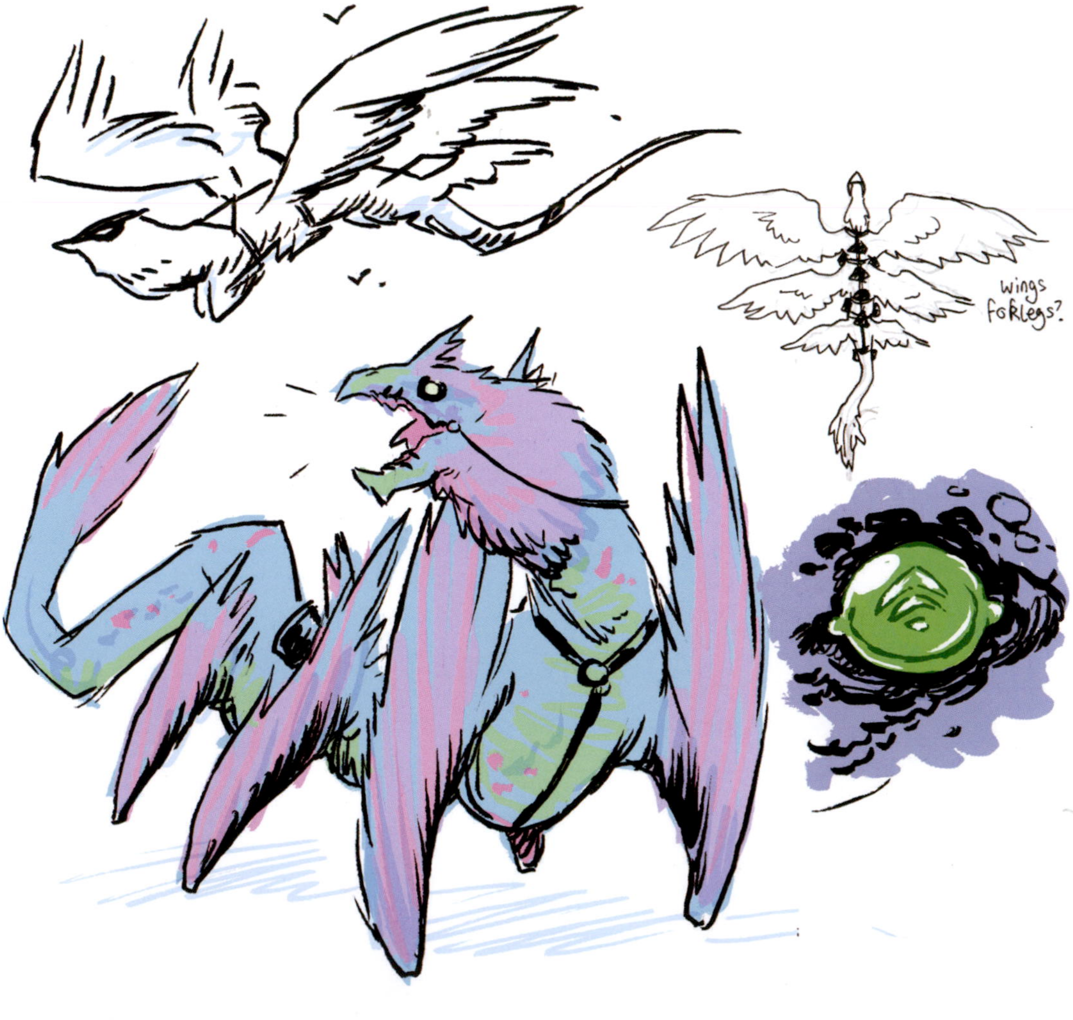
wings
for legs?

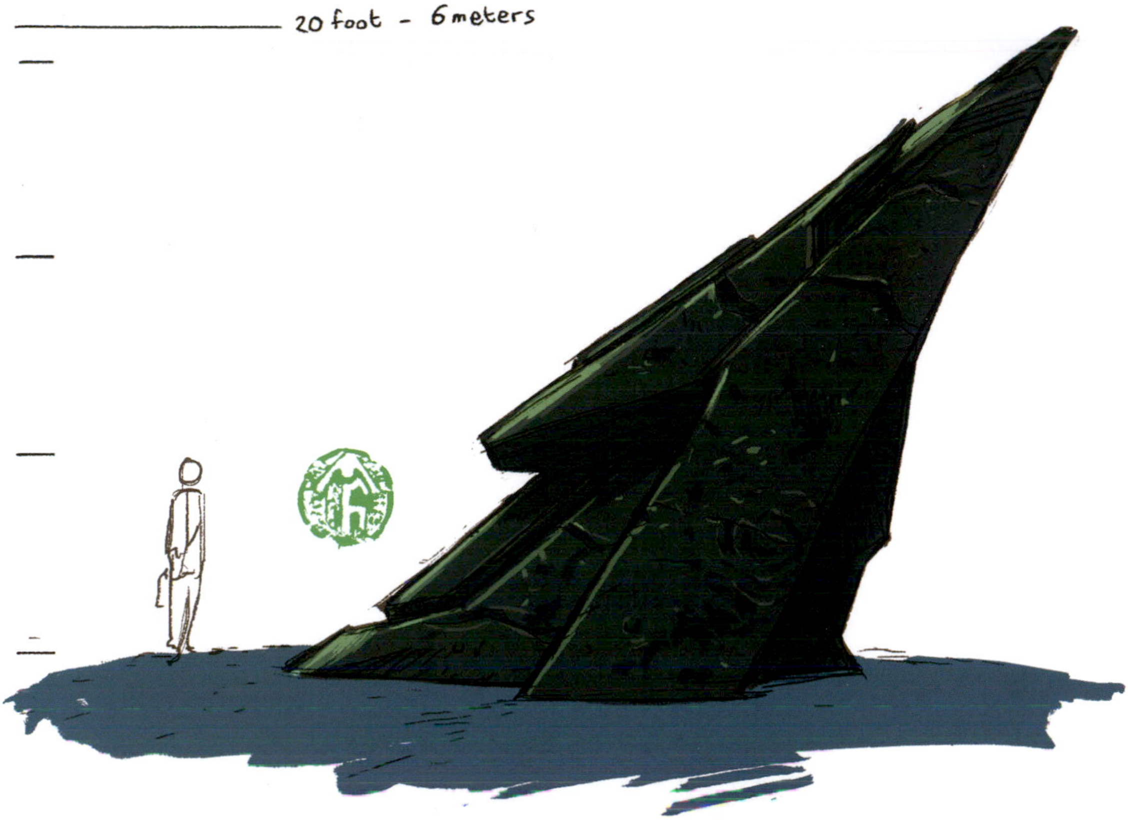
20 foot - 6 meters

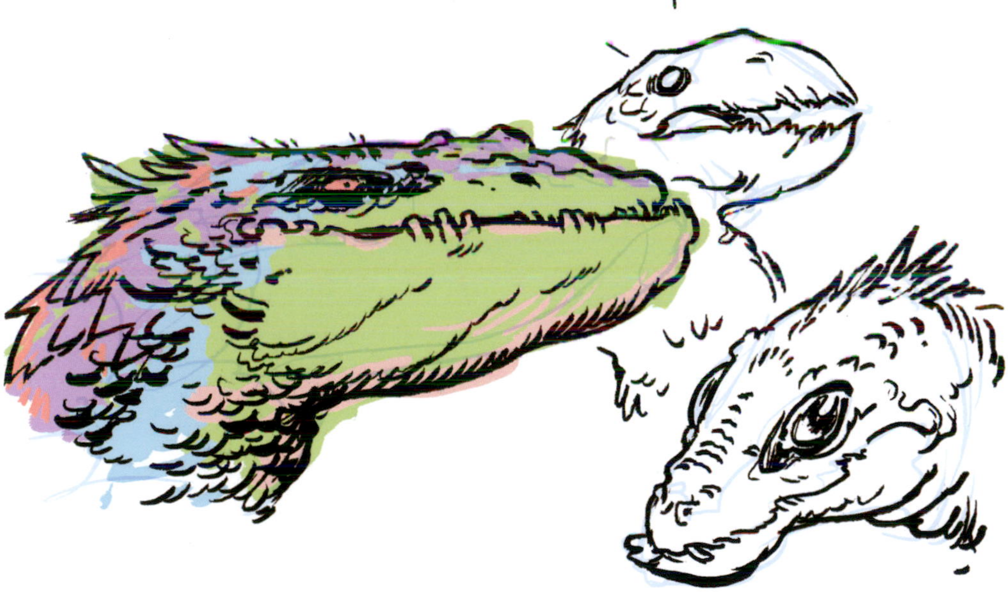

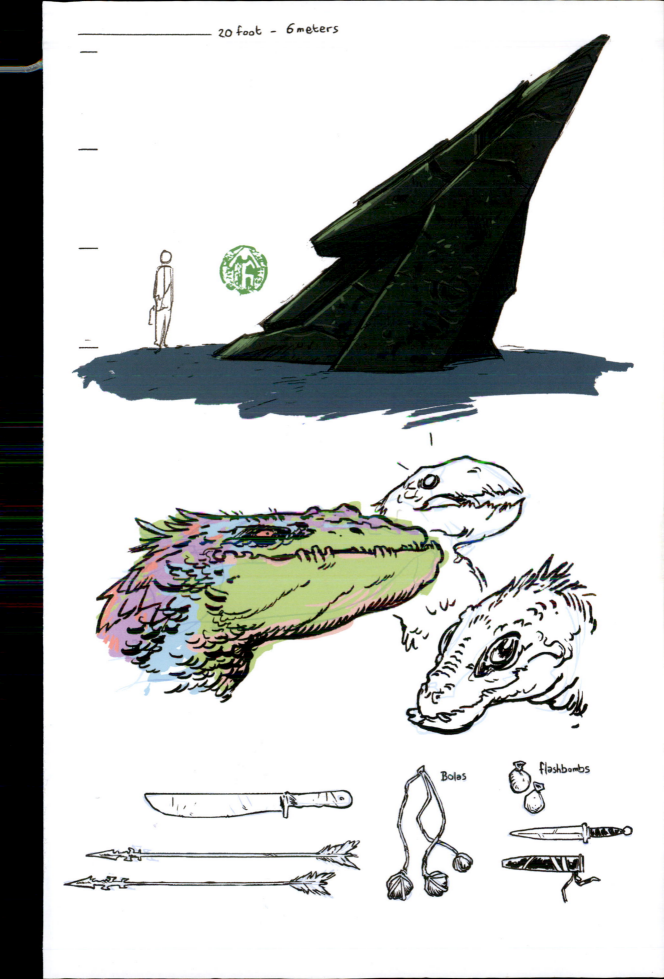

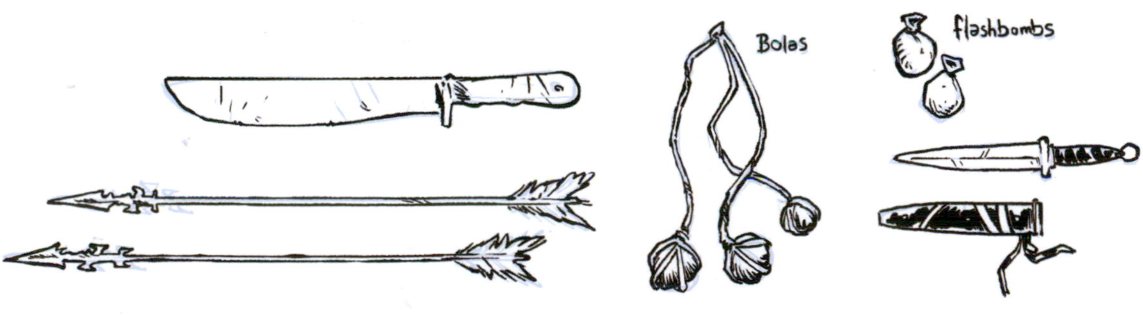
Bolas
flashbombs